$70 —

THE MARCOS FILE

Was he a Philippine Hero
or Corrupt Tyrant?

Charles C. McDougald

San Francisco Publishers

MASS MARKET EDITION

ISBN: 0-940777-06-1
LCCN: 86-062969

87 88 89 90 91 10 9 8 7 6 5 4 3 2 1

Library of Congress Cataloging-in-Publication Data

McDougald, Charles C., 1940–
   The Marcos file.

   Bibliography: p.
   Includes index.
   1. Marcos, Ferdinand E. (Ferdinand Edralin),
1917–   2. Philippines--Politics and government.
3. Philippines--Presidents--Biography. I. Title.
DS686.6.M35M37 1987 959.9'046'0924 [B] 86-62969
ISBN 0-940777-05-3

In Memoriam

Joan Fabian Whittle

1944-1981

Acknowledgments

I want to thank the many people who helped me throughout the adventure of writing this book. They cannot, of course, be held responsible for anything I have written, but they have my profound gratitude.

Emanuel V. Soriano, former president of the University of the Philippines and a member of the steering committee that advised Corazon Aquino during her campaign for the presidency, served as my mentor through this entire project. To him goes a special thanks for his supreme patience, understanding, and guidance no matter how hectic or dangerous the situation.

Lou Pritchett, then head of Proctor & Gamble in the Philippines, stood by me in the difficult times while other people were advising me that a book about Marcos wasn't a healthy pursuit. On numerous occasions he made his staff available when I requested guidance or assistance. Despite their duties in running one of the largest corporations in the Philippines, these people were always warm and accomodating.

Chief Justice Claudio Teehankee, who was an associate justice at the time, and Father Joaquin Bernas, S.J., president of the Ateneo de Manila University, critiqued the part of the manuscript regarding the law and the legal system in the Philippines. Archbishop Jaime Cardinal Sin was kind enough to review and advise me on the role of the church. Minister Teodoro Locsin, Jr., now Special Councel to President Aquino, but then vice-president of one of the local banks in Manila and an accomplished writer in his own right, reviewed and edited my original manuscript in 1984.

Doreen Fernandez at the Ateneo de Manila University in Manila, and Steve Psinakis in San Francisco always took time out of their busy schedules to help me when I would come calling no matter how busy they were. Boni Gillego was also particularly helpful with his expertise and advice regarding Marcos' military exploits.

Ador Porcioncula, secretary at the College of Business, University of the Philippines, was my girl Friday throughout the project. When I was abroad and needed an obscure fact, she always responded.

I am grateful to all those people and to the people whose names follow. Some are familiar, and some are not, but all are very important to me:

Jose Burgos, *We Forum;* John F. Doherty, S.J.; Colonel Gustavo Ingles; Colonel Jose Lukban; Senator Raul Manglapus; Colonel Narciso Manzano; Frank Quesada; J.G. "Johnny" Quijano; Pablo Q. Samson, director, national accounts staff, National Economic and Development Authority; John Sharkey, *Washington Post;* David Joel Steinberg; Marsh Thomson, American Chamber of Commerce in the Philippines; Irene Tienzo, director, international research department, Philippine Securities and Exchange Commission; Bernardo M. Villegas, Center for Research and Communication; and Edgar Zialcita, chief of economic research, Central Bank of the Philippines.

In addition, there are many of my sources who choose to remain nameless. To all of you go my heartfelt thanks. If anyone has been left out of this acknowledgment I hope they call and remind me so that amends can be made somehow.

Lastly, thanks to the Office of the Chief of Military History in Washington, D.C. for allowing me the use of the maps regarding the Battle of Bataan. The only other map used—Map 3—is copyright free.

Before you proceed I wish to point out two semantic peculiarities. This book is divided into three parts. In Part I, which is about Marcos as a soldier, I have used the military form of day-month-year when quoting dates. For example, Marcos won his first medal on 15 January 1942. In Part II, I return to the normal format of month-day-year. For example, Marcos was born on September 11, 1917.

The second pecularity is that in Part I most of the times of day are defined, again, in military terms. For example, a battle may start at 1430, which, translated, means 2:30 in the afternoon. For those uninitiated in militarese I ask forgiveness, but it isn't difficult to understand. The first hour in a day is 1:00 o'clock in the morning, or 0100 in the military. Noon is 1200, or 12:00 o'clock; and 6:00 in the evening is the 18th hour of the day, or 1800.

Salamat Po!

CCM
SAN FRANCISCO

Contents

	Preface	1
Part I	**Soldier**	**5**
1	Introduction	7
2	Lieutenant Marcos	13
3	The U.S. Medals	25
4	The Medal for Valor	31
5	The Final Battle of Bataan	45
6	Subjugation and Resistance	55
7	Guerrilla	65
8	Claims of the Maharlika	79
9	Marcos Joins the 14th	87
10	Escolta Guerrilla	97
Part II	**Statesman**	**109**
11	Introduction	111
12	The Politician	115
13	Constitutional Authoritarianism	123
14	Imelda	133
15	The Church	147
16	The Military	159
17	Expression	175
18	The Grand Coalition	187

Part III	Shaman	193
19	Introduction	195
20	Cronyism	201
21	The Capitalists	207
22	A Controlled Economy	217
23	The Coconut Monopoly	225
24	The Sugar Monopoly	233
25	The State Visit	239
26	Blitzkrieg	249
Epilogue	**Assassination**	**259**
27	Martyrdom	261
28	The Non-Event	269
29	Aftermath	273
30	Contrition	289
	Notes	**305**
	Index	**331**

Preface

WORLD WAR II. THE PHILIPPINES. CORREGIDOR. BATAAN. GENERAL DOUGLAS MACARTHUR. FERDINAND MARCOS. SCHOLAR. SOLDIER. STATESMAN. MARTIAL LAW. GROWTH. PROSPERITY. RECESSION. CRONYISM. STATE CAPITALISM. CORRUPTION. VIOLENCE. MURDER. REVOLUTION. WHY?

The whump-whump-whump of the American helicopters can barely be heard over the screaming and yelling of the crowd. A loud cheer engulfs the palace grounds as the choppers pull away. There is pandemonium at the gates. The hysterical crowd clambers over the wall and surges forward. Another deposed dictator has played out his last act in a scenario that could only be described as Shakespearean. If it were a play the curtain would descend and the story would end.

However, this is no fictional melodrama. Ferdinand Marcos may be a psychiatrist's dream but he is very real. Now it is up to the historians to analyze this Machiavellian character who in 20 years managed to rival the Spanish, oppressors of the Filipino for more than 300 years, in the wealth his regime stole and the people imprisoned, tortured, and killed. The most incredible part of his reign is the fact that he departed without a bloodbath. Such characters usually kill themselves off or end their rule in some obscene gesture understood only by the depraved mind of the dictator.

Why did he leave? It is easy to say that, considering the circumstances, it was the rational thing to do. But Marcos was not a paragon of logic in the last years of his rule. Perhaps he was finally too tired, too sick, and too scared to reckon with things any longer. Perhaps, cringing there in the palace surrounded by his thousands of body guards, he was thinking back to the time when his father was hacked to death with a bolo* and hung in a tree as an example of a traitor to his own people. Now, 41 years later, listening to the fury of the crowd outside, the same thing happening again may have become to him a very real possibility.

Perhaps he had received a sign. It is well known that Marcos believed in the mystical and supernatural. During the presidential campaign he told one crowd of his "special angel" who warned him when he was in danger, and another crowd that "voices" had urged him not to quit. Imelda alluded to his powers when she warned former Senator Aquino about coming to the Philippines, saying "...the president is sort of a clairvoyant."[1]

Visions and signs are one thing. A miracle is another. That is the way "People's Power" has been described. Those last days in February 1986 will never be forgotten when the people, cheated of one election, decided to cast another vote. Only this time no ballots were involved. A million people put their lives on the line when they stood up against Marcos' soldiers and tanks which had been called out to force them back into submission. The whole world was watching. There would be no fraud this time. Flesh against steel is one thing, but the spirit of a nation against a dictator's tanks is another. There was no contest. The people won their victory, and Marcos made a hasty departure.

The Filipino did himself proud during those dark days. It's the kind of story that every parent will pass on to his children and his children's children. It will be repeated in every pulpit throughout the land for many years to come. Good triumphed over evil in a remarkable fashion. The miracle on E. Delos Santos Boulevard will never be forgotten.

How Marcos came by such power and why he was allowed to use it so abusively is a despicable, but fascinating, story. Marcos

---

* A long, heavy single-edged knife.

was a master of illusion. He desperately wanted people to believe that he was the consummate soldier and leader. As a soldier he wanted to be a hero of biblical proportions. As president he wanted to be known as the supreme statesman who exercised political leadership wisely and benevolently. His government printing presses worked overtime, laboriously and meticulously turning out millions of pages of propaganda toward this end. There was no room for doubters. Anyone who dared to question his government was asking for trouble of the most serious kind; and anyone who questioned his personal achievements was in even worse trouble. Because of this, for a long time it was difficult to separate fact from fiction. About the only thing in his official biography that is real is his date of birth—September 1b, 1917. The rest of it is a cleverly woven tale of myth mixed with a few facts.

The truth is that he never was what he seemed to be. Marcos as soldier and statesman was only an illusion. In reality he was mostly unreal—a Shaman—a mystical creature who believed he was all powerful and able to control events, who hid his own greed and lust for riches until he brought about his own downfall by his inability to divine the will of his own people. In the end, when the aging and sickly dictator was at his weakest, in his paranoia he believed that Ninoy Aquino was coming to expose him for all that he was. For this reason Ninoy was murdered in front of 1,200 soldiers in broad daylight at a busy airport. That was the beginning of the end for Marcos, for it was the first time in a long time his powers didn't work. Of course, he didn't go quietly. He raged and stole until, in the end, he was sitting in that palace, mostly alone, facing reality, and perhaps realizing for the first time who he wasn't.

Imelda had always been an enigma, but her attempts to create a new past for herself were the most transparent of illusions. The fact that she really expected everyone to believe her is both tragic and comic. Perhaps by then, with her, illusion had become reality.

Who was Ferdinand Marcos? The reality began over half a century ago with another political contest and another killing on a rainy night in September. Some people handle defeat badly. Very badly.

PART I
Soldier

CHAPTER ONE

Introduction

In 1934, at the age of 17, Ferdinand Marcos entered the University of the Philippines in Manila as an undergraduate. According to his biography, he majored in liberal arts and was active in sports, winning a place on the all-university wrestling, boxing and swimming teams.[1] It also mentioned that, after spending two summers hunting in Davao in 1933 and 1934, Marcos won the small-bore and pistol championship of the Philippines.[2] He verified this in an interview that appeared in the September 29, 1975, issue of *Sports Illustrated.* However, then Senator Ambrosio Padilla, who was vice-president and then president of the Philippine Amateur Athletic Federation from 1972 to 1974, stated that there was no record of his ever competing in or winning such a championship, and that Teddy Kalaw had actually won that title. Padilla also stated that there was no record at the University of the Philippines Physical Education Department of Marcos lettering in any sport.[3]

In 1935, his father, Mariano Marcos, was defeated in an election for congressman of the Second District of Ilocos Norte, the province on the northeastern tip of Luzon, the main island of the Philippines. Mariano Marcos had been elected in 1924 and 1928, but lost in 1932. In 1935, in its new status as a self-governing commonwealth, the people of the Philippines had to choose its first president. In addition, all assemblymen had to face reelection. Mariano Marcos, a member of the Aglipayan Party, decided to run again. Manuel L. Quezon of the Nacionalista Party was elected president. Julio Nalundasan, also a Nacionalista, beat Marcos. Both were from the village of Batac and lived only a few hundred meters apart. Nalundasan could never be classified as a gracious winner. A mock funeral cortege paraded through Batac carrying a coffin with Marcos' name. The moonless night of September 20 was dark and stormy. Rain lashed the village as Nalundasan, delayed by friends congratulating him on his victory, took his supper later than usual. He was standing by the dining room window brushing his teeth when a shot rang out, and he fell mortally wounded.

Four years later, Ferdinand Marcos, about to finish law school at the University of the Philippines, was arrested for the murder of Nalundasan, tried, and found guilty. He had taken his bar examinations during the trial and scored the highest of everyone taking the test. He was the bar topnotcher in 1939, which carried great significance in the Philippines. This event, plus his murder trial and conviction, made Marcos front-page news.

A year later, in 1940, the Supreme Court overturned Marcos' conviction and made him a free man. The justice that penned this decision was Jose Laurel, who may have been somewhat impartial. In 1912, he had also been convicted of murder. At the age of 18 he had stabbed a man in a fight over a girl. His conviction was later reversed by the Supreme Court. Marcos had turned 18 just nine days before Nalundasan was murdered. The similarities went deeper. Laurel had also attended the University of the Philippines law school, and had also been the bar topnotcher.

The Supreme Court decision once again put the young Marcos on the front page of every newspaper in the Philippines. Marcos was somewhat of a celebrity when the war came to the Philippines in December 1941.

The presidential palace is called "Malacanang," which is a Tagalog contraction meaning "there is a man of nobility there." It has been the seat of power in the Philippines since 1863 during Spanish colonial times. The Spanish gobernadors resided there, as did the American governors general. The first president of the

Philippines, Manuel L. Quezon, moved in sometime in the month of November 1935. Malacañang survived the almost total destruction of Manila at the end of World War II and has been the official residence ever since. All the portraits of past presidents now hang there. Of all these, one portrait is unique because the man was never elected president, nor did he succeed as vice-president. The plaque below it says simply "President Jose P. Laurel."

Jose Laurel received his law degree in 1915. He then attended Yale University in the United States and received his DCL in 1920. He was appointed Secretary of the Department of the Interior in 1923 at the age of 32. He resigned that post and ran for the Senate. He won and served from 1925 to 1931, becoming the floor leader. In 1936, he was appointed associate justice of the Supreme Court and served until 1941, when the war broke out. In 1938, he received a Doctorate of Jurisprudence honoris causa from Tokyo Imperial University. He had sent one of his sons, Jose III, to Japan for military training and had represented a large number of Japanese firms in his pre-war law firm. He was known to be favorably disposed to the Japanese and their institutions.

When the Japanese occupied the Philippines, Laurel was invited to serve on the wartime Philippine Executive Commission. He held various posts on the Commission until he was shot while playing golf on June 6, 1943, probably by an anti-Japanese guerrilla. He recuperated from his wounds and was offered the presidency of the Japanese-sponsored republic. He accepted and was inaugurated on October 14, 1943. He served as president from then until the American liberating forces returned, and the Japanese flew him to Tokyo on March 19, 1945.

After the war Laurel was indicted on more than 100 counts of treason. Some thought he had served the Japanese a little too willingly; others remembered that Supreme Court Justice Jose Abad Santos chose to die by firing squad rather than serve the enemy; and still others claimed he had to cooperate with the Japanese, and risked his life to do so. William Manchester, who wrote *American Caesar*, a biography of General Douglas MacArthur, noted: "Collaborators were more complex because their motives varied. Some were frightened of the Japanese, some preferred Oriental rulers to Occidental, some thought they could best serve their countrymen by cooperating with their conquerors, and some were outright opportunists hankering for personal gain. Probably most were a blend of all these."[4]

Nevertheless, Laurel was accused of "collaboration," a highly pejorative term at the time. Ironically, the head of the People's Court which prosecuted the collaborators was the Solicitor General, Lorenzo Tañada, a former law student of Laurel's at the University of the Philippines.[5] Laurel was still a very popular man in the Philippines, and the issue divided the nation. Tañada, who had been a guerrilla in the resistance and was captured and tortured by the Japanese, insisted on a conviction. Laurel's lawyer, Vicente Francisco, maintained that he had only done his job and had saved many lives by cooperating. Many prominent lawyers of the time joined Francisco at the defendant's table to support Laurel and offer their services free.[6]

Manuel Roxas was elected president in 1946 and, strangely, did very little to assist Laurel in his predicament. It was strange because Laurel had saved Roxas' life several times during the occupation. Roxas had been a former speaker of the house and then President Quezon's Secretary of Finance and protegé. He also held a brigadier general's commission in the U.S. Army. When Quezon went into exile, Roxas politely refused the offer to accompany him and remained behind. During the occupation he refused to serve the Japanese in any official capacity, claiming ill health, and was secretly a member of the underground resistance. On several occasions the Japanese came to the palace and demanded that Roxas be arrested, but Laurel was able to thwart each demand. Roxas went on to be elected president and died in office in 1948. He was succeeded by his vice-president, Elpidio Quiriño.

As Laurel's trial wore on, the stigma gradually wore off, however, and he was eventually pardoned in 1948 by a general amnesty proclamation. He went on to be elected a senator, and was nearly successful in the presidential contest of 1949, losing a close race to Quiriño. Historian Teodoro Agoncillo noted that Laurel would have won in 1949, "were it not for the rampant cheating, especially in Mindanao where monkeys, trees, and other forms of the flora and fauna were made to vote for the incumbent president."[7] When Laurel died in 1959, the country mourned the loss of a true patriot.

About this time another son, Salvadore, following in his father's footsteps, was finishing up at Yale after getting his law degree at the University of the Philippines. He would also soon enter politics.

Jose Laurel and Manuel Roxas were men of stature during the war years and the young Ferdinand Marcos knew both. He was not associated with the Laurel presidency, nor was he a part of the Roxas spy network, but just the fact that he was in and around Manila during most of the occupation and was acquainted with both Laurel and Roxas, would have a tremendous effect on his life both during and after the war. As early as 1947, U.S. Army officers investigating Marcos' wartime exploits would comment about his political prestige.

CHAPTER TWO

Lieutenant Marcos

Ferdinand E. Marcos joined the Army in November 1941 as a third lieutenant. He served until February 1946. Not until 18 years later would he lay claim as the most decorated Filipino soldier of World War II, receiving more decorations — 32, 33, or 34, depending on which government literature was read — than Audie Murphy, who received 27 and was the U.S.' most decorated soldier. Of all the medals he claims, some are duplicates, but almost all have been disputed. Three things are noteworthy about his awards: first, all are based on affidavits after-the-fact; second, no source documents of that period can substantiate his claims; and, third, there are people and documentation that dispute his claims.

Anyone who ever served in the military quickly becomes aware that every activity has a "standard operating procedure," or "S.O.P." in military parlance, from field stripping a carbine to awarding medals. The proper procedure for receiving an award is a numbered General Order (GO) or Special Order (SO), from the appropriate headquarters or command, that contains the date and place of the action, a description of the action, and the role the awardee played. When there is an action deserving of an award, an officer or non-commissioned officer is appointed to investigate, take statements from participants and witnesses, and forward the information to the appropriate command. Almost all citations for bravery or wounds received in action are awarded within weeks of the action. None of Marcos' were. For someone as well known as Marcos to do something exemplary on the battlefield without immediate recognition is to strain the bounds of credibility. However, he was awarded two U.S. medals and numerous Philippine medals based on affidavits alone.

Four books treat the Marcos military exploits with exceptional care. Most of the exploits are based on records and documentation by the Armed Forces of the Philippines (AFP), which must be considered questionable. The AFP, at the time, did not follow the same thorough investigation procedures after an engagement as the U.S. Army with regard to proper documentation, especially with regard to the Marcos war medals, as will become obvious.

The first book to declare Marcos a war hero was his campaign biography published in 1964 by Hartzell Spence, entitled *For Every Tear a Victory, The Story of Ferdinand E. Marcos,** which was re-released in 1979, under the title *Marcos of the Philippines.*** The release in 1964 came at a propitious time. Marcos was running for president. His war exploits were trumpeted throughout the book, but it failed to mention that almost half his medals had been awarded the year before, in 1963. The book has been dismissed by critics as a fantasy.

Bonifacio Gillego served his country in World War II as a guerilla in Bicol. Afterwards the Bicol Brigade was officially recognized by the U.S. Army. He retired in 1961 after 21 years' service and later became an elected delegate to the Constitutional Convention in 1970. He has conducted extensive research on Marcos' war exploits. His articles for the *Philippine News* in San Francisco were the first to cast doubt on Marcos' war record. They were reprinted later in the *We Forum* in Manila, and resulted in the paper's being closed down in 1982 and its editor and staff arrested for subversion.† Gillego explained that the AFP had to lobby in Congress annually for appropriations and for confirmation of the promotion of officers to the rank of general. One unfailing technique was to give awards to selected members who would champion their cause. Marcos was such a champion.

---

* New York: McGraw Hill, 1964.
** Copyright, 1979, by Ferdinand E. Marcos.
  † The charges were dropped on March 5, 1985, for lack of evidence.

Another book *Filipino Heroes of World War II,** written by Philippine military historian Colonel Uldarico Baclagon features Marcos as one of the bravest of all the heroes. Baclagon graduated from the Philippine Military Academy in 1940, served in World War II, and was a guerrilla during the occupation in Negros. Because of his background and experience he is well qualified to write about Philippine military history. However, it is surprising that he didn't check the facts about Marcos' war exploits more thoroughly. Baclagon first published this book in 1965 under the title *They Served with Honor*, and apparently used the same AFP documents which Spence used so prodigiously as the basis of his accounts. His book was then re-released in 1980 under the new title but with a few additions. There were an additional 17 paragraphs interspersed throughout describing Marcos' war exploits in even grander terms, and an additional six pages at the end which describe Marcos' winning of the Philippine Medal for Valor and his recommendation for the U.S. Congressional Medal of Honor. For some reason this heroic deed was not even mentioned in the first release of his book, nor is it mentioned in the first release of Spence's book although the Medal of Valor was awarded in 1958.

Another book which doesn't headline Marcos, but mentions his heroics, is *They Never Surrendered,* by Gerald S. Snyder.** It is about Colonel Jesus Villamor, who was called "the most decorated Filipino soldier *during* the war," by John Toland, who wrote the introduction. Toland had written several highly regarded books himself: *The Rising Sun†*, and *But Not in Shame: The Six Months after Pearl Harbor,‡* which he wrote after interviewing almost 800 soldiers, sailors, and prominent personalities in the Philippines, including Jose Laurel, then President Carlos P. Garcia, Secretary of Defense Alejo Santos, and General Carlos P. Romulo. Toland delivered a graphic account of the day-to-day action in the Philippines right up to the surrender, but Marcos is never mentioned.

* Makati, Metro Manila: Agro Printing & Publishing House, 1980.
** Quezon City, Philippines: Vera Reyes, Inc., 1982.
† New York: Random House, 1961.
‡ New York: Doubleday, 1970.

Villamor was a captain in the Air Corp in December 1941, when he won two Distinguished Service Crosses in two days for his extraordinary heroism. (It should be noted that they were awarded by GO 48, dated 21 December 1941, for deeds done on 10 and 12 December 1941.) He was evacuated to Australia in early 1942, but returned with five men by submarine the following December on a secret mission code-named Planet Party. Landing on the island of Negros in the southern Philippines, he set up a network of 46 agents and for 11 months provided MacArthur with intelligence data. He returned to Australia in October 1943.

The book attributes daring deeds to Marcos. However, Villamor's after-mission report is a matter of record, and Marcos is never mentioned.* The fact is that Villamor started the book, but died in 1971 before finishing it. Snyder then took the half-finished manuscript and completed it in 1976. However, lack of financing prevented its publication until 1982, the year of Marcos' state visit to Washington. The acknowledgments in the book thank Marcos and others "for their generous financial assistance." The bibliographies list, among other sources, the books of Spence and Baclagon.

The most recent book to be published about Marcos' war exploits is *Valor*,** in 1983, by Baclagon and Jose M. Crisol. It is a further embellishment of Marcos' heroics, complete with photographs. The foreword is by Carlos P. Romulo, former foreign minister of the Philippines and the dean of United Nations ambassadors. It speaks of Marcos' bravery in glowing terms, and of how Major Emigdio Cruz, after his spy mission, reported to President Quezon that Lieutenant Ferdinand E. Marcos "deserved the highest commendation" as a resistance fighter, and of how General MacArthur referred to him as "an Army of one man." Cruz was the aide and personal physician to Philippine President Manuel Quezon at the time of the invasion. They were evacuated later, first to Australia, then back to Washington, D.C. Quezon then asked Cruz to return to the

---

* Volume II of the Army Study Group, GHQ, Pacific Series, Intelligence Activities in the Philippines During the Japanese Occupation, Assessment of Villamor Mission.
** Metro Manila: Development Academy of the Philippines, 1983.

Philippines on a clandestine mission to determine the loyalty and extent of collaboration of the officials whom Quezon had ordered to remain. Cruz landed by submarine on the southern island of Negros on 9 July 1943, and was met by Villamor. He made his way to Manila and contacted scores of people. Japanese intelligence knew he was in the Philippines, but through sheer luck and daring he managed to elude them and returned to Australia in February 1944. He was awarded the Distinguished Service Cross for this mission. His after-mission report is a matter of record,* and makes no mention of Marcos. Nor is there any record of Marcos being decorated by MacArthur or even mentioned by Macarthur in any of his writings.

Forty years before, when Ambassador Romulo wrote several books about the war, such as *I Saw the Fall of the Philippines* and *I Walked With Heroes*, he never mentioned Marcos. Romulo, who was then a major and the executive press relations officer of General MacArthur, was promoted to general and appointed as MacArthur's aide-de-camp because of his work on Corregidor as the "Voice of Freedom" which broadcast the exploits of the heroes of Bataan and Corregidor. Marcos was never mentioned in these broadcasts. It is obvious that the authors overstepped the bounds of decency when they asked Ambassador Romulo, an elder statesman who served his country longer and more honorably than Marcos, to try and give some credibility to Marcos' exploits.

Ferdinand Marcos' first assignment was with the 21st Infantry Division (PA) in the G-2 section. There were usually four sections at division headquarters: G-1 (Personnel/Administration), G-2 (Security/Intelligence), G-3 (Operations/Plans), and G-4 (Supply/Logistics). The Table of Organization and Equipment (TOE) had an additional slot for G-5 (Civil Affairs) when it was needed. On a lower level each regiment in the division (there were three regiments in the 21st—21st Infantry, 22nd Infantry, and 23rd Infantry) and each battalion (there were three battalions per regiment), and each company (three or four companies per

---

* Volume II of the Army Study Group, GHQ, Pacific Series, Intelligence Activities of the Philippines During the Japanese Occupation, Personal Narrative of Major E.C. Cruz.

battalion) would have a similar staff, only their designations would be S-1, S-2, etc.

As a newly commissioned third lieutenant with limited military training and experience, but armed with a law degree, Marcos was assigned as an assistant to Captain Ismael D. Lapus, the G-2 officer. A war zone doesn't discriminate between the veteran and the greenhorn, and war came to Ferdinand Marcos very quickly. He was with the 21st approximately five months until it was overrun on April 5, 1942. During this period he allegedly won nine medals for bravery, but two are duplicates.

When the Philippines was attacked and overrun in December 1941, Bataan had been selected for the final stand against the Japanese. An officer in the U.S. Army Corps of Engineers noted that "the rugged terrain of the Bataan Peninsula, covered as it was by a thick jungle, concealed the works of the defender even when the enemy had constant air superiority and air observation."[1]

Militarily Bataan was divided into two sectors—the East Sector became I Philippine Corps, and the West Sector became II Philippine Corps. The boundary between the two corps bisected the length of the peninsula from Mount Natib to the Mariveles Mountains. The area south of the Mariveles was designated the Service Command Area. (See Map 1.)

The Mabatang-Mauban Line, or Abucay-Mauban Line as it was more generally called, was the initial main battle line. Right in the middle of it was Mount Natib, an extinct volcano, which left a five mile gap between the two corps, covered an area of about 15 by 15 miles, and rose to a height of about 4,000 feet. The east coast was flat and swampy with fish ponds and rice paddies that extended inland for about two miles. Then the hills, covered with cane fields and patches of bamboo for about five miles, gradually rose toward rugged Mount Natib, covered in huge trees, dense jungle growth, and innumerable ravines, precipitous crags, and cliffs.

The right side of II Corps was manned by the elite Philippine Scouts of the 57th Infantry. Their area of responsibility extended about 2,000 yards inland as well as down the coast to the little town of Balanga. The untried 41st Division manned the middle of the II Corps line, with its three regiments spread out abreast for

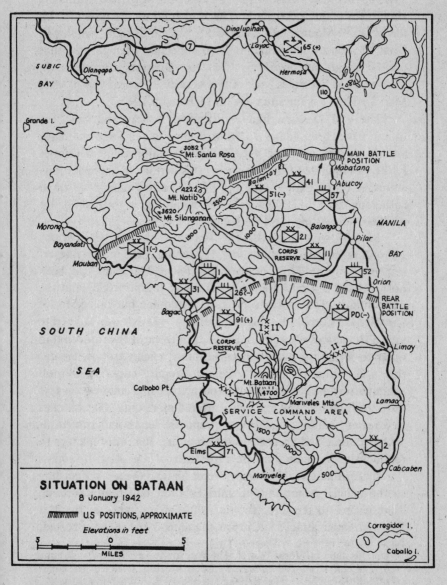

SITUATION ON BATAAN
8 January 1942

U.S POSITIONS, APPROXIMATE

Elevations in feet

MILES

Map 1

about 6,500 yards. The 41st Infantry was on the right, the 42nd
Infantry in the middle, and the 43rd Infantry on its left. The 51st
Division manned the left side of the line, with two regiments
abreast for about 5,000 yards. The 53rd Infantry was extended up
the slopes of Mount Natib and the 51st was to its right, running in
front of Abucay Hacienda, a small collection of nipa huts that
housed sugar cane workers. The 21st Division was placed in
reserve about five miles back of the Abucay Line near Guitol. (See
Map 2.) That was the situation on 15 January 1942.

The 41st Division had come under attack, and the 23rd
Infantry had been called up from reserve to reinforce the main
line of resistance of the 43rd Infantry. Major General George
Parker commanded II Corps during this period. In his operations
report he noted that "during the period 14-24 January, all three
battalions, 23rd Inf (PA) were singly committed to the main battle
position, supporting the 43rd Infantry (PA)."[2]

Marcos won a medal for bravery during this period.
According to his citation, on 15 January the main line of
resistance of the 23rd Infantry at Abucay Hacienda had been
pushed back several kilometers. The 31st Infantry (US) and the
45th Infantry (PS) tried to reestablish the line but failed. In his
capacity as "Combat Intelligence Officer," Marcos was ordered to
take a squad and reconnoiter the area in front of their position in
order to locate the main concentration of enemy troops. He did
this and, although under orders to report back to division
headquarters, he chose instead to participate in a counterattack of
the 23rd Infantry. The regiment suffered more than 300 casualties
as a result because of heavy aerial and artillery bombardment as
well as intense and accurate small arms fire, but it did manage to
reestablish the main line of resistance of the 41st Infantry.[3]

Unfortunately, this doesn't reconcile with the facts according
to the official history.* The 23rd Infantry had been called up
from reserve to reinforce the main line of resistance of the 41st
Division under attack, but it was the 43rd Infantry it supported,

---

* United States in World War II. The War in the Pacific Series. Volume
4. *The Fall of the Philippines,* by Louis Morton. Office of the Chief
of Military History, Department of the Army, Washington, D.C.,
1953.

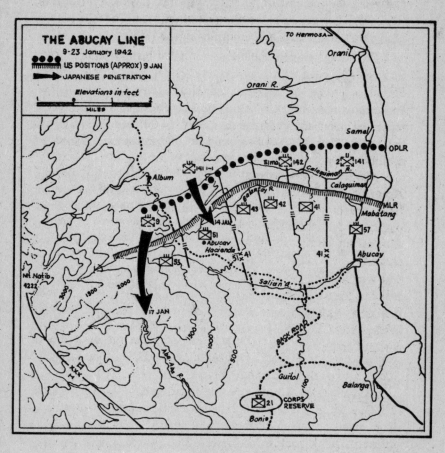

Map 2

not the 41st. In addition, the 31st Infantry (US), the only all-American regiment on Bataan, and the 45th Infantry (PS) referred to could not have "failed to reestablish the line" because they were not even on the front line yet. Both units, part of the Philippine Division, had been in USAFFE (U.S. Armed Forces Far East) reserve and were only called up on 16 January. The 31st arrived one mile east of Abucay Hacienda at 1900 on the 16th, and did not attack until the morning of the 17th. The 45th got lost and didn't arrive until early morning of the 18th.

With regards to the battle, the official history notes:

> Japanese pressure the next day, the 14th, was the heaviest on the left of the Abucay Line. Here the [Japanese] 141st Infantry hit the 43rd Infantry, forcing the outposts along the Balantay back across the river. The 51st Division to the left thereupon abandoned the main line of resistance and pulled back to positions on the south bank of the Balantay...It was here, at the boundary between the [43rd Infantry of the] 41st Division and the [51st Infantry of the] 51st Division that the main enemy blow came on the 15th with a strong attack by Imai's 141st Infantry. The reinforced 43rd on the left of the 41st Division, held firm...the fight continued throughout the day and at about 1600...Japanese troops crossed the river in the face of heavy fire and occupied a hill between the 51st and 43rd Infantry...The Japanese, at the end of the day, still retained their foothold on the south bank of the Balantay.[4]

There was no counterattack that day, and the main line of resistance of the 51st and 43rd Infantries had been forced back to the south side of the Balantay River.

The next day, 16 January, the Japanese continued the attack. The 51st Infantry regimental line gave way, but the 43rd Infantry to its right, according to the official history, "was now forced to refuse its flank back to the reserve line, where, under the calm guidance of Lieutenant Colonel Eugene T. Lewis, regimental instructor, it held against the repeated onslaughts of Imai's men."[5] There was no mention of Marcos or a counterattack.

For a citation to be fraught with so many inaccuracies is inexcusable. Regarding the S-2 and G-2 designations, there is no

such military occupational specialty (MOS) as "Combat Intelligence Officer." Although such an embellishment is dramatically
descriptive, the term does not exist in the military.

Nevertheless, Lieutenant Marcos was awarded the Philippine
Gold Cross Medal.* In fact, he was awarded it twice for this one
action, (GO 154, dated 20 December 1947, GHQ AFP, and GO
154, dated 20 December 1963, GHQ AFP), even though the
citation states, "The basis for this recommendation has not been
used for any previous award and will not be used for any future
recommendation."

---

* The US and Philippine medal equivalents are as follows:
  Congressional Medal of Honor — Medal of Valor;
  Distinguished Service Cross — Distinguished Conduct Star;
  Silver Star — Gold Cross

CHAPTER THREE

The U.S. Medals

In *Valor*, Baclagon commented on the alledged battle in which Marcos and the 23rd Infantry took part. He stated that "the battle action lasted for six days, from 15 to 21 January 1942. During most of the period Marcos was in the midst of the fight, so conspicuous in his display of courage that he was awarded the Silver Star and the Philippine equivalent of the Gold Cross Medal (sic)."[1]

However, he has somewhat confused the issue. Marcos supposedly won the Philippine Gold Cross for a battle on 15 January, but the action for which he won a U.S. Silver Star and its Philippine equivalent, the Gold Cross, did not take place on the main line of resistance. It was for an action back at the 21st Division reserve position, five miles to the rear, in Guitol, on 16 January. Assuming he was able to extract himself from the fighting at the main line of resistance and make it back to division headquarters, on that day he and three men "attacked and dislodged a greatly superior force which had captured the outpost and machine gun emplacements of the 21st Division in reserve, culminating in driving the enemy that were able to infiltrate in the bivouac area."

The quote is from an affidavit signed by Major Aurelio Lucero, and dated 1 February 1946. At the time of this action Lucero was a first lieutenant and the assistant to the G-1 officer in the 21st Division, and Marcos was a second lieutenant and the assistant to the G-2 officer. Four years after the action stated above, Lucero swore that the action did take place and that "in the latter part of Feb 42, Major Ferdinand E. Marcos, then a lieutenant, was awarded the Silver Star Medal in General Orders for gallantry in action in Guitol, Balanga, Bataan, on or about 16 Jan 42..."[2] This was Marcos' first U.S. decoration. Strangely, this action doesn't appear in either version (1965 and 1980) of Baclagon's first book. It appears in his book *Valor*, but in a somewhat confusing manner as described above. Marcos' biography also only mentions that he won a Silver Star but gives no details of the action.

The truth about Ferdinand Marcos and his war record is difficult to ascertain. However, after (1) reviewing documentation from Department of the Army; the U.S. Army Military History Institute at Carlisle Barracks, Pennsylvania; the MacArthur Memorial Archives in Norfolk, Virginia; the National Records Center; the U.S. Center of Military History; and the National Archives in Washington, D.C.; (2) reading scores of books and articles by and about the guerrillas in the Philippines in World War II; and (3) interviewing dozens of witnesses, the true story gradually emerged. Boni Gillego's pioneering research, along with that done by John Sharkey and Alfred W. McCoy in the National Archives, helped to clarify and resolve a lot of the mystery surrounding the medals.

At the U.S. Army's Carlyle Barracks in Pennsylvania, Sharkey found a typewritten manuscript entitled "History of the 21st Division." On its cover was a pencilled notation: "From General Capinpin but not necessarily by him." Brigadier General Mateo Capinpin was commanding officer of the 21st Division. This manuscript contradicts Marcos' claim and Lucero's affidavits. Marcos is mentioned several times, but no heroic deeds are attributed to him. In one instance it states that "Then Captain Ismael D. Lapus and then Lt. Ferdinand A. (sic) Marcos met the 31st Inf. (USA) at the Balanga Cadre and guided the American troops to the firing line."[3] The official history notes that the 31st Infantry (US) was moved into position near the Abucay Hacienda, about 6,000 yards north of Guitol, on the evening of 16

January, to assist the 51st Infantry.[4] (The 31st is the unit referred to in the citation for the Gold Cross Medal, which stated wrongly that the 31st was on the front lines on the 15th.)

This would seem to conflict with Marcos' claim; or, if it didn't, such a deed deserved at least equal mention as guide duty. Yet no action regarding Marcos' brave deed is mentioned in the History. Colonel Ray M. O'Day was the senior American instructor with the 21st Division. After the war he also prepared a history of the 21st, which covers the period from 1 December 1941 to 9 April 1942. It was submitted to the Office of the Chief of Military History, U.S. Army, and used by Louis Morton in writing the official history.[5] There are two brief references to Lieutenant Marcos but no mention of any heroic deeds or medals for heroism.[6]

Two days later, on 18 January, Marcos allegedly won his second U.S. medal. A battalion-size enemy force had infiltrated the USAFFE lines and caused a large number of casualties. According to the citation, artillery shells, mortars, and grenades falling in the area were threatening to disorganize the troops who were already in a state of confusion. Marcos and three men were ordered to locate the enemy position. They found it and, in the ensuing action, destroyed the artillery pieces, blew up the ammunition dump, and left behind 50 casualties, including eight officers.[7]

If that weren't enough to win the medal, the same citation noted that, on another occasion, Marcos took two men and somehow made it to the rear of the enemy lines to determine their strength. While crawling back, they were overpowered and taken prisoner, and, according to the citation, "While a prisoner in the enemy camp, he gathered valuable information from enemy sources. Having killed the guard, he released his two scouts and returned to his unit to submit the information he had gathered."

The medal is based on another affidavit submitted by Major Lucero and is also dated 1 February 1946. "For these actions," Lucero stated in his affidavit, "sometime in the latter part of March 1942, Major Ferdinand E. Marcos was awarded in Special Orders from Hq, USFIP [U.S. Forces in the Philippines], Fort

Mills, Corregidor, the Distinguished Service Cross..."[8]

This was truly an amazing feat deserving of a Distinguished Service Cross. However, the reason for Major Lucero's affidavit in 1946 was that somehow the orders got lost, just as the orders for the Silver Star had also gotten lost. So in 1946, Marcos wrote and inquired about the matter and included Lucero's affidavits. He received a letter back from U.S. Army Forces Pacific, dated 6 July 1946, that stated: "Based on your statements and the affidavits of witnesses, the validity of your claim for the award is acknowledged."[9]

A letter from the Department of the Army, dated 21 November 1985, confirmed that the only proof submitted for the awards were the affidavits executed by Lucero. Another letter from the Department of the Army, dated 12 December 1985, stated that "there are no General Orders or Special Orders from USAFFE confirming Marcos' entitlement to the Silver Star and Distinguished Service Cross. I have enclosed the only documents we have available which apparently confirm his entitlement."[10]

Sharkey's research found two official lists of 120 American and Filipino soldiers who were awarded the Distinguished Service Cross, which had been transmitted to the War Department in Washington, D.C., by General Wainwright on 11 and 12 April 1942, before he surrendered. Marcos' name does not appear. Also, after the war the machine records unit of General MacArthur's headquarters in Tokyo compiled a "List of Recipients of Awards and Decorations Issued Between Dec. 7, 1941, through June 30, 1945." Marcos' name does not appear.[11]

General Capinpin's history does not mention this action, but it does mention Marcos. After referring to the date of 18 January, it states that "on or about the same time, mortar and artillery shelling hit the bivouac camp, resulting in heavy casualties...The G-2 officer, then Captain Ismael D. Lapus and then Third Lieutenant Ferdinand A. (sic) Marcos led successive patrols to locate the enemy artillery but continuously failed."[12]

Colonel O'Day's history doesn't mention the action either. Nevertheless, Lieutenant Marcos was also awarded a Philippine Distinguished Conduct Star for this action (GO 24, dated 16 July 1956, GHQ AFP).

Thus far he had won a Gold Cross medal on the 15th, a Silver Star on the 16th, and a Distinguished Service Cross and Distinguished Conduct Star on the 18th. His next brave deed would win him his country's highest award for bravery—the Philippine Medal for Valor—and a recommendation for the Congressional U.S. Medal of Honor...supposedly.

CHAPTER FOUR

The Medal for Valor

This action allegedly took place from 22-26 January 1942, at the junction of the Salien and Abo-Abo Rivers. Marcos had reconnoitered the area and located the Japanese 9th Infantry Regiment which had skirted the left flank of the 51st Division (PA) on Mount Natib and encircled the left flank of II Corps. The 51st had been routed and forced to withdraw three miles south to Barrio Guitol, Balanga. They attempted several counterattacks with the support of other units but failed to regain their position.

According to the citation, Marcos "...realizing that the defense of the Salien junction was crucial to the entire USAFFE strategy and that it was unprotected because all units in accordance with plans and orders were withdrawing to a new line of defense along the Pilar-Bagac road...without awaiting orders from his superiors, hastily organized a company-size blocking force from remnants of the 3rd Battalion, 21st Infantry, 21st Division, and stragglers of the 51st Division."[1]

The citation went on to state that Marcos and his men held off a Japanese force of about 2,000 men for five days and "delayed considerably the fall of Bataan." A book published by the Philippine government entitled *Documents on the Marcos War Medals*, contains a map of the alleged action. (See Map 3.)

The citation is based on another affidavit prepared by the same Aurelio Lucero, dated 14 June 1946. In it Lucero claims that General Capinpin received a call from General Wainwright on 2 April 1942. After the conversation Capinpin informed Lucero

that all officers recommended for promotion had been confirmed, which included the promotion of Ferdinand Marcos to
Captain. Capinpin also informed Lucero that General
Wainwright "had agreed to the suggestion of Gen. Mateo
Capinpin that the Division Commander recommend for the
award of the Congressional Medal of Honor then Captain (newly
promoted) Ferdinand E. Marcos." Lucero then drafted the
recommendation, had Capinpin sign it, and handcarried it to
General Wainwright. However, no action was ever taken on the
recommendation and all the records were lost during the final
days of fighting which led to the surrender of Bataan.[2]

There are military regulations for the awarding of medals
with which General Capinpin must have been familiar. These
regulations did not require that General Wainwright communi-
cate the agreement before the recommendation was made. The
delay of nine weeks, from 26 January to 2 April, before even
putting in the recommendation is inexplicable. Such an action
would have been a significant feat, bringing glory not only to
Marcos, but to the 21st Division and all Filipinos as well. Until
that time only two men had won the Congressional Medal of
Honor during World War II, and both were on Bataan.*

At the end of Colonel O'Day's history of the 21st Division,
under "Status as of April 9, 1942," all American and Filipino
officers are listed, along with their rank and position. Marcos is
listed as a "1st Lieutenant, Asst. G-2." If any officers in the 21st
were promoted, O'Day would have known about it.

According to the book, *Documents on the Marcos War
Medals*, Lucero actually made two sworn statements regarding
this action — one on 14 June 1946 and another on 15 June 1946.
Both state basically the same thing. However, the affidavits he
signed on 1 February 1946, attesting to the Silver Star and
Distinguished Service Cross actions, are signed by "Major Aurelio
Lucero, ASN 0-45818." The affidavits he signed four months
later, on 14 and 15 June 1946, attesting to the Medal of Honor
recommendation, are signed "Colonel Aurelio Lucero," and one

---

* Jose Callugas, Mess Sgt., Battery B, 88th Field Artillery.
  Alexander R. Nininger, Lt., 3rd Bn., 57th Infantry (PS).

Battle Action at the Junction
of Abo Abo and Salian Rivers
22-26 January 1942

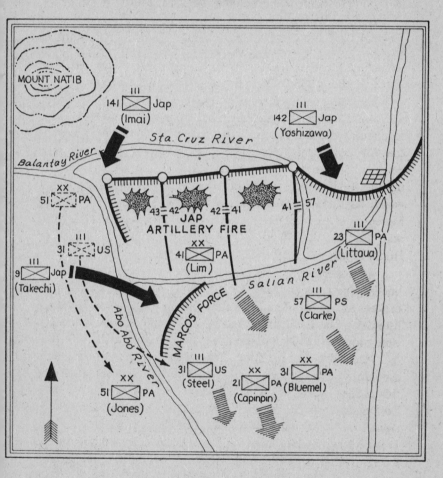

Map 3

of these gives his serial number as 0-2081. Lucero's serial number wasn't changed from a five-digit reserve number to a four-digit regular army number until 7 May 1950, and he wasn't promoted to lieutenant colonel until 1955. Not only that, he signed another affidavit three months later, entitled "Affidavit For Philippine Army Personnel," on 7 September 1946, as "Major, 0-45818."

General Wainwright survived the war, was promoted to full General, and awarded the Congressional Medal of Honor for his brave stand on Bataan and Corregidor. He wrote a book about his experiences* but Marcos is never mentioned.

Colonel John R. Vance is now 88 years old and living in Corte Madera, California. He was General MacArthur's finance officer and served on the awards and decorations board from early January 1942 until the surrender. Romulo, then a lieutenant colonel, was also appointed to the board by General Wainwright. Others on the board were a Judge Advocate officer named Lynch and a Major George Muzzey. In an interview, Colonel Vance stated that only two or three men were ever recommended for the Medal of Honor, and Marcos was not one of them. He couldn't recall Marcos' name ever being recommended for any award.[3] As already noted, Romulo's Voice of Freedom radio broadcasts and books never mentioned Marcos either.

This brave deed of 22-26 January 1942 went unheralded for 16 years until 1958, when Marcos was awarded the Philippines' highest award for bravery—the Medal for Valor (GO 167, dated 16 October 1958, GHQ AFP). There was no explanation as to why the Philippine government did not feel obliged to act on General Capinpin's recommendation for 16 years. By then both Wainwright and Capinpin had died.

The book, *Documents on the Marcos War Medals*, also contains a copy of a "Recommendation for Award of the Congressional Medal of Honor," signed by General Mateo Capinpin and dated 3 February 1946. This letter of recommendation was not referred to in Lucero's sworn statement that was the basis of the 1958 citation which stated:

---

* *General Wainwright's Story*, (New York: Doubleday & Co., 1946)

> ...in accordance with the records of this Headquarters, *including the recommendation of Brigadier General Mateo Capinpin, Commanding General, 21st Division, USAFFE (later USFIP), dated 3 April 1942, for the award of the United States Congressional Medal of Honor, which was reconstituted in a Sworn Statement, dated 14 June 1946, by then Major Aurelio L. Lucero...*

The intriguing question is: Why was it necessary in June 1946, to reconstitute a recommendation that General Capinpin made in 1942, when he was still alive and well in the Armed Forces of the Philippines, and had already made another recommendation in February 1946? It is also somewhat odd that General Capinpin would prepare a recommendation in 1946, for an action that occurred in 1942, when U.S. Army regulations require that such a recommendation be made within two years and awarded within three years.

Did Lieutenant Marcos and a hundred men hold off 2,000 Japanese for five days? An examination of documentation of that period will provide some insight as to what happened.

The U.S. Army official history noted that on 19 January 1942, Lieutenant General Akira Nara, commanding officer of the Japanese 65th Brigade, began reinforcing the 141st Infantry, led by Colonel Takeo Imai, in preparation for an all-out attack on 22 January, on the left flank of the II Corps line. In the meantime, the 9th Infantry led by Colonel Susumu Takechi, who had orders to circle around behind the American positions, continued his advance around the left flank. The 9th had already been observed on several occasions. On 18 January, artillery spotters reported a Japanese force moving southeast down the Abo Abo River valley. On 19 January, a patrol of Philippine Scouts from the 45th Infantry reported that an enemy force had already passed around the II Corps flank. Also, noted the official history:

> [On the morning of the 19th]...Patrols of the 21st Infantry attempted to hold up advance elements of the 9th but were easily routed...[That afternoon] the Japanese met and engaged elements of the 21st and 31st Divisions before Guitol. The former promptly withdrew, but the green untried

31st Division troops remained...The reason for the withdrawal of the 21st Division (PA) elements on the afternoon of the 19th is not clear.[4]

By 21 January, Takechi's 9th had seized the high ground along the Guitol Trail, running from Guitol to Abucay Hacienda, which dominated the left and rear of the II Corps line. All attempts to retake it were unsuccessful.

The 31st Infantry (US) and the 45th Infantry (PS) of the Philippine Division, had replaced the 51st on the left side of the II Corps line. These were elite troops. The 31st was the only all-American unit on Bataan, and the 45th was a Philippine Scout unit. Only the best of the Philippine soldiers was selected for enlistment in the Scouts. Numerous attacks were made to restore the left side of the II Corps line, but they were unsuccessful. The official history noted that "The terrain, dense vegetation, and the lack of accurate information about the enemy [was a big problem]."[5]

The II Corps Operations Report noted:

About 9:00 PM, 21 January, a Japanese force attacked the 31st Division (PA)* from the east and north. The 3rd Battalion, 21st Infantry (PA) was ordered to counter-attack at 7:00 AM, 22 January. The attack was launched but the enemy had withdrawn during the night.[6]

This withdrawal was probably effected in order to regroup in preparation for their next attack. The Japanese offensive began on 22 January with an air and artillery barrage. Colonel Imai's reinforced 141st Infantry then attacked. All of this concerted effort was against the 31st and 45th. They were gradually forced back, and by nightfall had formed a new line east and south of Abucay Hacienda, approximately the same place they had been five days earlier when they began their counterattack.

That night General MacArthur gave the order for a progressive evacuation of the entire front line back to the Pilar-Bagac road, beginning on the evening of 23 January. The

---

* Not to be confused with the 31st Infantry (US).

heavy artillery and service installations moved back that night. The next night the combat elements began to move back, protected, according to the official history, by "...a covering force, led by General Lough of the Philippine Division."[7] This thin line of resistance extended from Balanga westward to Guitol, and was manned from right to left by "...remnants of the 51st Division, the 33rd Infantry (PA), a battalion of the 31st Infantry (PA), one-third of the 57th Infantry (PS), and one-third of the 31st Infantry (US)."[8]

These units were ordered to withdraw to this line starting at 7:00 P.M., 24 January, hold it until 11:30 P.M., 25 January, and then fall back. (See Map 4.)

General Nara actually had no suspicion the American line was being abandoned. He was simply acting on insistent orders from General Homma to finish the battle of Bataan at once.[9] The Japanese did not become aware of the withdrawal until later, on the night of 24-25 January. The official history noted:

> As the men began to move out of the line, heading east toward Abucay and the East Road, the Japanese hit the thin covering shell. Against determined Japanese onslaughts the shell held long enough to permit the bulk of the men to withdraw.[10]

Toland noted in his account that "The thin protective shell didn't break. Officers worked up and down the screen, encouraging the men."[11]

The official history continued:

> At about 0300 of the 25th, the last of the Americans of the 31st Infantry, covered by heavy fire from the 194th Tank Bn, staggered out of their positions, looking "like walking dead men"... the withdrawal continued throughout the night of 24-25 January, all the next day and on through the night, with the Japanese in full pursuit. On the 25th Japanese aircraft were out in full force, bombing and strafing the retreating soldiers. From early morning until dusk, enemy planes bombs and diving low to spray the road with machine gun bullets...[12]

Captured enemy documents translated after the war by the Allied and Translator Section (ATIS) of the U.S. Army provide

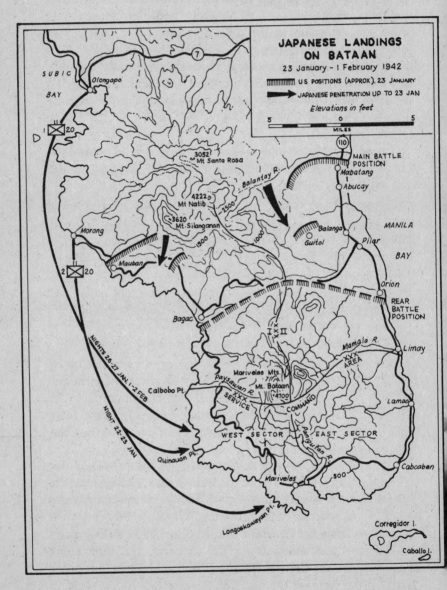

Map 4

an insight into what was happening on the other side. A report of General Nara's 65th Brigade noted on 24 January:

> As night fell, both front line flank units again resumed their fierce attack. At 1930 hours the right flank unit finally broke through the enemy positions on the front and, shouting their battle cries in the moonlight, pursued the retreating enemy. They evicted the enemy from every position, and their attack became an heroic night pursuit...[13]

Colonel O'Day noted in his history that the 21st Division had been assigned a position on the Pilar-Bagac road, the final line of resistance:

> We designated the 22nd Infantry for the right and the 23rd Infantry for the left of our sector, with the 21st Infantry in division reserve. McCafferty, Wappensteinl, and Mead [American instructors of the 22nd, 21st, and 23rd Infantries respectively. All were lieutenant colonels] were informed of the plan and I believe each managed to make a quick reconnaissance before evening...by night of the 25/26th all our battalions had gone into position.[14]

The last of the II Corps units were moved into position on 26 January. They were covered by two tank battalions stretched out along the north-south Back Road near Bani, and supported by 75 mm guns. They came under heavy attack by the Japanese 141st supported by artillery and low-flying aircraft, but held until the units had a chance to dig in.

The evidence for the action described in the Medal for Valor/Medal of Honor recommendation just isn't there. The official history doesn't mention it. The II Corps Operations Report noted that the *3rd Battalion, 21st Infantry Regiment* was attached to Brigadier General Clifford Bluemel's 31st Division on 21 January, and attacked on 22 January, but they didn't encounter anyone. Colonel O'Day noted that all battalions of the 21st Division were on the new line of resistance by the night of 25/26 January. The only delaying force mentioned in all accounts was led by General Lough and manned by *remnants of the 51st*

Division, the 33rd Infantry (PA), a battalion of 31st Infantry (PA), one-third of the 57th Infantry (PS), and one-third of the 31st Infantry (US). The blocking force that Marcos supposedly organized — the 3rd Battalion, 21st Infantry and stragglers of the 51st Division — were with Bluemel and Lough respectively. The Japanese after-action report didn't mention any blocking force that delayed their advance any longer than a day or so, nor is it mentioned in Capinpin's history or Toland's book.

The action described in Marcos' citation sounds very brave, but from a military perspective it doesn't make much sense. Junior officers don't go around grabbing men from other units to go on missions; and no one goes off on any mission without orders from a higher authority. As a lieutenant, Marcos did not know the overall situation in II Corps. Indeed, as a junior officer he could not even question the reasons for an order to withdraw or attack.

A general, Maxon Lough of the prestigious Philippine Division, had been ordered to take charge of a delaying force which had already been selected. A retrograde movement of this magnitude is very complex, and no job for a lieutenant with limited military training and experience. A line from Balanga to Guitol had already been selected for Lough and his men to try and hold during the withdrawal. This location had been selected by general officers at corps level, not lieutenants at division level.

If Lieutenant Marcos and his small band had been at the junction of the Abo Abo and Salien Rivers, as alleged, they would have run into two very elite units — the 31st Infantry (US) and the 45th Infantry (PS) — falling back on the 24th, as ordered. Toland noted on the 24th that "the two regiments of the Philippine Division [the 31st and 45th] retreated thankfully. They knew they had been outflanked and would have been surrounded. The remaining stragglers of Jones' 51st Division also were slogging back, wondering how they had escaped almost certain destruction."[15]

How Lieutenant Marcos and a hundred men would expect to keep from being outflanked — something that two elite regiments couldn't prevent — is beyond comprehension.

There was no blocking force at that junction on 22 January

or during that period. The 3rd Battalion, 21st Infantry were on their way to their new defensive position, and the 51st remnants were falling back. General Lough's thin line of resistance held for about 30 hours, not five days, and that was a Herculean effort. It was General Maxon S. Lough and his men, along with General James R.N. Weaver and his tanks, that prevented the decimation of the withdrawing troops, not Lieutenant Ferdinand Marcos.

By 26 January, the new line of resistance was manned along the Pilar-Bagac road,* running east-west across Bataan. On that morning General Bluemel walked up Trail 2** and inspected the forward area of the II Corps main line of resistance he had been assigned to hold. It was designated Sector C, about two and one-half miles wide in the center of the main line of resistance (MLR). To his amazement he found a ghostfront. No one was there. General Parker, the II Corps commander, had pulled out half of Bluemel's troops and put them in other positions miles to the east. Bluemel was supposed to have been informed but was not because of a snafu. He frantically ran around searching for men to plug this gigantic hole that existed on the right side of Trail 2. By midnight he had found enough troops to fill each foxhole They were thinly stretched but the gap was plugged.

Toland noted that "Every foxhole on Trail 2 was filled and excited young Filipino officers crept from foxhole to foxhole passing on Bluemel's dramatic exhortation: 'Here you stay and here you die!' Even so, this area should have been held by a Division. Every one of those men would have to do the work of three."[16]

The next day, at 3:00 P.M., Colonel Takechi's 9th Infantry attacked down Trail 2, and Colonel Imai's 141st attacked on his right. They were stopped. Another attack that night also failed. The 41st Infantry Regiment arrived during the night to reinforce Bluemel's thinly stretched line. The next day, 28 January, at dusk,

---

* A four-mile-long branch road, or cutoff, had been constructed from Orion to the Pilar-Bagac road, and the eastern portion of the II Corps line actually extended along this cutoff rather than along the road itself.

** An ingenious network of trails just wide enough for a truck was cut through the jungle.

after a one-hour artillery bombardment, there was another attack down Trail 2. Again the line held. And again they attacked. This went on for three days. Japanese reinforcements were brought up and were also stopped with the aid of artillery. Bluemel counterattacked on 2 February, and the Japanese broke off their attack and pulled back during the night. It was the end of the attack on Trail 2. Toland noted: *Bluemel's thin, stubborn line had momentarily saved Bataan.*[17] Somehow this sentence was paraphrased in Marcos' 1958 award for the Medal For Valor. The last sentence reads in part "...Major Marcos prevented the possible decimation of the withdrawing USAFFE troops and delayed considerably the inevitable fall of Bataan."

Two other battles were taking place besides the one on Trail 2. About the same time as the Trail 2 attack, I Corps was attacked and about 1,000 Japanese troops managed to break through the main line of resistance. Because of the jungle and mountainous terrain, they went undetected for three days. Called the Battle of the Pockets, it took more than a week to drive them out. On 10 February, 400 Japanese survivors slipped away during the night. Farther south, on the tip of Bataan, several Japanese boat landings had put about 1,200 troops ashore. Called the Battle of the Points, it finally ended on 8 February, when the last of the group was isolated near Quinauan Point and destroyed.

After the attack on Trail 2 enemy activity diminished considerably. A stalemate continued throughout February. The front line was strengthened and patrols probed the enemy. During this period Lieutenant Marcos supposedly won another medal. The only account of this action is in Baclagon's book, but it is too vague to determine the exact time or place of the action which he describes:

> ...Marcos led several patrols that penetrated deep into enemy territory. It was the report of Lt. Marcos on the strength and disposition of Japanese forces in Bataan that first brought out the precarious situation of the enemy...The intelligence reports submitted by Lt. Marcos were obtained under hazardous conditions for which reason he was awarded the

Gold Cross for gallantry in action. (GO 123, dated 20 March 1948, HNDF.)[18]

In the biography by Hartzell Spence, Marcos is mentioned as having a "sporty Oldsmobile," with which he "ranged up and down the north highway [gathering intelligence] as the USAFFE gave way" during the retreat to Bataan in the early days of the war.[19] Again there is no reference to such an activitiy in any other publication. However, Toland does mention another member of the 21st Division who drove his yellow convertible to Bataan during the retreat. Antonio Aquino was the son of Benigno Aquino, the sugar-cane king, Speaker of the Philippine Assembly, and President Quezon's Secretary of Commerce and Agriculture. "Tony" had recently been admitted to the bar when the war broke out, so he joined up as a third lieutenant with the 21st Division. When they were ordered to Bataan he took his convertible with him. By February 1942, it was somewhat battered and showing signs that it had been in a war, but it still ran so he used it on what he considered an important mission. He drove it to the tip of Bataan and, just before dark, hired a fisherman to take him to Corregidor. About a mile off the island the fisherman refused to go any further, thinking he might get shot as an infiltrator, so Aquino dove in and swam the rest of the way. He made this dangerous trip to see President Quezon, who was a friend of the family, to complain that the Americans vere getting better food than the Filipinos. He was able to see President Quezon and General MacArthur, and the rations were improved. Tony Aquino had a brother, Benigno, Jr., who was only eight at the time.[20]

CHAPTER FIVE

The Final Battle of Bataan

During this period General Homma asked for artillery and infantry reinforcements. At the same time, at Imperial General Headquarters in Tokyo, another attack on Bataan was planned. It would be a concentrated air and artillery bombardment on a two and one-half mile front in front of Mount Samat. It was planned to begin in early April.

On March 11, General MacArthur reluctantly made his daring escape from Corregidor by PT boat. Wainwright was promoted to lieutenant general and took over as Commanding General, USFIP. After the lull in February enemy activity increased in March. There was intermittent shelling and daily reports of large truck and materiel movements. Aerial activity and artillery bombardments increased. Enemy patrols became more aggressive. Skirmishes began flaring up along the outpost line. The enemy was seen massing in front of Sector D. On 28 March, a regimental-size force probed the lines in front of the 42nd Infantry. The second, and final, Battle of Bataan was about to begin.

On 3 April 1942, Good Friday, the main line of resistance (MLR) was mostly along the Pilar-Bagac road. The Pantingan River bisected this line, and II Corps' responsibility was on the right (eastern) side. The II Corps MLR was split into four sectors—A,B,C, and D. Sector D was on the extreme left, from the Pantingan River to Kilometer Post 136, a distance of about 5,000 yards. This sector was commanded by General Lough, and

consisted of the 41st Division, commanded by Brigadier General
Vicente Lim, and the 21st Division, commanded by Brigadier
General Mateo Capinpin. The 41st contained three regiments —
the 41st, 42nd, and 43rd Infantries — and controlled about 2,500
yards of the left side. The 21st also contained three regiments —
the 21st, 22nd, and 23rd Infantries — and controlled the other half
of Sector D, in front of Mount Samat. (See Map 5.)

General Homma had chosen the area in front of the 41st
Division as the main thrust of the attack. The Japanese 65th
Brigade, commanded by Lieutenant General Akira Nara, would
head the assault. Nara knew he was facing General Lim, the first
Filipino graduate of West Point, class of 1914. They were old
friends. Both had attended infantry school at Fort Benning,
Georgia, and graduated in 1928. Nara had also attended Amherst
College and was a classmate of President Coolidge's son.

The final assault began at 0900. The Japanese artillery began
to register their guns. At 1000 they fired for effect. For five hours
the 41st Division and part of the 21st Infantry endured a
devastating air and artillery barrage. At 1500, the 65th, led by
tanks, attacked. At the same time the Right Wing of the Japanese
4th Division, led by Lieutenant General Kureo Taniguchi and
consisting of tanks, the 61st Infantry, and a battalion of the 8th
Infantry attacked the middle of Sector D between the 41st and
21st Divisions. By that evening Taniguchi had advanced about
1,000 yards.

The assault the next morning, 4 April, began with another air
and artillery bombardment. There is no doubt the men of the 41st
and 21st Divisions fought bravely. But such devastating bombardments, followed by tank-led infantry assaults, began to take
its toll on the tired, sick, and starving soldiers who had held their
own for three months. That morning the 21st Division was forced
to pull back. First the 21st Infantry, next to the 43rd Infantry, was
forced back. Noted the official history:

> On the left the 21st Infantry fell back in disorder before the
> crushing attack of the Japanese tanks...the 23rd Infantry,
> already under pressure from the tank column to the
> west...began to fall back at about 1000. The 22nd...followed
> suit soon after.[1]

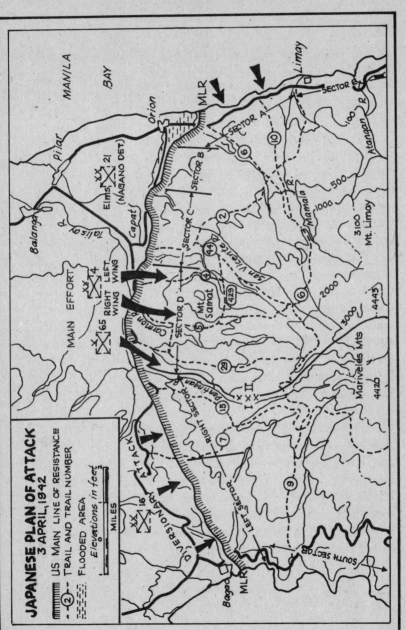

Map 5

By nightfall on Saturday, 4 April, the entire Sector D main line of resistance was in Japanese possession, and Taniguchi's Right Wing was in the foothills of Mount Samat.

On 5 April, at 1000 on Easter Sunday, after another air and artillery bombardment, the Japanese Right Wing's 4th Division and the Left Wing attacked down Trail 4. This trail ran north-south for about two and one-half miles. From the Pilar-Bagac road it skirted the eastern side of Mount Samat and ended at the junction of the east-west Trail 429. Part of the Right Wing, led by Colonel Gempachi Sato, secured the top of Mount Samat at 1250. Taniguchi continued his attack down Trail 4, and Sato continued down the southern slope of Mount Samat. At 1630 the headquarters of the 21st Division was overrun by Sato, and Capinpin was captured. The rest of the men retreated down Trail 429. By nightfall Sato and Taniguchi joined forces and set up their command post at the junction of Trails 4 and 429. (See Map 6.)

The Operations Report of USAFFE-USFIP noted on 5 April:

> Hostile pressure continued, direction of attack southeast. The 21st Division, which had withdrawn, broke in complete disorder and the entire Divison ceased to exist as a unit.[2]

Lieutenant Marcos supposedly won another medal that day. According to the citation, after sustaining a shrapnel wound in his abdomen, Marcos gathered together some stragglers on Trail No. 4 at Mount Samat and led the men back to the new main line of resistance. Through his insistence that this line be maintained he was able to persuade all regimental commanders to abandon their earlier plan of withdrawing from that line.[3]

That action is inconsistent with official accounts of what happened during that period. There was no "new main line of resistance" after the command post had been overrun. Not only did all regimental commanders of the 21st Division not maintain their resistance line on 5 April, the entire division had broken in disarray during the withdrawal.

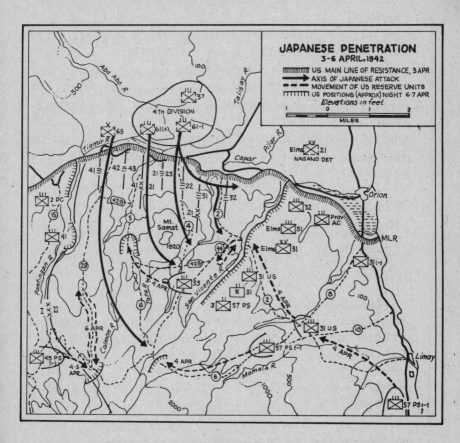

Map 6

Colonel O'Day noted in his history on 5 April:

> It was felt advisable to get in rear of the artillery positions.
> Marcos said he knew of a trail leading around to the east of
> the positions to in rear of Trail 6 (sic).[4]

This would have placed Marcos somewhere to the south and
west of the junction of Trails 4 and 429 on the afternoon of April
5, after the command post had been overrun. They were
retreating, not attacking. Despite the inaccuracies, he was
awarded the Philippine Gold Cross Medal for this action 12 years
later (GO 131-051, dated 21 January 1954, HNDF).

For some unexplained reason he was not awarded the
Philippine Wounded Personnel Medal for the shrapnel wound he
incurred during this action until 1963 (GO 155, dated 20
December 1963, GHQ AFP). This particular general order
awarded him three Wounded Personnel Medals—one for the 5
April action, another for an action on 7 April, and another for an
action on 17 March 1945.

There is a lot of confusion surrounding Marcos' promotions
and wounds, in addition to the confusion surrounding his awards.
One document obtained from the Department of the Army,
entitled "Affidavit for Philippine Army Personnel," which
Marcos executed and signed on 6 February 1946, claimed the
following promotions:

Organization	Rank	Authority	Effective Date
21st Division	3rd Lt.	Orig. Rank	15 Nov 41
21st Division	1st Lt.	SO 39, Par 2	10 Feb 42
21st Division	Capt.	Unknown	1 Apr 42
Maharlika Guer.	Major	Unknown	1 Dec 42
Maharlika Guer.	Lt. Col.	Unknown	1 Jan 44

As already noted, Colonel O'Day had Marcos listed as a first
lieutenant on 9 April 1942. There are no records of any other
promotion, other than the sworn statement of Marcos. The
promotions to captain, major, and lieutenant colonel were
self-promotions and will be explained later.

The same affidavit, under "Record of Wounds and Illnesses," lists a mortar wound on 7 April 1942, gastric ulcer-malaria-
beriberi during the period April to June 1942, a bullet wound of
the right thigh sometime in February 1943, a gastric ulcer in June
1943, and black water fever. The date for the black water fever is
illegible on the affidavit as is the exact date of the bullet wound in
February 1943.

Under "Decorations, Citations, and Awards," Marcos listed
the Distinguished Service Cross, Oak Leaf Cluster DSC (which
means a second Distinguished Service Cross), and a Silver Star.
The second DSC has never been accounted for. He also claims a
second Silver Star which was not listed in the affidavit. It should
be noted that such an affidavit is not proof of his promotions,
wounds, or awards. It is a sworn statement by an individual,
under penalty of courts-martial for false swearing, who claimed
service in the Philippine Commonwealth Army or the recognized
guerrillas during World War II in the Philippines. These claims
would have to be authenticated from official records.

There is no mention in the affidavit of any wounds received
on 5 April 1942 although Marcos' Gold Cross citation states, "Un-
mindful of the shrapnel wound in his abdomen." However, in the
book, *Valor,* while describing the action around this time, it states
that "At the height of the battle, Captain Ferdinand E. Marcos
was hit by a mortar shrapnel which tore into his right side. By a
freak of fate, a bullet from a sniper smacked into the wound
itself...At this time he learned that General Capinpin had been
captured by the enemy."[5]

Since there is no specific time mentioned, it is difficult to
determine whether this refers to a wound on 5 April, 7 April, or
two wounds on the same day. He may have been wounded on 7
April since this was a period of total disintegration in II Corps,
but the citation for his Wounded Personell Medal does not
reconcile with the facts. It states that on 7 April "Col. Marcos,
then a Major, was leading a group of soldiers in the vicinity of the
Division Command Post of the 21st Division at Mt. Samat,
Bataan, to rescue Brig. Gen. Mateo Capinpin from the enemy
when he was wounded."[6]

Marcos was not a major, and there was no 21st Division

command post after 5 April 1942. The site of the last command post, at the junction of Trails 4 and 429, was now occupied by the enemy for at least a thousand yards in every direction. (See Map 7.) Waiting two days, until 7 April, before attempting a rescue at a time when almost all of II Corps was being overrun is inconceivable.

The official history noted on 6 April:

Encircled and isolated, the Filipinos sought desperately to break through the Japanese ring and make their way to safety. Most were killed or captured, but some escaped. Of these a small number reached the American lines. The news they brought of the disintegration of the 21st Division and the strength of the Japanese on Trail 4 was disquieting.[7]

And goes on:

The story of the last two days of Bataan is one of progressive disintegration and final collapse.[8]

By 7 April, the Japanese attack had become an onslaught. At midnight of the 8th, Major General Edward P. King, Luzon Force Commander, decided that to continue would only lead to the needless slaughter of more brave men. Bataan surrendered on 9 April. General Wainwright held out for another month on Corregidor and finally surrendered on 6 May.

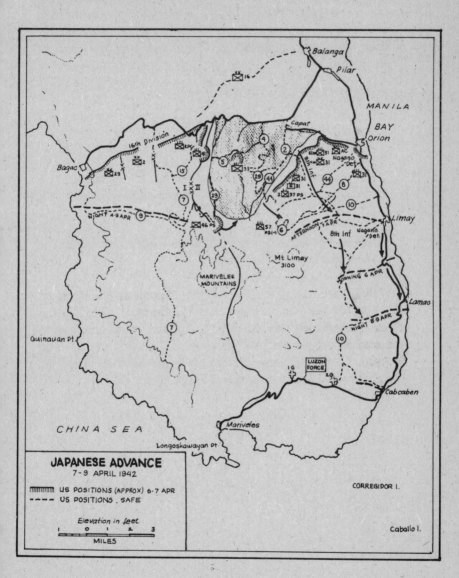

Map 7

CHAPTER SIX

Subjugation and Resistance

The infamous Death March began the day after General King surrendered Bataan on 9 April 1942. Of the 76,000 that surrendered, 12,000 were Americans. About 70,000 made the march—55 miles from Mariveles to San Fernando. From there they were herded into freight cars and taken to Capas, Tarlac, 25 miles further north, and then marched 8 miles west to Camp O'Donnell, an unfinished Philippine Army camp which was supposed to have been for the training of recruits. (It was located about 13 miles north of present-day Clark Air Base.) The whole trip took about 10 days. Seven to 10,000 died on the march, including about 2,330 Americans, from malaria, exhaustion, starvation, beatings, or execution.[1] Another 29,000 Filipino and American soldiers would die before the camp was closed around March 1943.

The camp was a terrible place. To quote the officer that had been placed in charge of burials:

> There were no sanitary facilities, no utilities, no water supply, no trees. Most of the prisoners had to live in the open spaces, without protection from the heat of the sun and occasional rain. It was truly Hell...Men started dying like fleas. By July, more than 500 daily were being buried...Everybody was sick. There were insufficient men with enough strength to carry the dead to the cemetery. The Japanese found a solution. They issued the order I called "Parole home to die." The order directed that all "seriously sick but could stand up" would be

sent home (to be buried by his family). Those who were so sick that [they] could not stand up would remain in camp to wait for their death and burial. Those who were not seriously ill would also remain in camp to constitute the burial details.[2]

Twenty-one years later Marcos would be awarded the Distinguished Conduct Star (GO 158, dated 20 December 1963, GHQ AFP) for a series of events that supposedly transpired from 4 August 1942, the day he was released from Camp O'Donnell, to December 1944.

He was released because he suffered from a gastric ulcer, malaria, and beri-beri. The next day, 5 August, according to the citation, he was arrested by the Kempetai and taken to Fort Santiago and, "was subjected to the most incredible forms of human torture."[3]

There is in existence in the Philippines a group which calls itself the Association of Survivors of Japanese Prisons. Its members were all incarcerated in Fort Santiago by the Japanese Kempetai. Just the mention of the word back then conjured up all that was evil and terrible about the Japanese. One of their duties was "preparing" prisoners for trial by "questioning" them until they procured the information they were seeking. Such preparation might go on for days, weeks, months, or longer. Many never made it to trial, having died in the preparation of their case.

The prisoner was then usually taken to the Old Bilibid prison where he was incarcerated during his trial and sentencing. Afterwards he was taken away to New Bilibid prison (now the present-day Muntilupa prison) to begin serving his sentence...if he were lucky. For some the judge would announce at the trial that the prisoner would be sentenced later. This usually meant that he would be taken to the cemetery that night for execution, usually by bayonetting or decapitation (beheading). Such a form of execution may sound ghastly but efficient. For some it was just ghastly. Not all Japanese soldiers knew how to wield a sword, and not all swords were sharp. When an execution didn't go well the word got around. The Japanese would know and so would the prisoners.

In interviewing some of the survivors, several pictures

emerge. One is awful—of beatings, torture, rape, and other inhuman cruelties; another is despicable—of Filipino informers making their weekly visit to the offices of the Kempetai to collect their Judas money; and still another is of courage almost indescribable—of men and women lying in their own pools of blood, the pain of their torture mixed with the shame of their degradation, and the agony of the certainty that they were going to die. Later they would be called patriots, but such a name doesn't begin to describe their bravery or the horrors they endured. Some broke. Others didn't. The survivors are kind to both. Their message: If you weren't there, and didn't go through it, then don't judge.

In this other-worldly setting the prisoners became bound to each other in a way that cannot be explained to those who never suffered their ordeal. In this brotherhood of human suffering they established their own system of communication. One prisoner, Raul Manglapus, received a warning from Fort Santiago three days before his arrest that the Kempetai were looking for him. But he decided not to run away. They would just arrest his mother instead if he did. So he waited. Manglapus had been a law student at Ateneo when the war broke out. Already known as a brilliant orator, and poet and songwriter as well, he went to work as a radio broadcaster for then Major Carlos P. Romulo, executive press relations officer to General MacArthur. When MacArthur and his staff retreated to Corregidor, Manglapus stayed behind and published an underground newspaper. He was arrested in August 1942, tortured, tried, and sentenced to 10 years imprisonment. He managed to escape in a daring jailbreak on 25 August 1944, involving 88 prisoners, and joined the Hunters Guerrillas for the duration of the war. After the war he continued serving his country, and today Senator Manglapus is a widely respected politician. As a former prisoner and member of the Association he has a list of all prisoners who were tried and sentenced. Marcos is not on the list, but the senator pointed out that Marcos supposedly escaped before he could be tried and sentenced. However, he still doubts that Marcos was ever incarcerated in Fort Santiago.

Another former prisoner who escaped with Manglapus, a

Jesuit priest now living in Honolulu, Father Jaime Neri, helped plan the jailbreak. He recalled the day when Colonel Straughn was brought in. It wasn't announced but word got around. He also remembers Lieutenant Colonel Nakar. Both were later executed. Father Neri said that very little went unnoticed at Fort Santiago. Very little. And no one recalls Marcos being there.

At Fort Santiago today there is a plaque placed on the remains of an old building destroyed by allied bombers during the liberation of Manila. It states:

> Ferdinand E. Marcos, Captain, USAFFE, was detained here August 5, 1942, to August 12, 1942. He escaped August 12, 1942, while on work detail in Tayabas, Tayabas, now Quezon Province.

The Association did not put up the plaque, and the donor's name isn't stated.

On a visit to Fort Santiago in 1986, Colonel Gustavo Ingles reminisced about his capture and imprisonment in Fort Santiago. He was beaten and tortured but never admitted that he was a member of the Hunters Guerrillas that he helped found. He pointed out the back entrance where the prisoners were brought in and the location of the buildings where they were detained while awaiting their fate. Across the compound, on the other side of the fort, were the ruins of the offices of the Kempetai. That is where Marcos' plaque is placed. Colonel Ingles also managed to escape in a daring pre-dawn raid staged by the Hunters on 25 June 1944. This raid and escape gave Father Neri and the others the idea for the 25 August 1944 escape.

After supposedly undergoing eight days of torture, Marcos then, in the guise of relenting, led a Japanese search party to a boat anchorage where, as surreptitiously arranged, it was ambushed by elements of the President Quezon's Own Guerrillas (PQOG) guerrilla group. Marcos then joined them and, though suffering badly from malnutrition and disease, took an active part in their activities against the enemy.

These activities are further explained in a Distinguished

Service Star (GO 435, dated 24 April 1945, HPA, and duplicate GO 152, dated 20 December 1963, GHQ AFP) awarded for meritorious service. The citation noted that Marcos, despite his illness, remained at the headquarters of the PQOG and "actively supported ex-Mayor Vicente Umali, later known as General Umali..." by guiding both the staff and combat-echelons. Marcos then refused the rank of general offered by Umali and organized his own guerrilla group with former USAFFE officers as leaders. He called it Ang Manga Maharlika (The Noble Ones).[4]

Lieutenant Colonel Charles W. Willoughby joined General MacArthur's staff in 1939 as his G-4, but was switched to G-2 before the war. He rose to the rank of major general and remained with MacArthur as his intelligence chief throughout the war. Afterwards he published a book, *The Guerrilla Resistance Movement in the Philippines: 1941-1945*.* The corpus of this work is actually a compilation of official Army documents, including Volumes I and II of the Intelligence Series, produced by the G-2 staff of MacArthur's command, which details the guerrilla movement in the Philippines.

The PQOG was formed in mid-1942, under Colonel Hugh Straughn, a fat, jolly U.S. Army officer. Vicente Umali, the former mayor of Tiaong, Tayabas, was its leader. Under Straughn's guidance, several guerrilla organizations were formed in the Bulacan-Rizal-Manila area. (Metro Manila now encompasses the Manila and Rizal areas.) Marking's Guerrillas and the Fil-American Irregular Troops operated east of Manila; the Hunters operated in Cavite; and the PQOG around Laguna, Batangas, and west-central Tayabas. According to Willoughby, Straughn's organization was the largest and best organized resistance movement in that area. After his capture in August 1943, there was no coordinated command of any consequence left.[5]

Marcos' supposed activities with the PQOG are not mentioned by Willoughby. Willoughby listed Vicente Umali as a lieutenant colonel and colonel, but never a general. It seems

---

* New York: Vantage Press, 1972.

unlikely that Colonel Straughn, who was still alive and active in the resistance during the period Marcos was supposedly with the PQOG, would have authorized Colonel Umali to offer the rank of general to a lieutenant.

Marcos himself apparently recognized Umali as a colonel and not a general. In a nine-page letter to the Commanding General, PHILRYCOM, Attention: GAD [Guerrilla Affairs Division] dated 2 December 1947, which he wrote seeking recognition for his Maharlika, Marcos referred to "Col. Vicente Umali and Col. Primitivo San Agustin, Jr., the highest ranking officers of the President Quezon's Own Guerrillas."[6]

The prestigious incident of Marcos being offered the rank of general may have been borrowed from another real-life situation. Lieutenant Colonel Wendell Fertig, a guerrilla leader in Mindanao, was offered the rank of general by Luis Morgan, another guerrilla leader who had been a former policeman in the area and had formed his own guerrilla unit. Morgan thought he could add prestige to his unit by having an American general as the head, with him as chief of staff. He even passed the word around that "General Fertig" had been sent by MacArthur. Morgan and Fertig didn't get along, but the ruse worked and helped insure Fertig's success on Mindanao.

The affidavit that Marcos executed in 1946 listed his duties and activities chronologically:

1. 15Nov41, Camp Ord, Called & inducted USAFFE
2. 16Nov41-8Apr42, Mt. Samat, Bataan, 21st Div. Assistant G-2
3. 9Apr42-4Aug42, Camp O'Donnell, POW released
4. 5Aug42-12Aug42, Fort Santiago, Captured-Escaped
5. 13Aug42-15Oct42, Tayabas-Manila, Hiding-Ill in bed
6. 16Oct42-12Dec44, Manila, 'Maharlika' Guer Unit

Marcos elaborated about his duties and activities under "Remarks:"

Re line 1. Called and inducted to the USAFFE as 3rd Lt.

Re line 2. Assigned as assistant G-2 of the 21st Division. Wounded in action on 7 April 1942 but remained with the unit. Captured on 9 April 1942 while on mission to recapture Gen. Capinpin.

Re line 3. As POW released.

Re line 4. I was arrested on suspicion of attempting to go to Australia. Concentrated at Fort Santiago. From Fort Santiago I was brought by the Kempetai to Tayabas to identify the boat which is going to leave for Australia. While there I escaped, and from that time I keep hiding.

Re line 5. While hiding we were living on the lands.

Re line 6. Ang Manga Maharlika, a guerrilla organization of which I was the CO was organized inside Camp O'Donnell although roster was formally drafter 1 Dec 42...

There was no reference to his service with the PQOG, and his reference to his "mission to recapture Gen. Capinpin" on 9 April doesn't reconcile with his Wounded Personnel Medal citation (see page 51).

A few weeks after Marcos was released from Camp O'Donnell, the officer who had been in charge of burials in the camp was released. If the Japanese had known who he really was—on Bataan he had torn off his rank insignia just before he surrendered and claimed he was a Filipino clerk—they would have surely put him in charge of his own burial. Lieutenant Colonel (later Colonel) Narciso Manzano was the highest ranking Filipino on active duty in the U.S. Army during World War II.* He had been charged with an official mission by General Wainwright before the surrender. He was to develop an intelligence net on Luzon as soon as possible. This he would do, and do extremely well.[7]

Manzano's background, education, experience, and intelligence made him a natural for the role he was about to play. Of Spanish descent, he had been one of the select few to be chosen, through competitive examination, and commissioned as a second lieutenant in the U.S. Army Corps of Engineers in 1921. He was sent to the Engineer School at Fort Belvoir, and then back to the Philippines. His last two assignments before the outbreak of the

---

* Colonel Manzano now lives in San Francisco. He graciously allowed the use of his memoirs for this material.

war was to map the Bataan Peninsula and then prepare it for the war — building docks, warehouses, roads, and a water supply. As topographical inspector his name appeared on those maps which were used by the troops. Copies fell into enemy hands. The Japanese were very interested in finding this "Captain Manzano," who probably knew more about Bataan than anyone else, but they never found him even though he was right under their eyes.

At the war's outbreak he was made executive officer of MacArthur's chief of engineers, Lieutenant Colonel (later Major General) Hugh G. "Pat" Casey. His first job was to blow all the bridges during the retreat to Bataan. At Calumpit his own retreat was cut off when the bridge was blown before he could cross over. He had to evade the Japanese troops as he made his successful escape back to Bataan, along with his American counterpart, Captain Major, who was promoted to Major for this daring maneuver. (Yes, there was a real Major Major in World War II.)

On Bataan, the G-2 section of USAFFE set up the Military Intelligence Section (MIS) in January 1942. Headed by Major General Simeon de Jesus, about 60 agents were sent on clandestine missions behind enemy lines to collect, evaluate, and disseminate information about the enemy. In March, Manzano volunteered to try and reach Cavite to knock out some Japanese artillery which was blasting Corregidor. His group was intercepted by a Japanese patrol boat and almost got wiped out. The mission failed but he made it back to Bataan.[8]

After his release from Camp O'Donnell, Colonel Manzano set about fulfilling his mission. He learned there were two important organizations in the Manila area. One was an intelligence unit whose nucleus was made up of intellectuals who came from the Civil Liberties Union, and was called the "Free Philippines." The board of directors was composed of Lorenzo Tañada (later a senator), Jose B.L. Reyes (later a Supreme Court justice), Rafael Roces (a columnist of the prominent Roces family, later killed), Tony Bautista (a prominent lawyer, also killed), Ramon de Santos, Jesus Barera, Cipriano Cid, R. Marino Corpus, Anselmo Claudio, and Amando G. Dayrit. The other group was composed of Colonel Manuel Roxas (President Quezon's confidant, Secretary of Finance, and later president of the Republic), Juan Miguel Elizalde (of the prominent Elizalde family, later killed), Senator Jose Ozamis (of the prominent Ozamis family in Mindanao, later killed), and Enrico Pirovano (an Italian businessman, later killed).[9]

Manzano became the military member to both boards, and was put in touch with agents of all subversive groups in the Philippines. He found many irresponsible, bragging about the size of their organizations and boasting of the fact that they were spies. However, some were well organized and acquired a certain amount of proficiency in their business: the "Hukbalahaps," a radical anti-Japanese group of communist origin; the "East Central Luzon Guerrilla Area" group, headed by Major Edwin Ramsey; Major Bernard Anderson's group; Terry Adevoso's Hunters Guerrillas; and those of Straughn, Nakar, and Enriquez, and the picturesque Marking and Yay Panlilio. Manzano never heard of Marcos or his Maharlika during the war.

CHAPTER SEVEN

Guerrilla

According to the Distinguished Service Star citation, Marcos remained with the PQOG until December 1942. He then formed his own group, the Ang Manga Maharlika and "in October 1943...heading a party of four officers, sailed on two sailboats for Mindanao...Colonel Marcos finally contacted Colonel Wendell W. Fertig, head of the Mindanao guerrillas, in Agusan..."

However, Marcos' biography stated that he departed Manila in March 1943, accompanied by Primitivo San Agustin, Vicente Raval, and Leonilo O'Campo, and located Fertig in January 1944. Neither version is correct. He was not the leader of the party that sailed for Mindanao if he went with San Agustin; he was not a colonel; and he never contacted Fertig personally. Baclagon's book, *Valor*, states that the trip started in March or April 1942, and that he established contact with Fertig in January 1943. This cannot be correct either since Marcos was captured on Bataan in April 1942.

Curiously, there is very little record of Marcos' movements or activities from 4 August 1942, the day he left Camp O'Donnell, until November 1943. His biography, Baclagon's books, and his citations are all contradictory, and his affidavit doesn't give his movements.

His 1946 affidavit states that he was in Manila General Hospital from June to August 1943, with malaria and a chronic ulcer. (In fact, Marcos was a very sickly person throughout the war, suffering from a variety of ailments.) Jose Laurel was recuperating in the hospital from his assassination attempt at this same time.[1] Laurel, it will be recalled, was the associate justice of the Supreme Court that penned the decision that reversed Marcos' murder conviction, and later became the puppet president in October 1943. Other than this, Marcos' activities and whereabouts are somewhat of a mystery until his approximate location became known in November 1943.

Primitivo San Agustin was formerly a lieutenant, assistant G-3, in the 21st Division, where Marcos was an assistant G-2. San Agustin made at least two trips to Fertig's headquarters—one in August 1943 and the other in December 1943. Major Bernard Anderson was a U.S. Army guerrilla leader operating in Tayabas near Batangas. He reported that "Nothing was known of the PQOG until late 1943, when Lt. Primitivo San Agustin went to Mindanao to establish contact with SWPA."[2] During this period Fertig's message traffic to SWPA never mentioned Marcos' name and only mentioned the Maharlika in a negative context.

Wendell Fertig was a successful civilian mining engineer in the Philippines when the war broke out. He was already a captain in the reserves and had worked for another engineer, Major Narciso Manzano, on occasion. When the Japanese attacked he was promoted to major (and later to lieutenant colonel) and made the executive officer to Colonel Stickney in the Department of Engineers, Philippine Department. Before the surrender of Bataan he escaped to Corregidor, and was ordered to join MacArthur in Australia, but the flying boat that evacuated him crashed on landing in Mindanao. So he remained there, established his guerrilla organization, and was soon in touch with MacArthur in Australia by radio.[3]

Willoughby noted that "The success of [Fertig's] organization was well known throughout the Philippines, and many guerrillas and intelligence organizations sent representatives to obtain advice and support. Best known of these was Captain Primitivo San Agustin who made several trips from Batangas to Mindanao and took back to Luzon the first radio with which successful contact was made."[4]

In his letter to the Guerrilla Affairs Division, dated 2 December 1947, Marcos claimed "the smuggling of the first radio equipment from Mindanao to Luzon in 1943."[5] This is disputed by Willoughby, who stated that San Agustin took back the first radio, and "by June 1944 had established radio contact between Batangas and Mindanao."[6]

A close examination of the message traffic between SWPA (General MacArthur's headquarters, Southwest Pacific Area, in Australia) and the Philippines, which is available in the National Archives in Washington and the MacArthur Memorial Archives in Norfolk, Virginia, helped to clarify some of his movements.

The journey to Mindanao was long and arduous, more than 500 miles mostly by boat, island-hopping in Japanese-controlled waters. On his first trip contact was finally made by San Agustin in northeastern Mindanao, in the Province of Agusan del Sur, in August 1943.[7]

On 29 August, Fertig sent MacArthur a radio message:

Report from Lt. P. San Agustin to inform Quezon/ MacArthur that they are carrying on fight for freedom. Desire Fertig act as adviser.[8]

MacArthur replied to San Agustin via Fertig on 6 September 1943:

I have instructed Col. Fertig to extend to you every possible facility and assistance and relay on to me such information as your group may obtain and believe to be brought to my attention until such time as some direct means of communication are established.[9]

On 11 September, Fertig radioed MacArthur:

Primitivo San Agustin still here and will question. He is with President Quezon' Own Guerrillas. He states that Marcos Villa San Agustin at Marking (no relation to Primitivo) is the CO of the largest group guerrilla in Rizal and Manila. He was responsible for political assassination in Manila.[10]

None of these messages mention Marcos or the Maharlika. If Marcos were on this trip with San Agustin, they had to have split up before Mindanao. Only in November was Marcos mentioned in the message traffic, but not by Fertig.

Major (later Lieutenant Colonel) Edwin D. Andrews was an American-mestizo guerrilla operating on the island of Negros, between Luzon and Mindanao. He had graduated from the Constabulary Academy in 1927, and then went on to the United States and studied at the FBI school. He returned to the Philippines and worked in the intelligence section of the Philippine Constabulary. He became a pilot in 1937, and was commanding officer of Zablan Field when the Japanese attacked.[11] He and Captain Jesus Villamor were good friends before the war and worked together when Villamor arrived on his intelligence mission. When Villamor departed on 20 October 1943, he left Andrews in charge of his network.[12] On 17 November 1943, he sent a message to SWPA, which stated in part:

> Above info is from Ferdinand Marcos who is reported by my Bohol man as claiming to be in charge of former Nakar and Enriquez units in northern Luzon, since capture and surrender of last two. Marcos reported going to Tenth Military District [Fertig's headquarters] to arrange recognition of his units by higher authority and render intelligence reports based on above data. Copy of said report now on way here. Believe above info is reliable.[13]

So Marcos was either on the island of Bohol, between Negros and Mindanao, or on Negros. Another document discovered in the National Archives in Washington was a history of the Maharlika written by Marcos in an attempt to gain recognition. Although it mentions seeing Major Ingeniero in Bohol, there are so many discrepancies in the document that it must be considered spurious.

The "info" Andrews was referring to gave the Japanese troop strength for Luzon and its provinces and estimated its artillery. The interesting thing is that the message is almost identical to the one sent by Fertig to SWPA on 16 and 25 December 1943 (the message was in two parts). Andrews information came from Marcos. It reads in part:

Enemy strength in Luzon as of 31 October is 142,000. [It then
breaks this down by area or province.]...Ten grand [10,000]
of which are convalescent or wounded with five grand in
Manila and five grand at Baguio...Troops mentioned are all
infantry units except nine hundred as cavalry and personnel
manning the following [It then lists various artillery pieces]...[14]

Fertig's information is from San Agustin. It reads in part:

...One four two thousand troops distributed as follows...[It
then breaks this number down by area or province, but
Agustin's breakdown is in more detail. It lists 26 places;
Marcos listed 7.]...Of the above five are hospitalized as sick
or wounded in both Manila and Baguio...All used as infantry
except nine hundred cavalry...Artillery [It then lists various
artillery pieces and their location. Marcos' message didn't list
their location, but he estimated the number of tanks, cars,
trucks, and aircraft, while Agustin did not.][15]

The information is too identical not to have come from the
same source. The message from Andrews is enlightening from
several standpoints. First, it is proof that Marcos had not yet been
to Fertig's headquarters; second, it states that he was in charge of
former Nakar and Enriquez units, possibly during the period he
was not heard from; and, lastly, he was providing information to
Andrews that San Agustin would provide to Fertig in Mindanao.
It is a mystery as to why Marcos would split from San Agustin
and give this information to Andrews if he wanted to see Fertig
and obtain recognition. The December message traffic implies
that Marcos never did make it to Fertig's headquarters and that
Fertig did not trust Marcos.

On 16 December, Fertig radioed SWPA information about
the enemy's strength which had been provided by San Agustin.
The message began:

Resume of military intelligence brought by Primitivo San
Agustin...

San Agustin was eventually provided a radio, as already
noted, but apparently not yet. On the same day another message

was sent to SWPA, assigning code names:

> Use as code names in future messages. General Roxas is
> Amigo. Peping Ozamis is Pemco. Fertig is Alfredo. King
> Negat or KN is Kangleon while item George is Inginiero of
> Bohol; Priming is Primitivo San Agustin.[16]

On 20 December, Fertig radioed SWPA:

> ...Ang Manga Maharlika guerrilla organization in Iloco,
> Ilocos Sur and Mountain Province who claim to be under my
> command. Never authorized but can do nothing about it
> now. Military info forwarded...[17]

These messages cast serious doubt on the authenticity of a
letter, dated 16 December, which Marcos presented as part of the
proof of his Maharlika in order to gain recognition. It is from
Fertig and congratulates Marcos for the intelligence report sent
through San Agustin. Marcos claimed in his Maharlika history
that he had an extensive intelligence network "spread over the
entire island of Luzon," but he gave no evidence of such a
network except for the letter.[18] Fertig's message, plus a report
from a U.S. Army officer after the war, investigating Marcos'
claim, appears to refute his claim. Captain Elbert R. Curtis, in a
report dated 25 July 1947, noted that it was only a photostatic
copy and could not be verified. He further stated:

> The unit claims a vast amount of intelligence coverage by
> submitting reports to Col. Fertig, Col. Peralta, Col. An-
> drews, Col. Marking, and Major Ingeniero. One letter from
> Col. Fertig is the only supporting evidence to substantiate
> these claims.[19]

For whatever reason, San Agustin, who was probably still
with Fertig at that time, did not vouch for Marcos and his
Maharlika.

Marcos not only wasn't assigned a code-name, the Maharlika
was obviously disclaimed by Fertig, who may have been
suspicious of Marcos for another reason. The previous April he

had sent a message to SWPA which listed the names of Philippine Constabulary and Philippine Army officers who had surrendered and then agreed to serve with the Japanese Bureau of Constabulary (BC). The list contained the name "P.V. Marcos."[20] There were many typographical errors and several names were misspelled but that name was there. In any event, the Maharlika never did get recognized by Fertig or "Free Philippines" in Manila, as confirmed in another message sent to SWPA on 16 February 1944:

> List of guerrilla groups submitted by Free Philippines: Manriquez in Mountain Province, Cushing (not Walter) in Pangasinan, Maguire in Zambales, Ramsey in Central Luzon, Around Manila: Marking's, Terry's Hunters, Anderson in Tayabas, Escudero and Vinzon's groups in Bicol out of contact.[21]

There was still one unresolved matter regarding Andrew's message of 17 November 1943. Was Marcos in charge of former Nakar and Enriquez units as he claimed?

After the Japanese invasion, but before the fall of Bataan, some of the American forces in northern Luzon became isolated by Lieutenant General Masaharu Homma's advancing army. Following the rapid Japanese advance and the USAFFE retreat into Bataan, they independantly continued to harass the Japanese troops. Lieutenant Colonel John P. Horan was the senior American officer on northern Luzon and commander of Camp John Hay in Baguio, Mountain Province. When he was cut off he decided to stay in the mountains and fight. He disbanded his troops from the 43rd Infantry Regiment (PS), and gave them the authority to try and make it to Bataan on their own where General MacArthur was regrouping. But 184 officers and men elected to remain with him.[22] He withdrew further north to Kiangan in Ifugao Province and organized into a guerilla regiment called the 43rd Infantry. On 15 January 1942, he assumed command of all friendly forces in Mountain Province and adjacent areas.[23] He then planned to organize another guerrilla outfit, so he sent one of his officers, Lieutenant George M. Barnett, to La Union

Province to organize some disbanded soldiers and reservists. This unit was designated as the 121st Infantry on paper.[24]

A few days after the Japanese landing at Vigan on 9 December 1941 a miner in Ba-Ay, Abra, by the name of Walter M. Cushing, gathered about 200 of his Filipino workers together and formed his own guerrilla outfit.[25] He ran into Lieutenant Robert H. Arnold, a signal air-warning company commander, who had been cut off with 32 of his men.[26] They joined together. Cushing's exploits soon became legendary. In January 1942, he heard of Lieutenant Colonel Horan in Mountain Province and went to see him. He returned to his own outfit with a U.S. Army commission and the rank of captain.[27] Cushing's group then joined with Horan. About this time Arnold was wounded in an ambush. When he recovered in April, he and a few of his men set out to join with Horan, but ran into another guerrilla outfit, the 14th Infantry. With USAFFE's permission he joined them.[28]

Captain (later Major) Ralph B. Praeger, commanding officer, Troop C, 26th Cavalry (PS), was on patrol in the Cagayan Valley in Mountain Province when the Japanese landed and cut him off. He immediately formed his own group—two U.S. officers and 59 Filipinos—into a guerrilla outfit. He and his men joined with Horan for awhile and then decided to move down to Nueva Vizcaya and operate on their own.[29]

General MacArthur's USAFFE headquarters had now been moved from No. 1 Calle Victoria in Manila to Corregidor. He promoted Horan to full colonel on 7 April 1942; Bataan surrendered on 9 April; and on 10 April, USAFFE officially constituted Horan's outfit the 121st Infantry Regiment, encompassing Barnett's and Cushing's outfits.[30]

General Wainwright surrendered Corregidor on 6 May 1942. One of the conditions forced on him was that he had to surrender all of the Philippines. Thus he ordered Horan and other commanders to surrender. Horan did so on 14 May.[31] However, his men decided to continue the resistance,[32] but not without setbacks.

Cushing was captured in September* and Arnold a few

---

* Willoughby reported he was captured. Volckmann's book claimed that Cushing shot himself rather than be captured.

months later. Captain William D. Peryam took over, only to be
captured in January 1943. He was followed by Captain Vicente
Abaya, who was captured a few days later. Command eventually
passed to George M. Barnett, by then a major.[33]

In early January 1942, Captain (later Lieutenant Colonel)
Manuel P. Enriquez, of the 11th Infantry (PA) at Camp Holmes
near Baguio was cut off and was organizing disbanded troops in
Aritao, Nueva Vizcaya, when he ran into Captain (later
Lieutenant Colonel) Everett L. Warner. Warner had been the
Provost Marshall under Lieutenant Colonel Horan at Camp John
Hay but was unable to join the troops when the Japanese
attacked, reputedly because he was inebriated.[34] However, he was
now determined to make amends, and joined up with Enriquez.
They, in turn, met up with Captain (later Lieutenant Colonel)
Guillermo P. Nakar, who was commanding the 1st Battalion, 71st
Infantry, when the Japanese attacked. Also cut off and
surrounded, he and his men crossed the Cordillera Mountains and
came down to Aritao. The groups joined together a force of about
800 and called themselves the "1st Provisional Guerrilla Regiment." They initially operated in the Cagayan Valley, ambushing
supply trains and patrols.[35] When General Wainwright surrendered, Warner, like Horan, was also ordered to surrender. Nakar,
now a lieutenant colonel, assumed command. Willoughby noted
that "As the most prominent USAFFE officer in the area, Colonel
Nakar also coordinated the remnants of other USAFFE forces."[36]
On 30 June 1942, he was contacted by General MacArthur in
Australia:

> Lt. Col. Nakar the courageous and splendid resistance
> maintained by you and your command fills me with pride and
> satisfaction STOP It will be my privilege to see that you and
> your officers and men are properly rewarded at the
> appropriate time STOP My affection and best wishes
> MCARTHUR[37]

Nakar reported back to MacArthur his unit's strength: 62
officers, 960 enlisted men, and 143 attached PC personnel,
including three officers. On 14 July, his unit was designated the

14th Infantry, U.S. Army, and serial numbers for 100 officers and 1,000 enlisted men were issued.[38] Nakar continued his active resistance until he was captured on 29 September 1942. His radio was also destroyed in this raid.[39] He was a leader and an example to his men to the very end. He refused to sign his surrender papers and, when forced to speak at Japanese "peace" rallies, he defied them and urged the people to continue the spirit of resistance. He was finally taken to Fort Santiago, tortured, and executed on/about 2 October 1943.[40]

Command of the 14th passed to Enriquez when Nakar was captured. Willoughby called his leadership "the most colorful of all guerrilla activities."[41] He was able to coordinate under one intelligence command almost all guerrilla units in the southern part of northern Luzon, including the 43rd, the 121st, and the 14th.[42] He was forced to surrender on 14 April 1943, when the Japanese took his wife and children hostage. Command then passed to Major Romulo Manriquez, a 1936 graduate of the Philippine Military Academy.[43] This was a difficult period for the 14th,* with some members being killed or captured and others surrendering, but Manriquez, a career soldier as well as an able leader, kept the unit together. He would eventually build up its strength to almost 1,900 officers and enlisted men.[44] Enriquez was released in October 1943, under a general amnesty when the Japanese granted "independence" to the Philippines. He resumed directing the intelligence activities of his group, which ran its operation out of a sari-sari [small neighborhood grocery] store in Baguio. A Filipino con-man turned Japanese spy, Franco Vera Reyes, betrayed him in early 1944. (Many prominent members of the "Free Philippines" and General Roxas' secret organizations were also betrayed at the same time by Reyes, including Senator Jose Ozamis, Juan Miguel Elizalde, Tony Bautista, and Enrico Pirovano. They were tried and executed.)

Thus Enriquez was arrested again, and this time he

---

* After the war there was a minor scandal when it was discovered that some of the officers and men of the 14th had engaged in "racketeering"—the buying and selling of steel cable and other war materials to the Japanese—from about mid-42 to mid-43. The problem was cleared up soon after Manriquez took over.

disappeared.[45] Reyes was also later killed by the Japanese when his usefulness ran out. On 24 November 1943, the 14th officially came under the command and control of USAFIP NL.

When Colonel Horan surrendered in May 1943, two lieutenant colonels became the senior American officers operating in northern Luzon as guerrillas. Martin Moses and Arthur K. Noble were both graduates of West Point, 1927 and 1929 respectively. They were originally with the 12th Infantry, a unit that had been activated only 10 days when the Japanese struck.[46] After being cut off, they were able to rejoin the USAFFE forces and ended up commanding regiments of the 11th Division on Bataan. When Bataan surrendered, they didn't. They escaped and made their way back to northern Luzon. On their way north they were able to contact many of the Americans still operating as guerrillas. They arrived at Captain Praeger's headquarters in February 1943. Since Nakar had been captured the previous September, with the help of Praeger, as senior officers they gradually assumed the coordinated command duties that Nakar and Enriquez had set up. On 1 October 1942, Lieutenant Colonel Moses announced he was assuming the command of all guerrilla units in northern Luzon. He named the command "U.S. Forces in the Philippines, Northern Luzon," or USFIP NL.[47]

Captain Parker Calvert commanded the 43rd Philippine Scout Battalion at Camp John Hay, where Lieutenant Colonel Horan was camp commander, when the Japanese attacked. Calvert did not join Horan's guerrilla outfit. He chose instead to try and go south to link up with the USAFFE forces.[48] He was unsuccesful and returned north to try and link up again with Horan. On the way he gathered about 40 disbanded Philippine Scout and Philippine Army soldiers, but by the time he reached Bontoc, where Horan was supposed to be, Horan had surrendered. A short while later he ran into Moses and Noble and joined them. As the word got around, more of his Philippine Scouts joined him. He called his unit "Detachment, 43rd Infantry (Philippine Scouts)."[49]

In June 1943, Moses and Noble were captured. The Japanese tried to force them to induce other guerrillas to give up, but they refused to cooperate. They also disappeared.[50] Praeger suffered the same fate in August.[51] This was a terrible blow to the guerrilla movement in northern Luzon, but resistance continued.

The next senior officer in northern Luzon was Captain (later Colonel) Russell W. Volckmann, West Point, 1934. He had arrived in the Philippines in August 1941, and was assigned to the 11th Infantry, Philippine Army, at Camp Holmes near Baguio, the same outfit as Captain Enriquez, as senior instructor. After the invasion he was transferred to the 11th Division on Bataan, the same as Moses and Noble, as the intelligence officer.[52] It was here that he learned of the guerrilla units of Horan, Cushing, Barnett, Praeger, and others already in northern Luzon. When Bataan fell, he and another captain, Don Blackburn, slipped away and made their way north to the mountains where they joined Moses and Noble. That had been a year earlier. Now Volckmann was the senior officer in command.[53]

Over the next 18 months he organized the widely dispersed guerrilla units into an effective organization with improved coordination and communication (mostly bamboo telegraph) between units. He also changed the name of the organization to U.S. Armed Forces in the Philippine, Northern Luzon, or USAFIP NL.[54] Initially the USAFIP NL was divided into seven geographical areas, called "districts," with a commander assigned to each. Further reorganization resulted in five commands by December 1944: Major Parker Calvert's 66th Infantry (which comprised elements of the 43rd, 11th, and 12th Infantries) in the 1st District (Benguet and Mountain Provinces); Major George M. Barnett's 121st Infantry in the 2nd District (La Union, Ilocos Sur, and Abra); Major Robert H. Arnold's 15th Infantry in the 3rd District (Ilocos Norte and Abra); Major Don Blackburn's 11th Infantry in the 4th and 7th Districts (Cagayan, Apayo, Kalinga, Bontoc, and Ifugao); and Major Romulo Manriquez' 14th Infantry in the 5th District (Isabella and Nueva Vizcaya).[55]

Major Manriquez was the only Filipino in this elite group. The 6th District, which comprised parts of Nueva Vizcaya and Pangasinan, was commanded by Major Robert Lapham, but he stopped acknowledging Volckmann's authority, so the 6th was dropped from the area of responsibility of the USAFIP NL. Calvert eventually became Volckmann's chief of staff, and Dennis

Molintas took over the 66th. Major Arnold was originally with
the 14th and then assigned to USAFIP NL headquarters as the
signal officer in October 1944. He took command of the 15th
Infantry the following December, relieving John Patrick O'Day.

John P. O'Day (not to be confused with Colonel Ray M.
O'Day, Senior Instructor of the 21st Division, who was captured
on Bataan) was an Irish mining man who had been in the
Philippines 14 years when the Japanese invaded. He originally
joined the 121st under Barnett. Not every American guerrilla in
the Philippines was cut from the mold of John Wayne. Some
preferred the Filipina women to fighting. Others preferred whisky
to warfare. Still others used their guerrilla guise to rape, plunder,
and murder with little or no military motive. O'Day was reported
to be the worst of the lot. Barnett had a somewhat similar
reputation, but he still controlled the largest outfit in the USAFIP
NL, with more than 2,000 men. There was also a Filipino in the
121st, Emilio Escobar, known as "Sagad," or "the broom." He is
reported to have killed more than 4,000 of his own people. Most
of the killings were random acts of terrorism, done just for the
sake of killing.[56]

In spite of some misguided elements, the value of the
resistance effort and intelligence-gathering capability of the
USAFIP NL cannot be overestimated. It had grown from 2,000 to
more than 8,000 guerrillas,* with an organized reserve of an
additional 7,000, plus 5,000 more organized into service units.
Thus when General MacArthur's army landed on Leyte on 20
October 1944, and then on Luzon at Lingayan Gulf on 9 January
1945, Volckmann had 19,660 officers and men waiting.[57] The
Japanese retreated into the mountains of northern Luzon for their
final stand. It would take seven more months of fighting, but the
cease-fire order finally came on 15 August, and surrender on 2
September.

Colonel Volckmann survived the war and wrote a book

---

* In December 1944, the size of the USAFIP NL, broken down by unit,
was as follows: 11th Infantry—66 officers, 1,800 enlisted men; 14th
Infantry—83 officers, 1822 enlisted men; 15th Infantry—7 officers,
917 enlisted men; 66th Infantry—54 officers, 1202 enlisted men; 121st
Infantry—92 officers, 2,246 enlisted men.

about his experiences with the guerrillas in northern Luzon entitled *We Remained*.* Lieutenant Marcos and his Maharlika are never mentioned.

---

* New York: W.M. Norton, 1954.

CHAPTER EIGHT

Claims of the Maharlika

There is no evidence to support Marcos' claim that he was in charge of former Nakar and Enriques units. To the contrary, the only evidence is that he had no association with the 14th until December 1944, and that he may have attempted to form a guerrilla unit but it only got as far as the "paper" stage.

Major (later Lieutenant Colonel) Romulo Manriquez took over the 14th after Enriquez surrendered, and ultimately became part of Volckmann's USAFIP NL. This is confirmed by Willoughby and Volckmann in their books, and in a master's thesis, The Resistance Movement in Northern Luzon (1942-1945), written at the University of the Philippines in 1962 by then Captain Cesar P. Pobre, a graduate of the Philippine Military Academy, class of 1952. He devoted two years of research to the study of this guerrilla movement.[1]

In his preface, Pobre thanked the many people who helped him in his research and in preparing his thesis. One of these was Professor Teodoro A. Agoncillo, the noted historian. In a letter to Boni Gillego in 1982, he wrote:

> In my 2-volume work, The Fateful Years: Japan's Adventure in the Philippines, 1941–1945, I never mentioned Marcos, a fact which made him blurt out in a meeting with the Philippine Historical Association, as reported to me by a friend, that some historians — apparently referrring to me — did not do justice to his alleged exploits. I've pored over thousands of documents on the war in the Pacific, including

my good friend and U.P. contemporary, the late Major
Conrado B. Rigor's work on the North Luzon guerrillas, but I
never found any mention of Marcos' exploits.[2]

Major Conrado B. Rigor was a guerrilla in northern Luzon,
and commanding officer of the 3rd Battalion, 121st Infantry. He
was well known for his heroic leadership, especially for his role in
the bloody Battle of Bessang Pass.

In defending his claim that the Maharlika did exist as a unit,
Marcos referred to Willoughby's book, which listed the Maharlika as one of the guerrilla units of northern Luzon. This mention
did not give the Maharlika credibility. It was merely listing all
units reported to be in northern Luzon. In fact, the mention of the
Maharlika by Willoughby is the first indication that the
Maharlika was not what it claimed to be.[3] It stated that its
strength was 8,200 as of April 1944, but that "Many of the
personnel belonging to the Maharlika seem to belong to
Volckmann's organization."[4] One example of this was Lieutenant
Colonel Manriquez, who was listed as the commanding officer of
the third district of the Maharlika. Manriquez denies ever
belonging to the Maharlika, and only met Marcos when he joined
the 14th in December 1944.

In his book Willoughby listed 64 people whom he cited as key
figures in staff or operations in the guerrilla movement in the
Philippines. Fertig and San Agustin were on this list but Marcos
was not.[5] Also included were Captain Jesus Villamor and Major
Emigdio Cruz, whose daring clandestine missions have already
been noted. Neither of their after-mission reports mentioned
Marcos or the Maharlika.[6]

Marcos' Distinguished Conduct Star citation (GO 158) stated
that, after meeting with Colonel Fertig, he returned to Luzon to
unify all guerrilla units into one single command "pursuant to
SWPA's instructions." There is no record of such instructions. To
the contrary, in a report to SWPA, dated 20 November 1944,
Volckmann stated that he was prepared to take over the Second
Military District (Luzon) "If Higher Headquarters so desires."[7] In
an internal memo (SWPA Check Sheet, dated 2 December 1944) it
was decided "that existing policy be adhered to," and no area

commander was appointed for Luzon.[8] Willoughby noted that, while accepting that "the guerrilla leaders were individualistic and bound to clash," some would emerge as really strong men, "as leaders will always emerge in time of stress and disaster."[9]

SWPA did, at one time, consider centralizing all intelligence activities on Luzon. A Memo to the Chief of Staff, dated 29 May 1944, and signed by Willoughby, included a "Revised General Intelligence Plan for the Philippines." It stated:

> The area not now adequately covered for intelligence at the present time is Luzon...The estabishment of independent intelligence nets has in fact been encouraged in the past...These nets can well be preserved, but the time has come to coordinate their activities...Manzano has the best contact with the Luzon guerrilla units and is well known to them.[10]

The memo recommended Manzano be appointed director and coordinator of Luzon intelligence activities. However, he was ordered to Mindanao before this centralization could be carried out.[11]

When Marcos actually returned from the southern Philippines is unclear. It was probably December 1943 or January 1944. His biography claims that he returned, tried to unify the guerrillas, and failed. Then "in April 1944, he staggered into his mother's house and collapsed."[12] He was taken to Philippine General Hospital suffering from malaria and stayed there until August. While in the hospital, according to his biography, he had chemists brew some nitroglycerine. This was given to members of his Maharlika,who used it to blow up two ships docked at Pier 7 in Manila Harbor.[13] According to his Distinguished Service Star citation (GO 435 and duplicate GO 152), "[the Maharlika] guerrilla unit was responsible for... harassment of the enemy and the burning of two ships at Pier 7 sometime in August 1944."

In his letter to the Guerrilla Affairs Division, dated 2 December 1947, Marcos contradicted the claim in the citation when he wrote that "no guerrilla unit has as yet outdone 'Ang Manga Maharlika' in its achievement of burning three Japanese war vessels in Manila in July 1944." Now he was claiming that the

event occurred in July and he added one more ship. His
Maharlika history also claimed responsibility for blowing up
three Japanese ships in Manila harbor on 16 July 1944, burning
another ship in the Pasig River a week later, and for setting fires
in shipyards, lumberyards, and supply dumps, and sabotaging
telephone lines.[14] These claims were investigated by the U.S.
Army, which reported that "Extensive sabotage is claimed in 1944
but no evidence is presented to substantiate these claims."[15]

Marcos was actually trying to claim the brave deeds of other
guerrilla units. Willoughby reported only two sabotage units in
the Manila area at that time. One was developed and supported by
Colonel Fertig on Mindanao, called the "LOD Sabotage Unit." It
had contacts with Major Anderson, Major Ramsey, and Captain
Primitivo San Agustin. The unit was reported to have burned
several ships and destroyed several oil and ammunition storage
areas.[16]

Anderson and Ramsey had originally worked together with
Colonel Claude Thorpe's guerrilla unit in east central Luzon.
Thorpe, a military policeman at Fort Stotsenberg, had organized
an intelligence net composed of Philippine Scout officers while on
Bataan. He was captured in October 1942, and the group split
up.[17] Anderson now operated out of Tayabas. (His executive
officer was Lieutenant Colonel Adriane Manzano, the nephew of
Colonel Narciso Manzano.) By mid-1944, he was in radio contact
with SWPA, and received several tons of supplies and equipment.
He established an intelligence net in central Luzon, and was in
touch with the Hunters, the PQOG, the Free Philippines (until
they were compromised), and a group called the Chinese
Anti-Japanese Guerrilla Force.[18]

The other sabotage unit was run by Ramsey and his East
Central Luzon Guerrillas (ECLG).[19] His report to SWPA, dated
15 May 1945, was divided into four sections: intelligence
activities, sabotage activities, propaganda activities, and combat
operations. His intelligence net, like Anderson's, was very
effective, covering Pangasinan, Tarlac, Nueva Ecija, Bataan,
Bulacan, Pampanga, Rizal, Cavite, and Manila. His report
included some of his sabotage activities: setting afire a tanker
loaded with gasoline in Manila Bay on 16 June 1944; setting afire

a steamship loaded with rice in the Pasig River on 25 July 1944;
burning parts of Piers 5 and 7 on 15 July 1944; raiding supply
dumps; burning bridges; and tampering with enemy communication lines.[20] Both Anderson and Ramsey's guerrilla outfits were
recognized. The Maharlika was not. In fact, Captain Elbert R.
Curtis, one of the U.S. Army investigators, stated in his report on
Marcos and the Maharlika after the war:

> Maj R B Lapham is familiar with the activities of the
> commanding officer of the Maharlika unit and attests to the
> following...It is quite obvious that Marcos did not exercise
> any control over a guerrilla organization prior to liberation.[21]

Another U.S. Army investigator, Lieutenant William D.
MacMillan, stated in his report:

> Colonel Ramsey, Maj Lapham an (sic) Maj Obana, all of
> whom operated in the area where this unit is alleged to have
> operated...heard his [Marcos] name in connection with the
> "buy and sell" activities of certain people...[22]

Marcos' Maharlika history also states that a company was set
up called TESCO (The Ex-Serviceman's Company), "for the
purpose of engaging purely in the commerce and trade of
materials not connected whatsoever with the war purposes but
actually to serve the double purpose of a front for a headquarters
and a continuous source of revenue."[23] Its location was the Regina
Building in Escolta, Manila, which was an odd place for a
guerrilla headquarters, considering the fact that it was known to
be one of the places in Manila most frequented by Japanese spies
and collaborators.[24]

It is possible that the Maharlika could have carried out
sabotage and intelligence activities in Manila, but it is unlikely
that such activities would have escaped the intelligence nets of
Ramsey, Anderson, and Manzano, among others. If Anderson
knew about this, he didn't mention it in his message traffic to
MacArthur. But what he did mention, in a message dated 19
August 1944, was that:

Lieutenant Ferdinand E. Marcos contacted undersigned with request he and his unit (as he says he is authorized by Colonel Fertig) come under this command. He also requests funds and other aid. Request verification authentication and instructions.[25]

Marcos was looking for an outfit to hook up with as early as August 1944, when U.S. planes attacked the Japanese at Davao, and it became obvious that MacArthur would fulfill his pledge to return to the Philippines. However, Anderson would deny his request, perhaps because he found out Marcos wasn't authorized by Fertig. Also, this message called Marcos a lieutenant. His biography claimed MacArthur promoted Marcos to major by radio when he arrived to see Fertig in Mindanao in January 1944.[26] This contradicts his affidavit of 6 February 1946, which states he was promoted on 1 December 1942. There is another affidavit, dated 15 February 1945, apparently executed while trying to seek recognition for his Maharlika unit, which only deals with his promotions. In it Marcos states:

That I was commissioned in the Philippine Army in 1937 with the rank of Third Lieutenant; That I was promoted to the rank of First Lieutenant in February, 1942, by the USAFFE headquarters in Corregidor; That on December 1943, my rank of Commanding Officer of "Ang Manga Maharlika," was recognized by SWPA through Col. Wendell W. Fertig, C.O., 10th Military District (Mindanao)...[27]

There is no mention of his promotion to captain or lieutenant colonel, which he claimed in his 6 February 1946 affidavit. His Maharlika history claimed that Lieutenant Jose Valera, who was brought from Australia via submarine on a clandestine mission, supposedly had a document identifying Marcos as a lieutenant colonel, so Marcos assumed that rank effective 15 June 1944.[28] This contradicts Marcos' 2 December 1947 letter to the Guerrilla Affairs Division, which states Valera's document referred to Major Ferdinand E. Marcos.[29] The only promotion that Marcos could actually prove by official orders was his promotion to first lieutenant. All others, in addition to being contradictory and confusing, appear to be spurious.

About a month before Anderson sent his message to SWPA inquiring about Marcos, he received a letter dated 26 July 1944. The letterhead stated "Ang Manga Maharlika." It requested arms, ammunition, a transmitter, money, and medical supplies. It also stated, "I regret that my illness prevents me from personally extending the message." It is signed "William Saunders, Commanding." The letter was found in the Whitney papers at the MacArthur Memorial Archives. On the back is handwritten "14 Aug 44, Req. fr Col. Fertig, Dec 43, Ferdinand E. Marcos w/Gen Capinpin." There is no known comment or reply, and no further reference to William Saunders.*[30] A month later, Marcos requested that he and his unit, the Maharlika, come under Anderson's command.

Saunders' letter and Marcos' request may have caused Anderson to become wary, and for good reason. After Marcos got out of the hospital in August, according to his biography, he donned the uniform of a Japanese BC officer and was taken by members of his Maharlika to Malolos, Bulacan, outside Manila, where he "spread his gear in a Japanese barracks and made himself at home."[31] The biography pointed out that he only did this as a cover while still recuperating from his sickness.

Willoughby noted that Anderson had "excellent contacts in Bulacan which is the center for Manila intelligence."[32] Marcos may have been seen in Bulacan in a Japanese uniform. It was also well known that General Capinpin, Marcos' former commanding officer, was now a military adviser to the puppet president, Jose Laurel. In the Philippines, a common trait is "utang na loob." As already noted, it means "debt of gratitude." If a favor is accorded to a person, that person is honor-bound to return the favor some day. Whatever obligation Marcos may have felt he owed Laurel can only be guessed. But now he was wearing a Japanese uniform.

This in itself was not necessarily bad. The problem of ascertaining why some Filipinos collaborated while others did not will always be a difficult one. Volckmann commented on this problem in his book. Many of the Filipino soldiers who had been

---

* Years later, in 1968 Ferdinand Marcos would open his first Swiss bank account, using the name William Saunders.

captured on Bataan were released only after they agreed to serve in the BC. They were vital to the Japanese as occupation troops. Before they joined, the Japanese subjected them to an intense reorientation program. As a result some grasped the Japanese cause and supported it fully. Others only pretended and were still loyal to the United States.[33] "Chick" Parsons, with G-2 making supply runs from Australia to the Philippines, made an intelligence gathering trip from February to July 1943. In his report he commented:

> Guerrilla groups throughout Luzon...are so afraid of Fifth Columnists and espionage agents (Filipinos) being used to a great extent by the enemy to track down and uncover [them].[34]

A pro-Japanese Filipino agent had infiltrated Anderson's unit in late 1943 and caused a wholesale purge, so he had cause to be wary.[35] In any event, Marcos never did join Anderson's group.

CHAPTER NINE

Marcos Joins the 14th

On 6 August 1944, U.S. planes attacked the Japanese at Sasa, Davao, in Mindanao. This was the first show of U.S. military might since 1942. On 1 September, the U.S. launched the first daylight air strike against the Philippine Islands. Admiral William F. Halsey's Third Fleet closed in on Mindanao, and carrier-based aircraft attacked on 9 and 10 September. On 12 September, they struck the Visayas. Radios and the bamboo telegraph secretly flashed the word all over the Philippines. The Americans were on their way. On 21 September, U.S. planes bombed the Japanese in Manila.[1] General MacArthur returned on 20 October, landing at Red Beach on Leyte.

On 12 December, Marcos appeared at the headquarters of the 14th Infantry and asked Romulo Manriquez, now a Lieutenant Colonel, if he could join them.[2] The puppet government moved to Baguio in the mountains of northern Luzon a few days before Christmas, and Laurel, Capinpin, and a few others escaped by air to Tokyo the following March. General Roxas decided to remain behind.[3]

Marcos' biography states that "[He] proposed, for the good of the service, to fuse his Maharlika units into Volckmann's command.[4] It also stated that "An official report shows that when American forces reached Lingayan Gulf in January 1945, the Maharlika greeted them with 3,450 men in Northern Luzon, 3,800 in Pangasinan, 1,650 in Zambales and Manila, and 300 in various espionage cells.[5]

The Maharlika would have been a welcome addition to the USAFIP NL, but Volckmann only claimed 8,400 in all five of his regiments, plus reserves and service elements. Such an addition would have deserved at least a mention in Volckmann's book, but there is none. The "official report" referred to in the biography is the mention in Willoughby's book, which, as already pointed out, noted that most of the men claimed by the Maharlika were already in Volckmann's command nine months before Marcos joined the 14th.

Romulo Manriquez, the commanding officer of the 14th at the time, has lived in the United States since 1950. He finished his law degree at George Washington University and now works for the Veterans Administration in Washington, D.C. Vincente Rivera, who was a captain and the regimental intelligence officer (S-2) at the time, now lives in Detroit, Michigan. He received his master's degree in psychology at University of Michigan. He has written a history of the 14th, replete with names, places, and dates, including what men were wounded in what battles. It is a tribute to his fallen comrades. In interviews both men recalled that Marcos arrived at the 14th with only one other man, a Sergeant Ventura (his first name was either Isidro or Iñigo). Ventura's brother had been with them but had gotten sick and stopped on the way. There were no Maharlika units. Rivera recalled that Marcos was very sick when he arrived.

After he reported to the 14th and his presense was reported to USAFIP NL headquarters, an order came down shortly afterward—to execute Ferdinand Marcos. There are conflicting stories as to the circumstances. Marcos' biography claims that he asked Lieutenant Colonel Manriquez to send a note to Colonel Volckmann and complain about abuses being committed by some of Volckmann's officers and men. When this note arrived at headquarters, an order came back down to execute Marcos.[6] However, Manriquez denies this version, as does Rivera.

Marcos chose the 14th by necessity. He was Ilocano but he chose not to join a guerrilla unit there. It seems there were relatives of Julio Nalandasan, the murdered political rival of his father, still looking for him. Some were reported to be in the 121st. Others, according to Rivera, considered many of his

movements and activities suspicious. In the investigation of the
Maharlika after the war the report of Lieutenant Pete C. Breaz
stated:

> Major Lapham states that in Dec 1944, Col Marcos came to
> Pangasinan and began soliciting funds for the construction of
> an airfield. The purpose of this airfield was supposedly to
> allow an airplane to land so that General Roxas and his
> family could be flown to SWPA; Col Marcos was apprehend-
> ed by the LGAF [Lapham's guerrilla unit] and released only
> upon word from Roxas.[7]

Marcos was arrested by Captain Ray Hunt, who commanded
one of Lapham's guerrillas units. This incident, plus the other
things — wearing a BC uniform, trying to join Anderson's outfit
under false pretenses, engaging in buy-sell activities — apparently
convinced someone that Marcos might be a Japanese collaborat-
or. It was already known that his father, Mariano, was visiting
villages in northern Luzon with a Japanese escort and giving
speeches on behalf of the Japanese. (In early 1945 he was finally
arrested and executed by the guerrillas. His body was hung in a
tree and left there as a message to other collaborators.) According
to Hunt, Marcos would have been jailed until the end of the war if
Manuel Roxas had not interceded. Marcos was subsequently
released.[8]

Afterward Marcos headed for Ambaguio, Ifugao, and the
14th. He had a law classmate there — Lieutenant Lino Patajo —
who was the S-2 of the 3rd Battalion. Patajo vouched for Marcos.
Manriquez knew the Marcos family, but he still requested verification and authorization from USAFIP NL headquarters. It was
standard operating procedure. That was when the order came
down to execute him.[9]

Stories abound as to who did what to whom and why. Exact
details are vague. It is known that Lieutenant Patajo prepared a
statement attesting to Marcos' loyalty, and asked his townmate,
Captain Rivera, to do the same, which he did. These were
delivered by First Lieutenant Venancio S. Duque, S-1 of the 14th,
to his uncle, Colonel Calixto Duque, the G-3 at USAFIP NL

headquarters, and the order was rescinded shortly afterward.

Colonel Volckmann was now ordered to create a civil affairs section in each of his regiments to handle civilian claims. Lieutenant Colonel Manriquez assigned Marcos to this position. However, Marcos' biography claims that he "was assigned as major of intelligence and adjutant general of the 14th Infantry under Manriquez."[10]

This was not true. There is no such military occupation as "major of intelligence." There is an S-2 slot, but Captain Rivera had that. There is no adjutant general's slot at regimental level. That is a division-level slot. The 14th had an adjutant, but that slot was also already filled. Marcos was the S-5, civil affairs officer of the 14th, and not the intelligence officer or the adjutant general. He would remain with the 14th in that position for four months.

Marcos' biography claims that he was quite busy in January 1945 going on patrol, blowing up roads, and evacuating an entire hospital to establish a military hospital in the mountains.[11] It also noted that he occasionally took over command of the 14th from Lieutenant Colonel Manriquez when he was sick, and that Volckmann gave him a commendation that credited him with "the total destruction of the hostile dispositions in the Provinces of Nueva Vizcaya, Isabela, and Ifugao."[12] No record of such a commendation exists, and Manriquez denies Marcos ever took over for him. He recalls that it was Marcos who was always sick. When he wasn't on sick call, he never did anything except staff work. In fact, Marcos was very busy in January, but it had little to do with the war effort.

In 1948, Marcos received another award—a Wounded Personnel Medal—for wounds received in action at Panupdupan, Kiangan, Ifugao, on 13 February 1945 (GO 303, dated 13 July 1948, HNDF). The only reference to this incident is in his biography. While on patrol Marcos supposedly shot a Japanese straggler, and, while checking the dead soldier, he, too, was shot in the back.[13] Marcos claims he was wounded a total of five times during the war. As already noted, according to his citations he received four Philippine Wounded Personnel Medals and a

Purple Heart for wounds received on 5 April 1942, 7 April 1942 (WPM and PH for this wound), 13 February 1945, and 17 March 1945. He may have forgotten but he also claimed a sixth. In his letter of 2 December 1947, he stated that "The undersigned was wounded in the right thigh in a gun fight with Japanese soldiers and undercover men in 1943." His 6 February 1946 affidavit mentions a bullet wound in "February 1943," but it isn't mentioned in any of his citations.

In 1963 he was awarded the Distinguished Conduct Star twice in two months for the same action (GO 124, dated 31 October 1963, GHQ AFP, and GO 157, dated 20 December 1963, GHQ AFP) which allegedly occurred on 17 March 1945. According to the citation, the 14th Infantry headquarters in Panupdupan, Kiangan, Mountain Province, came under attack by a battalion-size force. Though very ill in the infirmary at the time, Marcos single-handedly held the enemy at bay and then pursued them as they retreated. A counterattack proved futile. Then he and one enlisted man managed to sneak behind the lines and began firing at the enemy from the rear. Thinking it was a relief column, the enemy abandoned the attack, "withdrawing with two loads of dead and wounded."[14]

This action is not mentioned in his biography but it is mentioned by Baclagon. Manriquez and Rivera deny it ever took place. Rivera recalled the events of the day in a letter:

On March 17, 1945 [Marcos] was designated as Officer of the Day. I know this fact because I was the Regimental Supply Officer (S-4) and before he left for duty around the perimeter of the 14th Infantry HQ, he asked for food. Sgt. Sofronio La Rosa killed a small chicken and roasted half of it and gave it to Marcos. I was the CO of the Headquarters Co, being S-4 of the Regiment. At about three o'clock in the morning we heard indiscriminate shooting the firing of the Thompson sub-machine gun. The personnel in the regiment ran to the creek nearby and sent Major Dingcong to investigate the cause of the shootings. It was found that Marcos shot with his Thompson moving leaves. Marcos thought they were Japanese while in fact only moving leaves...[15]

However, Rivera's remarks contradict a signed statement by him, dated 1 October 1963, which states almost exactly the wording of the citation. He said he doesn't remember signing the document. He does know that is not his wording. He was adamant about the fact that the action for the citation never took place and that Marcos was never recommended for any awards while he served in the 14th because Marcos was never involved in any action. After the surrender, Rivera was appointed chairman of the Awards and Decorations Committee of USAFIP NL. He never came across any recommendations of any kind for Marcos.

Manriquez recalled that, during Marcos' state visit to Washington in September 1982, he was visited by one of the government ministers and a military attache of the Philippine Embassy, and asked to sign a statement attesting to the bravery of Marcos during the war. He said he did sign in a moment of weakness, and was presented with two gold Cartier watches—one for himself and one for his wife—and two books signed by the president. When he later recanted and said that Marcos didn't deserve his medals, he was visited again, and the watches and books were taken back.

Marcos' fifth Wounded Personnel Medal was awarded in 1963 (GO 155, dated 20 December 1963, GHQ AFP) for wounds received in action on 25 March 1945. On that day, Baclagon recalled in his book, the 2nd Battalion, 14th Infantry, had come under intense fire at an airfield. Marcos, commanding the combat and engineering companies, helped the 2nd Battalion put up a determined stand. After several days of battles, in which the airfield changed hands many times, the 2nd Battalion had to withdraw due to fatigue and lack of ammunition. Marcos was wounded in one of the firefights.[16]

Marcos' biography increased the number of enemy and changed the outcome of the same battle when it noted that "For nine days, fifty thousand of the Emperor's best troops contested with them the possession of a jungle airstrip, and nine times the field changed hands before the Japanese withdrew."[17]

Rivera has a different version. He was there when it happened. The Battle of Hapid took place from 25 March to 4 April 1945. Hapid was the site of an airstrip which C-47 aircraft used to deliver supplies to the 14th. The Japanese 10th Division and 2nd Tank Corps, numbering about 10,000, attacked 268 officers and enlisted men of the 2nd Battalion, 14th Infantry, commanded by Major Zosimo Paredes (the brother of Lieutenant Colonel Manriquez' wife). Rivera was Paredes' executive officer at the time. They fought for 11 days before withdrawing for lack of food and ammunition. The 14th had no "combat and engineering companies," and Marcos was not with the 2nd Battalion. He was assigned to company headquarters at Panup-dupan, as the S-5.

On 5 April 1945, Marcos supposedly won another Gold Cross and his second Silver Star. Bacalgon's book confuses the issue somewhat by giving no specific date, just "April 1945," and a few pages later states that "On April 5, Marcos won his second Silver Star, as a result of a singular action that saved the regimental command post of the 14th Infantry from being routed."[18]

Baclagon doesn't give any other details regarding the alleged second Silver Star. However, the book, *Documents On the Marcos War Medals*, does cite the 5 April 1945 action, and it is the same as Baclagon's "April 1945" action. Marcos' biography also cites the same action, noting that "On April 5, Ferdinand won his second Silver Star."[19]

The citation (GO 467, dated 22 July 1945, HPA) notes that Marcos was at 14th Infantry headquarters and volunteered to reconnoiter the surrounding area with one enlisted man after receiving a report that the Japanese had found their location. About one kilometer away he found the enemy debarking from some trucks and making their way to his headquarters. He then ordered the enlisted man to get back to headquarters and report this, and ambushed the enemy force by himself, holding them at bay for 30 minutes before the enemy retreated.[20]

The Gold Cross award for this action was made in July 1945, which makes it unique. It is the only award for valor that Marcos was awarded while still in the Army. Manriquez denies making any recommendation for the award and would like to see the supporting documentation. As Marcos' commanding officer at the time of the action he would have had to make the recommendation, and he didn't. Rivera also denies such an action took place. He stated that the best evidence against this claim is geography. "Panupdupan is very far from the road. You have to travel half day by foot to reach it. Marcos must have a good eye-sight to see [an enemy truck] one kilometer away."[21]

Marcos' biography mentions two other actions in which he allegedly participated. They are not mentioned by Baclagon. Although he won no medals for these actions, they appear to be every bit as daring and courageous as the others.

In late April 1945, the Battle of Bessang Pass was going on. Marcos was supposedly given command of a ranger company to head off a so-called "Japanese suicidal offensive" from the southern flank of General Tomoyoki Yamashita. Marcos out-flanked Yamashita and inflicted heavy casualties, thus opening up the Japanese lines which led to the final victorious battle of Bessang Pass and the surrender of General Yamashita.[22]

Also in late April 1945, the USAFIP NL supply base at Batac was supposedly attacked by another "Japanese suicidal offen-sive." Marcos was given command of another ranger team. They cut off the enemy's approach to Tirad Pass and, after severe hand-to-hand fighting in which heavy casualties were inflicted, Marcos' men enveloped their left flank.[23]

Just as there were no combat and engineering companies, there was no ranger company in the 14th, or in all of USAFIP NL. Rivera's history of the 14th does not mention either of these attacks, nor are they mentioned in Pobre's thesis, the USAFIP NL after-battle report, or the official Army history.* Both allegedly took place during the Battle of Bessang Pass. Only three units of the 14th took part in this battle. They were companies I, K, and M of the 3rd Battalion, and they were not assigned until 21 June. Rivera listed the names of the company commanders in his history: Second Lieutenant Panfilio P. Fernandez commanded I Company; First Lieutenant Teofilo Allas commanded M Compa-ny; and Captain Johny Sabalburo commanded K Company.

---

* United States in World War II. The War in the Pacific Series. Volume 11. *Triumph in the Philippines*, by Robert Ross Smith. Office of the Chief of Military History, Department of the Army, Washington, D.C., 1963.

During this battle the three companies were attached to USAFIP NL headquarters, and were not under the operational control of the 14th.[24] Marcos was not assigned to these companies and was not in the area at the time.

Both Manriquez and Rivera claim that Marcos was never involved in any patrol or combat operations while assigned to the 14th, and that he requested a transfer out of the 14th and departed on/about 28 April 1945, in a Piper Cub aircraft. The Japanese were getting closer to the 14th headquarters every day. All families of the soldiers had been ordered to evacuate the area. The only aircraft flying into Panupdupan was the single-engine Piper Cub, which made only one trip daily. The airstrip was too short for a bigger plane. The Piper Cub normally held only one passenger, but on 28 April, three passengers squeezed into the tiny cockpit — the wife of Major Zosimo Paredes, her daughter, and Marcos. They stopped by Calimag to say goodbye to her husband, and then flew on to Camp Spencer, USAFIP NL headquarters.[25] That was the end of Marcos' assignment in the 14th Infantry.

In 1954, Marcos was awarded another Distinguished Service Star (GO 196, dated 7 May 1954, GHQ AFP); and in 1963 he was awarded the same medal again (GO 153, dated 20 December 1963, GHQ AFP). The citation, for meritorious service, noted that from 29 April 1945 to 28 February 1946, Marcos had several positions of responsibility, serving concurrently "as Deputy Judge Advocate General and Deputy to AC of S G-5 (Civil Affairs Officer) and subsequently as AC of S, G-5..."[26]

Holding two somewhat diverse jobs at the same time would be difficult, but Marcos' affidavit, dated 6 February 1946, disagrees with this claim. It states:

7. 13Dec44-30Apr45, Kiangan, Mountain Province, 14th Infantry Attached to USAFIP NL

8. 1May45-6Jan46, Camp Spencer, Civil Affairs, GHQ USAFIP NL

9. 7Jan46-[Illegible] July46, Camp Spencer, Judge Advocate 2nd Inf. Div.

10. [Illegible]-5Feb46, [Illegible]

The last legible date is 5 February 1946, which contradicts the July 46 date in item 9. According to items 8 and 9, Marcos did not have "concurrent" jobs as stated in the citation. He was the AC of S, G-5, which means the assistant to the civil affairs officer in USAFIP NL, from 1 May 1945 to 6 January 1946; and Deputy Judge Advocate General, which means the assistant to the chief legal officer, in the 2d Infantry Division, from 7 January 1946 until he departed the Army, either on 5, 6, or 28 February 1946.

The citation also noted that Marcos, with many admirable talents, "[restored] the civil government in the entire area of operations of USAFIP NL, to include Abra, Cagayan, Ilocos Norte and Ilocos Sur, Isabela, La Union, Mountain Province and Nueva Vizcaya."[27]

When General MacArthur landed on Leyte, at the request of President Sergio Osmeña, the Army Service Command (ASCOM) was set up. This group had the task of going into an area after it was occupied by U.S. troops, and pacifying the area as soon as possible by settling civilian claims, constructing roads and bridges, setting up medical clinics, etc., and turning the area back over to the Philippine government as quickly as possible. General Hugh G. "Pat" Casey was appointed head of ASCOM. He, in turn, appointed Colonel Narciso Manzano as head of all civil affairs. Manzano doesn't recall Marcos restoring civil government to any province. In fact, he doesn't recall Marcos at all. Just as lieutenants had little to do with the retrograde movements of II Corps, Marcos had little to do with the civil affairs of fledgling governments. What he probably did was process legal claims for USAFIP NL. In *Valor*, it states that one of his duties was to try and determine those Filipinos who had served on active duty and not deserted or collaborated, thereby becoming eligible for back-pay and other benefits. This was done by obtaining affidavits and supporting proof whenever possible.[28] It now appears that Marcos spent a great deal of time obtaining such documentation, but not for others.

CHAPTER TEN

The "Escolta Guerrilla"

After the surrender in September 1945, Boni Gillego recalled the mood back then:

> After the war another battle raged in newly liberated Manila. The weapon was the typewriter. The battle-ground was Escolta [the main street]. The euphoria of liberation and the lure of night life enhanced under the table deals with American processors.[1]

The objective was to win back-pay and allowances, along with fame and glory. Out of this emerged the so-called "Escolta Guerrilla." Manzano voiced the same sentiments. He noted that everybody had his own list and wanted to get as many names as possible. All his friends were asked to join the guerrillas no matter what they had been during the occupation. Even Willoughby decried "the evils of 'bandwagon jumping,' in which literally thousands claimed guerrilla status and collected back-pay on it."[2]

Over a million Filipinos claimed guerrilla status after the war. The U.S. Army estimated that only about 250,000 had fought the Japanese. Because of the overwhelming paperwork involved, the Philippine-Ryukyus Command set up a special unit, the Guerrilla Affairs Division, to handle the claims.

Marcos was one of those trying to get recognition as a guerrilla and, in turn, receive pay and benefits accorded such status. However, based on the available documentation, it appears that he didn't wait until the end of the war. He started seeking recognition as soon as he arrived at the 14th Infantry headquarters in January 1945. It also appears that he was seeking a lot more.

Marcos had already been disclaimed by Fertig and turned down by Anderson. He had also just been arrested and released by one guerrilla unit, and then barely escaped being executed by another. In addition, his father was executed as a collaborator about this time. So, recognition meant a little more to him than just pay and benefits. He was trying to salvage the family honor and some respectability, and he didn't have much time. The Americans had landed. It was only a matter of time before the war would be over. So he must have decided that if he were going to make a case for himself as a soldier and a guerrilla, he had better start doing it now. It is highly probably that, as of January 1945, Marcos had not been awarded any medals nor had he been recommended for any. The elaborate attempt to prove himself the bravest soldier and the bravest guerrilla of all may have its origins in these somewhat sobering circumstances.

Although he had just been assigned to the 14th Infantry, Marcos prepared a letter on stationery with the heading "The United States Forces in the Philippines, 'Ang Manga Maharlika,' (Interior Force), Manila Sector," dated 25 January 1945, and addressed to "The United States Liberation Army Headquarters." In it he claimed "5,000 strong patriots ready for action," and added, "Furthermore, the unit wishes to solicit from the Liberation Forces an official recognition that the unit [is]...fighting for the cause of liberating the Philippines."[3] There is no known reply. About this time he also prepared a Maharlika "Unit Report," and backdated it to 26 July 1944. This report claimed the Maharlika numbered 8,300 troops and possessed 474 weapons and several thousand rounds of ammunition. A later investigation revealed that the Maharlika unit claiming these weapons didn't receive them until 1945, leaving no doubt that the report could not have been prepared before January 1945 and was, therefore, a fabrication.

As already noted, Marcos requested a transfer to the USAFIP NL headquarters which was granted, and he departed the 14th Infantry on 28 April. Almost as soon as he arrived he put in a request to Colonel Volckmann, asking to return to his Maharlika unit in Manila. Volckmann turned him down, stating that "his organization, Ang Manga Maharlika, is not among the guerrilla units recognized by higher headquarters."[4] It is somewhat ironic that his very first award—the Distinguished Service Star—was for "outstanding service as a guerrilla and underground leader in the Philippines in World War II." The date of the award is 24 April 1945, about a week before Volckmann turned him down because his Maharlika wasn't a recognized guerrilla unit. The awarding unit is Headquarters, Philippine Army (HPA), General Order 435. (As already noted, he was awarded this medal again in 1963.) Someone, during the war, had to make a recommendation for such an award. Two of the guerrilla leaders who supposedly would have been aware of his guerrilla service were Fertig and Umali, but neither made the recommendation. It could have been someone at Headquarters, Philippine Army, but this is unlikely as will be shown.

On 22 July 1945, Marcos was awarded a Gold Cross "for gallantry in action," that took place on 5 April 1945. Again the awarding unit was Headquarters, Philippine Army, General Order 467. It is not known who made the recommendation for this award either. In this case it would have had to come from Lieutenant Colonel Manriquez, his commanding officer at the time, but he didn't make the recommendation. Both awards—the Distinguished Service Star and Gold Cross—were supposedly awarded during the war, and both came from Headquarters, Philippine Army.

On 18 August 1945, three days after hostilities officially ended in the Philippines, Marcos wrote to the Headquarters, Philippine Army, Adjutant General, and asked for recognition as a guerrilla unit. He cited several instances of Maharlika missions in order to justify such recognition, but surprisingly he never mentioned either award, which would have certainly added to his credibility.

Instead, in citing the reason for joining another outfit, the 14th, while supposedly leading the Maharlika, he stated that the U.S. Army landings at Lingayan cut off his return to his unit. This letter may have been the first to cast suspicion on Marcos'

claims. It went through an official chain of command. Major
Harry McKenzie, in the first endorsement to the request, dated 16
September, stated:

> Par 3 b. is contradictory in itself. "Landings at Lingayen cut
> off my return to my organization." However, he attached
> himself to USAFIP NL 12 December 1944, only a few days
> after he arrived in the area. Landings a month later could not
> have influenced his abandoning his outfit and attaching
> himself to another guerrilla organization.[5]

Four days later Lieutenant Colonel James W. Davis, at
Luzon Area Headquarters, in the second endorsement, concurred
with McKenzie and turned down Marcos' request. On 1 October
1945, Major General Basilio J. Valdez, Philippine Army Chief of
Staff, in the third endorsement, made the following comment:

> 1. Basic communication pertains to a request for approval of
> an additional roster of the guerrilla unit known as "Ang
> Manga Maharlika." The only roster of the "Ang Manga
> Maharlika" received at this office is the roster of the
> Intelligence Section of said unit with a strength of 32 men
> under the command of Major Ferdinand Marcos.
>
> 2. As roster of guerrilla units have to be approved by GHQ,
> AFPAC, this is referred to that Headquarters...[6]

The fourth endorsement requested "documentary evidence in
the form of a certificate of attachment to a United States Army
unit."[7]

Over the next two and one-half years Marcos would attempt
to gain recognition. Beginning with Major MacKenzie's report,
numerous investigations regarding the Maharlika would be
conducted and would lead one investigating officer to conclude
that the unit was "fraudulent." Among other things, Marcos had
taken to inserting his name as commanding officer on the rosters
of units he wasn't associated with, thereby hoping to convince the
Guerrilla Affairs Division that they were a part of the Maharlika.
The insertion of his name on any roster other than the USAFIP

NL, the investigating officer concluded, was "a malicious criminal act."[8]

Although the war was over, Marcos was still in the Army, assigned to USAFIP NL headquarters in the Civil Affairs section, and still trying to get recognition. On 18 December 1945, he wrote again and asked why his Maharlika headquarters unit wasn't recognized while the "East Pangasinan Unit" and the "Special Intelligence Unit" were. These two units had been given official recognition, and Marcos claimed the Maharlika headquarters had planned and initiated their organization.[9] An investigation was conducted by Lieutenant William D. MacMillan, and a letter was written in June 1947 informing Marcos that "recognition of this guerrilla unit is not deemed to be warranted." It listed eleven reasons for the denial.[10]

Before he got out of the Army in February 1946, Marcos made certain his claims were a matter of record. In his 6 February 1946 affidavit, he stated:

> 6. 16Oct42-12Dec44, CO,Maharlika Guer Unit Manila.

He elaborated under remarks:

> Re line 6. Ang Manga Maharlika, a guerrilla organization of which I was the CO was organized inside Camp O'Donnell although roster was formally drafted 1 Dec 1942. As to [illegible] of work area and occupation: membership and recognition of Guer. unit see attached extract from page 45 "Guerrilla Resistance Movement in the Philippines," published by General Hq, SWPA on 31 March 1945. As to date organization, the endorsement of Chief of Staff, PA to the papers of recognition, acknowledgment of intelligence report and extract list of Luzon guerrillas from SWPA, June 1944(sic).

The SWPA report he refers to is the same "official report" referred to in his biography and, as already noted, is the mention in Willoughby's book he would always refer to when claiming his Maharlika did exist. The endorsement of the chief of staff he referred to was that of General Valdez. As already noted, this was not an endorsement to Marcos' so-called papers of recognition, but a comment that the only roster of the Maharlika received at his office showed a strength of 32 men commanded by Marcos.[11]

As already noted he stated in the same affidavit that he had been awarded a Silver Star and two Distinguished Service Crosses. Although no orders could be found to justify the awards, Major Aurelio Lucero executed affidavits on 1 February 1946, attesting to the awards. The following July the U.S. Army acknowledged Marcos' claims "based on your statements and the affidavits of witnesses." This must have spurred him to greater efforts in seeking recognition. It also may have given him a new idea.

When Marcos received word that he was turned down in June 1947, he was in Washington, D.C., on an official visit to lobby for Filipino veterans' benefits. He fired off a radiogram and protested strongly his denial of recognition. This set into motion more investigations by the U.S. Army and led Captain Curtis to conclude in his report of 25 July 1947 that "Marcos has enough political prestige to bring pressure to bear where it is needed for his own personal benefit."[12] When he returned from Washington, Marcos prepared for one last onslaught. To support his claim three bound books of documentation, including affidavits, accompanied Marcos letter of 2 December 1947.[13] Apparently his political prestige didn't bring enough pressure. There were no affidavits from Umali or Manriquez, two of the people he was supposed to have actually served under as a guerrilla. Also, one of the most important affidavits he could have included to substantiate at least one of his claims was missing. Manuel Roxas was now the President of the Philippines. An affidavit from him would give Marcos' Maharlika considerable credibility and also clear up the claim that he had been collecting money in Pangasinan to build an airstrip for Roxas. However, for some reason Marcos never submitted an affidavit from Roxas.

Now he had pulled out all the stops and was citing all manner of daring deeds already noted. Strangely, he still didn't mention the medals he had been awarded by Headquarters, Philippine Army, as a guerrilla although he did mention his U.S. awards in the Maharlika history included with this new request. It wouldn't have mattered anyway. The evidence proved to be his undoing. It was a mass of inconsistencies and contradictions impossible to reconcile.

In the letter dated 7 June 1947, one of the reasons given for denying one his earlier requests for recognition was that "Adequate records were not maintained."[14] In his last attempt Marcos stated that his records "were destroyed in the middle of 1944 to prevent the leaking of our secrets." He went on to state, "Any group of men who have an abundance of records are not true guerrillas."[15] However, in an earlier letter to the Adjutant General, Philippine Army, dated 18 August 1945, Marcos told a different story. "My request [for a transfer] was denied [in May 1945]...I had lost contact with the officers and men of my unit and the original roster and other papers of the organization were buried somewhere in Manila. I alone knew the location thereof."[16]

The Ang Manga Maharlika was supposedly composed of four units: The headquarters in Manila, commanded by Major Ferdinand E. Marcos; the Ilocos Norte Regiment, commanded by Major Simeon Valdez; the East Pangasinan Unit, commanded by Captain Donato Ancheta; and the Allas Intelligence Unit, commanded by Captain Cipriano Allas. This table of organization was a complete fabrication. Marcos attempted to make it appear as a fighting force commanded by him. In reality, they were never unified and most did indeed belong to Volckmann's organization. Valdez, Ancheta, and Allas did command units, and each one did ultimately receive recognition by the U.S. Army as a fighting force during a particular time, but Marcos and the Maharlika had nothing to do with the existence of the respective fighting forces.

Marcos' Maharlika history claims that his unit was formed on 1 December 1942, and that Major Simeon Valdez was with him from the start. Marcos supposedly sent Valdez to Ilocos Norte in early 1944 to form the Ilocos Norte regiment. This was done in April or May 1944. Because of intimidation from other guerrilla units in the area, Marcos ordered Valdez to join with the 15th Infantry Regiment. Most of the 15th came from Valdez' unit. Those are the facts according to the Marcos and the Maharlika history.[17] And they are also a complete fabrication. Captain Curtis noted in his investigative report of 25 July 1947:

> The Ilocost Norte Regt under the command of S M Valdez
> was not organized or contacted by Maj Ferdinand Marcos
> until after Nov 1944.[18]

Valdez did not organize his so-called Ilocos Norte regiment until November 1944, despite his and Marcos' claims to the contrary. Also, Valdez had written Colonel Volckmann, the USAFIP NL commander, and requested to join him.[19] He did so in November 1944, and joined the 15th Infantry Regiment, USAFIP NL. He commanded its 1st Battalion.[20] His unit served honorably and was recognized, but not as part of Marcos' Maharlika. Marcos joined the 14th Infantry of USAFIP NL a month later. Captain Curtis concluded:

> It is evident that Ferdinand Marcos and S M Valdez
> combined their forces in order to gain recognition and by so
> doing have created a very confused picture of the unit.[21]

Marcos claimed that the East Pangasinan Combat Unit, under a Captain Corrales, joined the Maharlika in April 1943, after the capture of Major Cushing, with whom the unit had served. This was the unit which Marcos claimed had possessed 474 weapons. On investigation, Captain Ancheta, the commanding officer of the unit, admitted that his East Pangasinan Unit was in existence prior to liberation but it was not active, nor did it have arms, until it was attached to the 128th Infantry, 32d Division, on 11 February 1945.[22] The unit served honorably and its 111 officers and men were recognized but not as a part of Marcos' Maharlika.[23] For some reason the recognized roster did not contain the name of Captain Corrales.

Captain Cipriano Allas claimed that he organized the Allas Intelligence Unit in August 1942. He was captured on 26 May 1943, and the unit disintegrated. He was released in early June 1943, and joined the Maharlika on 15 July 1943. He served with that unit until August 1945. With the arrival of the liberating forces he had himself and 29 men attached to the 25th Infantry Division on 25 January 1945. However, the investigative report of First Lieutenant Kenneth H. Neubauer stated that there was no evidence that the unit was ever active until it joined the 25th Division.[24] Another investigative report by First Lieutenant Hospicio M. Velarde revealed that Allas spent most of his time in 1943 engaged in nefarious trade with the Japanese.[25] However, his unit, composed of 30 men, was attached to the 25th Infantry Division on 25 January 1945, served honorably, and received recognition, but not as part of Marcos' Maharlika.[26]

Unfortunately, all of Marcos' political prestige couldn't bring him the one thing he craved—recognition as a guerrilla leader. The only unit in his contrived Maharlika not recognized was the headquarters that he supposedly commanded. Marcos claimed, in his letter dated 2 December 1947, that his Manila unit "of a little more than a hundred in number" was attached to the 5th Cavalry.[27] An investigation revealed that only six officers and 18 enlisted men had been assigned.[28] Furthermore, in a letter dated 31 May 1945, Major R.G. Langham of the 5th Cavalry recommended that even these not be considered for recognition due to the limited value of their duties.[29] This marked the ignominious end of the Maharlika.

If the war record of Lieutenant Ferdinand E. Marcos is to be believed, only one other man in history performed as many brave deeds. In 1918, during World War I, while serving with the 42nd "Rainbow" Division in France, Colonel Douglas MacArthur won a Silver Star and Croix de Guerre on 26 February. That was only the beginning. Over the next nine months he became a legend, winning the following medals for bravery:

9 March	Distinguished Service Cross
15 July	Silver Star
29 July	Silver Star
3 August	Silver Star and Croix de Guerre
11 September	Silver Star
26 September	Silver Star
15 October	Distinguished Service Cross
6 November	Silver Star

All told, in World War I he won two Croix de Guerre, two Distinguished Service Crosses, seven Silver Stars, two Purple

Hearts, a Distinguished Service Medal, and 19 other medals from allied nations. The total came to 33. He had also been recommended for a Congressional Medal of Honor in 1913 at Vera Cruz, Mexico, but it didn't go through. The war record of General MacArthur was well known in the Philippines. To the Filipinos he was almost a god. And, of course, many tried to emulate him.

Twenty-four years later, Lieutenant Marcos, with the 21st "Lightning" Division, is alleged to have performed such feats of daring as to make him his country's most decorated soldier. But the evidence just isn't there. No one heard of those deeds during the war. All are based on affidavits, and the citations don't reconcile with the facts.

When Marcos was turned down for the last time in March 1948, he switched his tactics and put in a claim for $594,900, claiming the Army had commandeered 2,366 head of cattle on the Marcos ranch in Mindanao. This claim was also rejected.[30] Then he decided if he couldn't get official recognition, he would write his own version of the war. This he did. His biography, *For Every Tear a Victory*, and later the book *Valor* had to fulfill all of his fantasies as a hero of biblical proportions, something he never was. And then there was the movie. In 1970, it was decided that a movie of President Marcos' war exploits should be made, entitled "MAHARLIKA." A beautiful American actress, Dovie Beams, was brought over to the Philippines to play the romantic lead. Marcos met her and they became lovers. He eventually tired of her, so she decided to play another part—that of scorned lover. She called a press conference and played a tape-recording for her audience. It was the sounds of their love-making. Needless to say, this created quite a stir. She flew to Hong Kong afterward and made the headlines there when she announced that several gunmen were sent by Marcos to kill her. She finally made it back to the states alive. Whether or not the movie was ever completed is not known.

Marcos the soldier was an illusion. His claims are so full of discrepancies and inconsistencies that it is difficult to believe he performed any of those alleged deeds. The claims appear to be part of an elaborate hoax perpetrated by someone who couldn't settle for just being brave. He had to be the bravest. Therein somewhere probably lies a key to a man who couldn't settle for just being president. He wanted more — a whole lot more.

PART II
Statesman

CHAPTER ELEVEN

Introduction

The Ethnic origin of the Filipino is an anthropological phantasmagoria. Its intricate social and cultural fabric is due in part to the trade that has flourished there for centuries, and brought it a constant stream of new knowledge. The monsoons that blew across the oceans filled the sails of early vessels plying the East-West trade routes more than 2,000 years ago, and the Chinese began to wander farther and farther from their coasts in search of more trade. Later the Arab traders arrived with their message of Islam, and these were followed by Europeans searching for the spices for which the region was renowned.

The earliest settlers were Negritos, a group of aboriginal people. They were followed by the Malay and the Chinese. The Islamic influence was not felt until about the fourteenth century, and the Spanish latecomers didn't arrive until the seventeenth century, but they stayed for more than 300 years until the turn of the century. During Spanish rule the trade route to the Philippines was via Mexico. Acapulco was the major trading port. From there Mexican Creoles (Caucasians born in Mexico) and Latin American mestizos sailed for the Philippines to find their fortunes. Many married and settled there.

The Philippines is one of the most beautiful countries in the world. Lush green tropical rain forests are criss-crossed by towering mountain ranges. More than 7,000 islands are spread over a half-million square miles of blue-green ocean. This tropical paradise has an annual average temperature of about 80 to 85 degrees. When the sun sets in Manila Bay, the strikingly brilliant colors can only be described as awesome.

The beauty is misleading, however. The ages will attest to this. Typhoons, earthquakes, and volcanic eruptions have reminded the inhabitants from time immemorial that nature rules this paradise. Typhoons are a common occurrence during the rainy season. There have been an average of 26 a year for the past 15 years. The volume of rain can exceed 160 to 200 inches during the rainy season, which is six months a year. (The annual average rainfall for New York City is about 45 inches.) The country lies on the Pacific seismic belt. Severe earthquakes occur occasionally. The most destructive in recorded history was on August 17, 1976, in Mindanao. A tidal wave rendered 90,000 homeless. Three thousand people were killed and another 3,000 disappeared. There are at least ten active volcanoes. One of them—Taal, on the island of Luzon—erupted on January 30, 1911, killing 1,300.

The country is also rich in natural resources. More than one-third of the land is under cultivation. Its primary crops are rice, maize, coconut, and sugarcane. It is almost self-sufficient in rice and corn. Coconut oil and coconut products are big dollar earners for the country. Sugar was until a few years ago. Tobacco, abaca (hemp), ramie, pineapples and bananas are also grown for export and local consumption. One-third of the U.S. market for pineapples comes from Mindanao in the southern Philippines. There are 50,000 square miles of mineral lands. There is gold, silver, copper, nickel, iron, lead, manganese, zinc, and the world's largest deposit of chromite. It is the sixth largest producer of gold. Copper is the biggest dollar earner in the minerals.

The country is truly rich, but, as with its beauty, the riches can also be misleading. How can so much wealth cause so much misery?

The Philippines has a history of violence due primarily to the fact that country after country has laid claim to this wealth. The Spanish brutally repressed the people for more than 300 years, and it took the Americans six years of guerrilla warfare to put down the insurrection at the turn of the century. After a brief respite, the U.S. set up the Philippine Army in 1936, just in time to participate in World War II. After the war the Philippines was granted independence in 1946.

David Joel Steinberg, one of the foremost American authorities on the Philippines today, noted that the war did something to the country: "[It] spawned a totally armed society, and the readiness to resort to force has been a disturbing feature of post-independence Philippine life.'" In 1946 Governor Rafael Lascon of Bacolod raised his own private army. They were called a "reaction and security force" to combat dissidence and banditry. The practice spread and other provincial governors soon had their armies. Then some business-politicians decided they needed more protection. Gradually the number of political warlords with private armies grew.

The Philippines is a developing country. It is transitional in the context that it is evolving from a traditional society steeped in the mores and traditions of more than 500 years of Spanish, Chinese, Catholic, and Islam influence, to a modern society characterized by the influence of the Americans for most of this century. Its value systems stem from traditional Old-World concepts mixed with a penchant for American food, clothes, and cars.

The "compadres" system is a personal relationship established between a person of whatever status in the community with a "patron," who can be anyone from a good friend to the head of a social enclave to whom all others owe loyalty and allegiance. By having him act as the godfather at a wedding, baptism, or confirmation, a certain degree of kinship is established between the patron and the honoree.

Inherent in the same system is a high regard for authority and an excessive concern for status in the community. This can be seen, for example, by the way people are addressed or introduced as "Engineer Valdez" or "Attorney Cruz." By the same token, high social value is placed on wealth. The wealthier the Filipino, the greater the status. Add to this a political dimension. Filipinos view a career in government or politics as a family opportunity for wealth and lifetime security.

A politician in the Philippines would quickly recognize how a network of ritual bonds could be developed. It is obvious that Marcos became aware of this very early in his political career. A patron dispensing political favors to relatives and friends, thus gaining their loyalty and allegiance, could go a long way in poliltics. A recipient of such favors would incur another Filipino trait—the "utang na loob," the debt of gratitude. The extent to which one carried this social networking would, to a great degree, determine how successful one could be in politics.

Marcos was an Ilocano, coming from Ilocos Norte. In the local dialect he was their "apo," the patron of all Ilocanos. All his trusted generals in the military, and many of his trusted advisors, were Ilocano. Just being an Ilocano during the reign of Marcos gave one a certain advantage over others seeking favors. However, his compadres network did not stop at the boundary of Ilocos Norte. It spread all over the Philippines.

CHAPTER TWELVE

The Politician

It was in this social atmosphere of compadres mixed with a political scheme that included warlords and private armies that Marcos went to work in post-war Manila in March 1946 in the prominent law firm of Vicente Francisco, the attorney who had defended him in the Nalundasan murder case, and had defended Laurel in his collaboration case. Another young assistant in the office was Arsenio Lacson, who would go on to fortune and fame as a newspaperman and then become the hugely popular mayor of Manila. Some think he would have become president instead of Marcos if he had not died of a heart attack in 1962. In addition to sharing political aspirations, they had at least one other thing in common. Both were notorious womanizers. In fact, Marcos would wind up marrying one of Lacson's girlfriends, Imelda Romualdez.

In 1948 Marcos reestablished his residency in his home province of Ilocos Norte and began his first political campaign. He won his first election in 1949 as a congressman (as did Lacson). During his first term in office he authored the Import Control Law and became chairman of its committee. Dollars were scarce and had to be regulated, so the law required that all requests for import licenses be screened and approved by the Central Bank Import Control Board.

At that time, J.G. "Johnny" Quijano was a successful Manila lawyer. He defended several prominent personalities of that era, including Teodoro Locsin of the Philippine Free Press, the nation's largest circulation weekly magazine, who was prone to the use of strong language in describing the local political scene. This occasionally got him in trouble. He was sued for libel more than a dozen times but, with the help of Quijano, was never found guilty. Another client was a Chinese who brought suit against the Import Control Board for malicious discrimination. Because of the suit Quijano was able to familiarize himself with the Board's practices, and in the process learned how Marcos may have made his first fortune.

The normal procedure was to submit an application to the Board and wait for approval. After several weeks or months the application might be turned down, or approved for only a fraction of the amount requested. However, there was another way to expedite the request. If ten percent of the amount requested were offered as an incentive, full approval could be had within ten days. The money, always cash, was delivered to a lawyer in Dasmariñas, downtown Manila. As a rule no receipt was given. Afterward a phone call was made to the Board and a notation made on that person's application: "Please expedite." Marcos was rumored to be the most notorious ten-percenter in this business. During this period he met a beautiful young mestiza (she was a former Miss Press Photography Philippines), Carmen Ortega, from Vigan, Ilocos Sur, working in the Import Control section of the Central Bank. Although they never married, they lived together until Marcos married Imelda. The union resulted in four children.

While Marcos was making a name for himself in Congress, the Secretary of Defense Ramon Magsaysay was busy putting down a rebellion that had sprang up in central Luzon, near Manila, after World War II. The Huks were the same guerrilla outfit that fought in the war. Now they had banded together to support the peasants who demanded agrarian reform. The rebellion was eventually crushed with assistance from U.S. counterinsurgency experts.[1] The leader of the Huks surrendered in 1952 to Magsaysay's young assistant, 18-year-old Benigno Aquino, Jr., "Ninoy" to his friends. Magsaysay would go on to become the next president of his country. Young Aquino's political career was just beginning.

Marcos continued to further his political ambitions as he rose in prominence. After three terms as congressman he was elected to the Senate in 1959, and became Senate president in 1963. It was during Marcos' campaign for Senate president that he was involved in a scandal. In the late 50's, Harry S. Stonehill was one of the most powerful Americans in the Philippines. He had a cotton plantation and his U.S. Tobacco Corporation was the country's largest cigarette firm. He also began the first land reclamation project in Manila Bay. His business practices attracted the attention of Senator Gil Puyat, chairman of the Budget Committee, who complained that people like Stonehill were ruining the economy. He requested the chief of the National Bureau of Investigation, Lieutenant Colonel Jose Lukban, to investigate him. Stonehill's phones were tapped and his companies examined. The investigation took over a year. Finally all his corporations and houses were raided at the same time on March 3, 1962. Some 25 truckloads of documents were confiscated. One of the items seized was the "Blue Book."

The Blue Book contained a list of names, including several politicians, of people who were entertained by Stonehill. If any of these people were going to New York, he would inform Ira Blaustein, his general manager there, of their visit. Upon arrival they would be entertained royally and their hotel accommodations taken care of. The Blue Book and other evidence was examined by both houses of Congress. Senator Oscar Ledesma's Committee on Elections and Privileges and Representative Jovita Salonga's Committee on Good Government looked into the reported involvement of congressmen. Many of them sheepishly admitted their guilt. Marcos' name was on the list but he vehemently denied any wrongdoing. He said he had received money from Blaustein but he had returned it, and presented a receipt for $2,000 as proof. The receipt was turned over to the NBI. Lukban's document officer examined it and found it to be fake. They were ready to testify in Congress about the matter but all of a sudden it was hushed up. Marcos had powerful friends even then.[2]

After 14 years in the Philippines, Stonehill was deported on August 4, 1962. In a radio-television address to the nation ten days later, President Diosdado Macapagal defended the deportation, stating that "graft and corruption has been contained and reduced to the minimum." Although no names were mentioned he went on to proclaim that "the causes of corruption such as licensing of dollars and imports" had also been removed during his administration. There was little doubt as to the target of such remarks but they had little effect. Marcos went on to become the Senate president and, in 1965, ran for president against Macapagal. His campaign biography, *For Every Tear a Victory*, printed that year, trumpeted his wartime exploits. The people loved it. He was elected. Lukban was removed as head of the NBI in 1966.[3]

A Central Intelligence Agency memorandum, entitled "Philippine Elections" described the political scene during the presidential race of 1965.

> The Philippine electorate craves efficient and honest government and increasingly feels it does not get it. There is a generalized condition of discontent and lawlessness in the Philippines that is fed by several basic and interrelated factors: widespread rural poverty; deep social and economic cleavage between upper and lower classes; extensive unemployment and underemployment; widespread graft, corruption, and favoritism in government and in business. In the cities, especially among the youth, there is frustration over the lack of political and economic opportunity...[4]

In the first year of the Marcos presidency the Philippine government signed the United Nations-sponsored International Covenant on Civil and Political Rights. Later, it backtracked. While stating that it fully subscribed to all rights enumerated in the Covenant, the government said it did not wish to ratify it. The reason given was that it considered provisions allowing states' parties to the Covenant to bring petitions against one another constituted a derogation from national sovereignty. This seemingly trivial objection was the first indication of a man who would abuse the power of his office more than any other in history. The truth was far more ominous. Marcos had his own ideas about political rights.[5]

He also had his own ideas about graft and corruption. On March 20 and 21, 1968, four bank accounts were opened by Marcos at the Swiss Credit Bank in Zurich. Two were in his name, one in the name of William Saunders, and one in the name of Jane Ryan. A total of $950,000 was deposited. Just three years earlier, in the first year of his presidency, Marcos had declared his assets to be $30,000, and his annual salary as president was the equivalent of $5,600.[6]

He ran again four years later and once again used his old tactic of trumpeting his wartime exploits. He may have gone a little too far when he reminded everyone that his opponent, Sergio Osmeña, had been convicted in 1947 of collaboration during World War II. Marcos won again. Osmeña called the campaign the dirtiest in his country's history.

As Marcos began his second term in 1970, he was confronted with the same issues that had confronted him four years earlier. The poverty was still there as was the widespread graft and corruption; and the enormous chasm between the lower and upper class still existed. There was little evidence that he had done anything to alleviate any of these problems. Against this backdrop of economic unrest were some 80 political warlords with private armies scattered across the country. According to the Philippine Free Press of November 15, 1970, "Six are members of the Senate, 37 members of the Lower House and the rest are provincial governors, city mayors and prominent individuals related to powerful politicians."[7] The Free Press article was a public outcry against the armies and the random violence and gunfights it produced that was so typical of the times. It got results...of sorts. Two months later the paper reported that the number of private armies was down considerably, but the number of licensed private security agencies had increased from 192 to 507 during the same period.[8]

No one was about to give up his army. They were needed. According to Steinberg, "Since the holding of office guarantees power and therefore the opportunity for wealth, the scramble to get elected in the years prior to martial law cheapened the electoral process through fraud, murder, and bribery."⁹ Guns and violence were as much a part of the electoral process as the stuffed ballot box.

Marcos had neglected his country's wellbeing in order to prepare for a more important task, that of perpetuating his dynasty. He had already begun putting together a political machine that would help perpetuate his rule. There were signs everywhere. A Constitutional Convention began rewriting the nation's constitution in 1970. Marcos tried every way possible to influence its writing, including outright bribery. In what became known as the "Payola Expose," Imelda was caught distributing envelopes of cash to delegates who might be convinced to write a Marcos version. One delegate, Eduardo Quintero of Leyte, exposed the corrupt practice.

Also in 1970 another scandal occurred. Two prominent newspapermen were kidnapped and forcibly taken to Taiwan. The Yuyitung brothers, Quintin and Rizal, published the *Chinese Commercial News*. They were highly critical of the Chinese Kuomintang faction from Taiwan, which was very prominent in local business. The leader was Antonio Roxas Chua, a Chinese-Filipino who was a big contributor to Marcos' campaign. For some reason the brothers were ordered deported after being given a cursory hearing by the Immigration Board. Johnny Quijano, their lawyer, appealed the decision to the Supreme Court. While waiting for a verdict, which everyone expected to be in their favor, the brothers were arrested, taken to the airport, and forcibly put on a plane for Taipei. That was the last place the brothers wanted to go. The Kuomintang were in power there. They were tried by a military court and sentenced, Rizal to two years and Quintin to one year in prison.

There was more political violence. On August 21, 1971, at Plaza Miranda in Manila, two grenades exploded in the middle of a political rally being held by several politicians running for reelection who were opposed to President Marcos. Nine were killed and many more injured, including all seven Liberal Party candidates. Among the wounded were Senator Gerardo Roxas

and his wife, Senators Jovito Salonga, Sergio Osmeña Jr., and
Eva Estrada Kalaw, and Senate hopefuls Ramon Mitra and John
H. Osmeña. Aquino, by now a senator and a presidential
aspirant, arrived late and avoided the tragedy. Newspapers
speculated that the grenades were intended for him alone. Marcos
publicly ordered an investigation, but after the excitement died
down, the clamor for justice gradually subsided. The perpetrators
were never identified or arrested.[10]

The year 1972 started with three months of monsoon rains
which destroyed the nation's rice crop, a staple in every
household. Marcos was getting blasted in the press for his failure
to fulfill any of his campaign promises and the rampant bribery
and corruption that still persisted. Senator Aquino, now the
prime candidate for the '73 presidential campaign, was Marcos'
number one protagonist. An eloquent orator, he was speaking
almost daily of Marcos' inept bureaucracy.

In the meantime random bombings in the urban areas,
especially Manila, were increasing. They were blamed on the
communists. Then a car carrying Minister of Defense Juan Ponce
Enrile was ambushed in September. Enrile survived but that
incident provoked Marcos into declaring martial law. At least that
is what he wanted everyone to believe. In reality it was a set-up.
Only years later would Enrile admit that Marcos had the ambush
staged in order to carry out his plans. The fact is his second term
was winding down. He couldn't legally run for a third term and
the constitution had not been changed according to his liking. The
only way to stay in office was through emergency powers. Some
of his opponents were aware of this possibility. Senator Jose W.
Diokno, in a speech to the Senate entitled "A Throne of
Bayonets," in mid-July 1972, warned that Marcos might attempt
such a move. He was rewarded when martial law was declared by
being arrested and kept in a military stockade until the Supreme
Court ruled in favor of the legitimacy of the new presidency.

In September 1972, Johnny Quijano was in Taipei arranging
for Quintin Yuyitung's papers to go to the United States. He had
just gotten out of prison and couldn't return to the Philippines. A

reporter from the Taipei bureau of Agence Free Press called Quijano, told him that martial law had been declared, and asked for an interview. Quijano acceded to the request and lambasted Marcos. It was published the next day in the *Stars and Stripes* newspaper. This infuriated Marcos, who ordered Quijano arrested as soon as he landed in Manila. Quijano was called in Taipei and warned not to return. As a result he departed for the United States with his friend and client, Quintin Yuyitung, who was also persona non grata in Manila. They became two of the first exiles.[11]

Constitutional Authoritarianism

On September 23, 1972, martial law was announced.* Marcos called it the birth of a "New Society." He protested about the oligarchic character of Fililpino society. A few families controlled most of the wealth in the Philippines, and he called for a "Democratic Revolution" to demolish them. He proclaimed: "Let no man invoke friendship or blood kinship to enrich himself or to enhance his position." The Tagalog phrase "Walang Palakasan" became his battlecry. Loosely translated it meant: no weight-throwing, no name-dropping, no favors asked or given, no undeserved attention and no influence peddling.[1]

At first everyone had hope. The *Philippine News* in San Francisco described the change as "A blare of slogans and promises that wafted like a breath of fresh air across a land made arid by influence peddlers, vested interests, political untouchables and sacred cows."[2] Sadly this didn't last very long.

Marcos called his version of democracy "constitutional authoritarianism," but the similarities between this and the "constitutional dictatorship" form of government Laurel had used as Japan's puppet president in World War II are striking. Steinberg's study of Laurel noted that while serving as president, his authoritarian tendencies began to emerge. Even before the war he had defended the emergency powers of President Quezon,

---

* The declaration of martial law was signed two days earlier, on September 21, but it wasn't announced until the 23rd.

saying that "constitutional dictatorship" was in keeping with a world-wide trend in which "totalitarianism is gradually supplanting democracy." He espoused the belief that Japan's "phenomenal rise...has been due, in the main, to its system of government which is characterized by massive powers, rigidly centralized, but exercised with wise benevolence."[3]

Laurel was attempting "to maintain the western style institutional forms of constitutional democracy while actually creating [a] modified dictatorship in order to effect needed reforms." One of his first moves after assuming the presidency was to get the appointed legislature to pass Act 39, which declared a state of emergency and authorized the "President of the Republic of the Philippines to promulgate rules and regulations to safeguard the safety, health and tranquility of the inhabitants of the Philippines." Noted Steinberg: "Laurel made maximum use of the powers granted to him by the 1943 Constitution and this legislative act to dominate all governmental activity."[4]

As president of the Japanese-sponsored mass political party, the Kalibapi, he supervised the only legitimate political organization permitted by the Japanese. In December 1942, the Japanese had dissolved all political parties, and a single party was formed for the National Service of the New Philippines, later called the Kalibapi. Membership was supposed to be voluntary, but anyone dealing with the government in any way whatsoever had to prove membership. Of course, under such a dictatorship, everybody had to deal with the government in some way.[5]

Laurel's espousal of "constitutional dictatorship" may have planted the seeds for Marcos' "constitutional authoritarianism" 30 years before martial law was declared. Like Laurel, Marcos made maximum use of his powers to dominate all governmental activity. However, unlike Laurel, he did not espouse the merits of totalitarianism and avoided any mention of the word "dictatorship." He knew what he could do with "massive powers, rigidly centralized," and it had little to do with effecting needed reforms. He also had plans for his own version of the Kalibapi.

General Order No. 1 was signed on September 22, 1972. It stated that Marcos would "govern the nation and direct the operation of the entire government, including all its agencies and instruments." In other words, Marcos assumed all the powers of government—executive, legislative, and judicial. General Order No. 2 followed quickly. It ordered the Minister of Defense to arrest named individuals who were said to be "active participants in the conspiracy to seize state power."[6] It ordered the arrest and detention "until otherwise ordered released by me or my duly authorized representative" of people who might have committed the crimes of insurrection or rebellion, crimes against national security, the law of nations, the fundamental laws of the state, public order, and crimes involving usurpation of public authority. Persons who had violated decrees and orders promulgated by the president or on the president's orders were also to be detained.[7]

It was a witchhunt and had nothing to do with communists, subversives, conspiracy, or rebellion. It was enemies of Marcos, not enemies of the state, who were rounded up. The "conspirators" all turned out to be his political opponents and journalists who were critical of his regime. Senator Aquino was picked up the same day the General Order was signed—Friday, September 22—at a speaking engagement at the Hilton Hotel. The roundup continued through the weekend. There were a lot of knocks on doors at midnight reminiscent of the Gestapo and KGB.

On Friday night all newspapers and radio and television stations were closed and journalists were detained. None were ever brought to trial but overnight 50,000 gainfully employed people were out of work.* Only a few were ever allowed to return to their jobs.[8]

The New Society did not allow criticism. The importance of this issue was shown when the first Presidential Decree—PD

---

* Closed in Metro Manila were 7 English dailies, 3 Pilipino dailies, 1 English-Pilipino daily, 7 English weeky magazines, 1 Spanish daily, 4 Chinese dailies, 3 business publications, 1 news service, and 7 television stations. Closed in the provinces were 60 community newspapers and 292 radio stations.[10]

1—created the Department of Public Information, and Letter of Instruction No. 1 ordered the immediate seizure and control of all media communications facilities and equipment.[9] Freedom of speech was controlled through General Order 19, which stated: "Any person who shall utter, publish, distribute, circulate, and spread rumors, false news and information and gossip...may be arrested or detained."

On Saturday night at 10:00 P.M., Marcos gave his initial martial law address to the nation. He knew he would need at least the passive support of the people if he were going to carry this off. He stated in his opening address that martial law was being proclaimed in accordance with the 1935 Constitution of the Philippines; that it was not a military takeover of the civilian government; that the operation of law and constitutional provisions not directly related to or affecting the state of emergency would continue; and that "this extraordinary power vested in me by the Constitution was to be employed in saving the Republic and in the reform of society."[11]

Marcos claimed he was doing everything in accordance with the 1935 Constitution. This could not have been true. He never had the authority to suppress or disband one branch of government, as he did with the bicameral Philippine Congress, while allowing others to function, like the Supreme Court. In Proclamation 1081 (the declaration of martial law) Marcos stated: "the rebellion and armed action undertaken by these lawless elements of the communists and other armed aggrupations organized to overthrow the Republic of the Philippines by armed violence and force have assumed the magnitude of an actual state of war against our people and the Republic of the Philippines."[12] There were many that would argue that the communists were that strong.

Former Senator and Solicitor General Lorenzo M. Tañada appealed to the Supreme Court to stop Marcos' obviously illegal attempts to take over the country. He pointed out in his petition "that martial law gave no new power to the president, and as the Constitution is the Basic Law, in times of crisis more than in times of normalcy, the national emergency merely affords the basis of reason for the exercise of a living power already existing or enjoyed; it does not create power, nor increase granted power to remove or diminish the restrictions imposed upon power granted or reserved. The declaration of martial law did not give President Marcos the authority to take away the power of the legislature, nor did it empower him to make laws."[13] The Supreme Court, controlled by Marcos' appointees, rejected the petition.

Marcos then amended General Order 2, which greatly expanded the police powers of the military. In addition to the crimes of insurrection, rebellion, and crimes against national security, they could now arrest and detain anyone suspected of robbery, kidnapping, illegal fishing, tax evasion, graft, forgery, fraud, drug offenses, crimes against public morals, and price manipulation. Later amendments would add such crimes as "spreading false news and rumors" and swindling and deceit.[14] This caused Archbishop Jaime Cardinal Sin to comment: "Daily we experience the increasing militarization of our lives; the pervasive surveillance of citizens, who express dissent democratically, by military intelligence; the lack of mercy and prudence shown by special military units against suspected military criminals; the use of torture to extract information; the unexpected wealth of many military officers."[15]

After defining the crimes for which the military could make arrests, Marcos then created military tribunals that had exclusive jurisdiction over certain offenses and concurrent jurdisdiction over others. They were defined as an agency of the executive rather than as a branch of the judiciary. In other words, they had greater authority than the civilian courts and were directly under Marcos. Each tribunal consisted of five military officers, only one of which was required to have legal training. One can only wonder at the influence Marcos had as Commander in Chief on the officers of these courts.[16]

Marcos then moved his attention to the Constitutional Convention. A number of delegates were arrested. Then a motion to suspend the convention while martial law was in force was defeated by the Marcos loyalists in the absence of the arrested delegates. The convention's proceedings were ordered to be speeded up. On November 29, 1972, a draft constitution was approved.[17]

The new constitution, drafted under pressure by delegates who had very little choice, envisaged the establishment of a parliamentary system, but incorporated a set of "Transitory Provisions" prepared by Marcos himself. These Provisions shored up the legalities of his one-man rule and the right to make laws on his own without approval of anyone. Thus, one of the most basic principles of democracy became the victim of martial law — the separation of powers among the legislative, judicial, and executive branches of government. Section 3(2) of Article 17, known as the Transitory Provisions of the 1973 Constitution, stated:

> All proclamations, orders, decrees, instructions, and acts promulgated, issued, or done by the incumbent President shall be part of the law of the land, and shall remain valid, legal, and binding, and effective even after lifting of martial law or the ratification of this Constitution, unless modified, revoked or superseded by subsequent proclamations, orders, decrees, instructions or other acts of the incumbent President, or unless expressly and explicitly modified or repealed by the regular National Assembly.

Thus, Article 17 gave Marcos the right to remain in office beyond his extended term as duly elected president and extended his rule indefinitely. However, the constitution still had to be ratified by the people. On November 30, Marcos announced that a plebiscite would be held on January 15, 1973, and called for a period of "free and untrammelled" debate during the campaign for ratification or rejection of his new constitutiion. In December, Senate President Gil Puyat presided over a caucus of senators and decided to convene Congress as usual in regular session on the fourth Monday of January. They also forged an accord with their colleagues from the House of Representatives to work against the ratification of the new martial law constitution which would only legitimize Marcos' dictatorship. When Marcos heard about this, he suddenly suspended the plebiscite and called for a referendum during the period January 1 to 15.[18]

Even with martial law in force, Marcos' term was due to expire on December 30, 1973. After that, if there were no newly elected president, only the Senate president would have the right to act as president. However, if the new constitution were ratified before Congress convened, and if the new constitution abolished the old Congress, then his one-man rule was assured. Marcos moved quickly to solidify his power. Adopting the Japanese wartime Kalibapi system, he had organized citizens assemblies in each village to create grass-roots organizations called barangays. Referendums were held in each barangay. The government claimed that more than 95 percent of the people had ratified the constitution, and on January 17 this was made official.[19]

However, a Supreme Court petition pointed out that the constitution had not been validly ratified since ratification called for a plebiscite, which required qualified voters at least 21 years of age to decide by ballot. Instead, the referendum had only called for a show of hands conducted by so-called "citizens assemblies," which had included those 15 years of age and older. The petition was correct, and even the Marcos Supreme Court must have felt troubled by the technicality. When they voted to strike down the presidential proclamation, they were only two votes short of the simple majority required. The decision was promulgated on March 31, 1973, and the constitution went into effect.[20]

After this ruling the Supreme Court relied thereafter on Section 3 (2) of the Transitory Provisions to rule that all presidential acts were now beyond judicial review. This section was judged by the Supreme Court to have put beyond doubt Marcos' legal authority to issue decrees.

The Transitory Provisions of the 1973 Constitution, which upheld the validity of the presidential decrees and orders issued since the imposition of martial law, provided that members of the judiciary, which included the Supreme Court justices, could continue in office only "until otherwise provided by law or decreed by the president." There was no longer an independant judicial branch of government. It was now controlled by Marcos. During martial law the Supreme Court never ruled against him. Perhaps it was because all but two of the judges were nominees and appointees of Marcos before martial law was declared; or perhaps it was the subtle form of intimidation he used.

Even before the Transitory Provisions, Letter of Instruction No. 11 was issued on September 11, 1972, requiring all judges except those of the Supreme Court to submit their undated resignations. Now Marcos could dismiss judges just by accepting these resignations or by appointing their successor.[21] Retired Supreme Court Justice Jose B.L. Reyes, former head of the Integrated Bar of the Philippines, protested to Marcos that inaction on the undated resignations held by him was a virtual "Sword of Damocles" held over their heads. In a letter dated November 21, 1973, Justice Reyes wrote, "The indefinite uncertainty as to the actual tenure of judges undermines the independence of the judiciary, which is one of the cornerstones of due process and the main guarantee that the people's liberties and rights will be protected." Marcos did not bother to reply.[22]

Amnesty International expressed its concern. It reported that both the Universal Declaration of Human Rights and the International Covenant on Civil and Political Rights explicitly recognize that there are times of national emergency when emergency powers may legitimately be invoked. However, the introduction of a state of emergency was subject to clear conditions and limitations. Article 4 of the International Covenant on Civil and Political Rights states:

> In time of public emergency which threatens the life of the nation, and the existence of which is officially proclaimed, the States Parties to the present Covenant may take measures derogative from their obligations under the present Covenantto the extent strictly required by the exigencies of the situation, provided that such measures are not inconsistent with their obligations under international law...

Article 4 made it quite clear that any restrictions regarding rights guaranteed by the Covenant were to be limited both in scope and duration "to the extent strictly required by the exigencies of the situation." However, it may be remembered that this is the Covenant which Marcos signed but then refused to ratify seven years earlier. He had announced that he "fully subscribed" to all rights enumerated in the Covenant, but it contained certain provisions that allowed states' parties to the Covenant to bring petitions against one another. This, Marcos claimed, was a derogation of national sovereignty. In any event, he did not let the Covenant stand in his way. He very obviously went far beyond restrictions required by the "exigencies of the situation."

Jovito R. Salonga is a twice-elected Senator (1965 and 1971), an academic (Harvard LLM, Yale JSD), a prolific author (several of his books are used as texts in Philippine law schools), and a survivor of the Plaza Miranda bombing in 1971. He was arrested and detained without charges in 1980. He was subsequently released and allowed to leave the Philippines. He came to the U.S. where he became an outspoken critic of the Marcos regime.

Salonga compared the American legal system with its Philippine counterpart during the Marcos reign. The Bill of Rights of the Philippine Constitution is heavily influenced by the U.S. Constitution. However, he noted, that there was a yawning gap between American law and Philippine law, especially with regard to "public order violators." In American law a person cannot be imprisoned without being informed of the charge or charges against him; in the Philippines a person could be detained without charges and without a trial. Many acts that were considered subversive in the Philippines are not even considered crimes in the U.S. In American law, guilt by association is condemned; in the Philippines that concept was deeply honored in practice. In American law dissent is tolerated, even encouraged; in the Philippines honest, principled dissenters were arrested because they "undermine the security of the nation." In American law courts are independant of the Executive Branch and judges enjoy security of tenure. In the Philippines there was no such security.[23]

Marcos was now in control of all branches of the government. He had his political opponents jailed, his media critics muffled, his military behind him, and his judges on a short leash. It is safe to assume that he was now firmly in power. There were at least five distinct elements that would determine his success as a martial law president: The people, to a great extent represented by the church; the government's enforcement of martial law, to a great extent represented by the military; the media, as to how the Philippines would be perceived in the eyes of the world; a Grand Coalition of friends, relatives, politicians, and assorted government and military personages, who administered the Marcos policies and reaped all the rewards; and Imelda, who would play an increasingly larger role in government.

CHAPTER FOURTEEN

Imelda

If the past 20 years of Philippine history were fiction instead of harsh reality, the story-teller would have probably invented a character- like Imelda just to make things more interesting. Imagine a beauty queen who grew up to become the wife of a president, jet-setting around the world, serving as ambassasdor plenipotentiary to her little country, returning just long enough to her other positions as the governor of her metropolis, a minister to the poor, and a member of the elite presidential Executive Committee. In addition, she takes the time to launch enormous social projects that eliminate poverty forever. The people, eternally grateful, elect her to the National Assembly. She climbs higher and higher, to the tune of "Don't Cry For Me, Argentina..." That was the image of Imelda that the government wanted people to swallow. But that background music had been chosen by the people and they kept playing it too loud. It was from a musical enormously popular in London and New York at the time. Entitled "Evita," it was about Eva Peron, a former prostitute who became the influential wife of the Argentine dictator and rose to power. Imelda hated it and banned the play from performances in the Philippines. "I'm not a whore," she would proclaim when someone, usually from the foreign press, would indelicately compare the two.

Imelda is an enigma — a study in contra-distinction. She was possibly the most controversial First Lady in the world during her time. She said one thing. She did another. She claimed to help the poor while spending lavishly on herself. By now everyone knows about her jewelry, her 4,400 pairs of shoes (2,800 were found at the palace and another 1,600 at her Leyte residence), 500 black bras, and racks and racks of furs and dresses bought but never worn. To some she was a folk hero; to others a monster. She was adored; she was hated. Some described her as larger than life; others as just large, as her size 40 and 42 girdles attest. Whatever she was, she left her mark on the Philippines. A character more out of Shakespeare than "Evita," a comparison to Lady Macbeth might have been more appropriate. Could the "Rose of Tacloban" have been the same person as the "Iron Butterfly"?

She was a Filipina. They rank among the world's most beautiful women. The country produced two Miss Universe winners in four years—Gloria Diaz in 1969 and Marjie Moran in 1973—not bad for a population of 42 million at the time. The beauty of the Filipina can only be matched by their charm. The first thing a visitor to the country notices is their warmth and friendliness. Filipina journalist and writer, Sheila Ocampo-Kalfors, noted other attributes: "Colonial experience under Spain and the U.S.—which might be described as 300 years in a convent and 50 years in Hollywood—has produced in Filipinas a dual personality. Torn between feminine and masculine values, the Filipina can be beguiling and sensuous, but in fierce competition with a male counterpart she can be relentless and ruthless...They are materially acquisitive, putting a lot of importance on personal belongings (jewelry and property) for their security."[1] This observation would prove to be somewhat of an understatement when describing Imelda.

No matter what her queenly pretentions were (she once compared Marcos to the King of Thailand, noting many similarities), Imelda was not of the aristocracy. She was born July 2, 1929, in Manila, the daughter of Vicente and Remedios Romualdez. It was Vicente's second marriage. His first wife had died and left him with five children. He then married Remedios and fathered six more—Benjamin, Alita, Alfredo, Armando, Conchita, and Imelda. Vicente was not very successful, and was always having financial problems. In addition, family squabbles caused his wife, along with Imelda and Benjamin, to move out of the house in San Miguel, Manila, near Malacañang Palace, and live in its converted garage, sleeping on long boards propped up by milk cartons. They lived there until Imelda's mother died in 1938. Imelda was nine. One can only imagine what effect this had on a young child who received little love from her father, scant attention from a mother who was always working, and who then found herself seemingly alone.[2]

Vicente, still unsuccessful and still in financial trouble, sold his house and returned to his home in Tacloban, Leyte. Imelda spent her teenage years there with eleven other children. She grew into a natural beauty and became known as the "Rose of Tacloban." Her father had two brothers: Norberto, who had a son—Norberto, Jr., who became Secretary of Labor; and Miguel, who had two sons—Eduardo, who became the Philippine Ambassador to the U.S., and Daniel, who became Speaker of the House of Representatives. Because of her cousin's success Imelda was able to return to Manila in her early twenties and live with Daniel and his wife. She worked, first in a piano and music store on the Escolta in Manila, and then as a clerk in the Central Bank. In 1953, she entered the Miss Manila beauty pageant and lost out to Norma Jimenez. The results were protested. (The mayor of Manila by then was Arsenio H. Lacson, Marcos' former associate in the law firm of Vicente Francisco. Lacson had sponsored Imelda in the contest.) As a compromise Imelda was awarded the title "Muse of Manila."[3]

According to her palace biography, Imelda was "dressed in houseclothes, wearing slippers, and crunching watermelon seeds" when she met Congressman Marcos in 1954.[4] Another version of this meeting is told in a biography written in 1969 by Carmen Navarro Pedrosa, who had been a staff member of the Manila Chronicle. It was entitled *The Untold Story of Imelda Marcos*. Imelda apparently preferred the palace version. She had the Pedrosa book banned after martial law was declared. Ms. Pedrosa, then in London, was warned that she would be arrested if she returned to the Philippines. The book recounted that in 1954, while working in Manila and staying at the home of her first cousin, Daniel Romualdez, Speaker of the House, Imelda accompanied Daniel's wife to the Capitol to pick him up. They were in the cafeteria in the basement when she was introduced to Ferdinand. A whirlwind courtship ensued, which included an invitation to a bank vault where he displayed his collection of stacks of $100 bills. Apparently it was love at first sight. They were married 11 days after they met, on May 1st, at the Pro Cathedral of San Miguel in Manila. It was called the wedding of the year. President Ramon Magsaysay was the principal sponsor. They honeymooned in Baguio, the honeymoon capital of the Philippines. Their first child, a daughter—Imelda, was born November 12. They would have two more—a daughter, Irene, and a son, Ferdinand, Jr.[5]

The marriage was a true partnership. Imelda and her husband seemed to be ideally matched in their quest for power. There was the occasional drawback. In 1960 she had a nervous breakdown due to the pressures of Marcos' demanding political career. But what she lacked in mental toughness she more than made up for in ambition. Some thought her even more ambitious than her husband. After Marcos became president there was a joke: Question: "What happens if death takes the chief from our midst?" Answer: "Then the president would have to run the whole thing himself."[6]

In 1968, serving her first term as First Lady of the Philippines, Imelda had said that she "... worried about the poor and suffering people of the country who had barely enough to eat while the rich wallow in such luxury."[7] Imelda wasn't worried about the poor then or at any other time. The truth of the matter was that she still felt like an outcast in Filipino society because of her poor childhood. Such taunting remarks were her way of getting even for not being accepted by them. There were also other ways. To reassure herself of her position, she drafted a group of wealthy matrons to serve as her assistants at official functions. They became known as "the Blue Ladies" because of Imelda's request that they all wear blue, thereby publicly acceding to their position and also serving as an elegant but somber background to Imelda, who always stood out in her more stylish fashion. After martial law was declared, her attempts to get even became less subtle. She proceeded with a vengeance. In childish glee she banned society columns from all newspapers. Now the rich couldn't read about themselves and their parties. Then she used her brother, Kokoy, to confiscate many of their assets without compensation. Years later, when the plight of her "poor and suffering" people still had not improved and had, in fact, gotten worse, Roy Rowan of *Fortune* Magazine asked her to explain the sudden affluence of her relatives and friends who were now wallowing in the same luxury she had criticized. Imelda replied that "Some are smarter than others." Nothing could be farther from the truth. With all the advantages her friends and relatives had in business, many of them still managed to fail time and again primarily because of bad management, leaving the banks with mountains of bad debt.[8]

William Sullivan, U.S. Ambassador to the Philippines from 1973 to 1976, in his book about his foreign service career,* described Imelda as "...an interesting woman, with a shrewd native intelligence, a certain physical charm, an earthy sense of humor, but a limited education."[9] Her desire for public acclaim, and the methods she sometimes used, could only be described as ludicrous. Sullivan described an incident in 1974. It was the anniversary of General MacArthur's return to the Philippines during World War II, which was celebrated every year. Imelda usually presided over the ceremonies since MacArthur had landed in Leyte, the home province of the Romualdez family. That year was the thirtieth anniversary so it was decided that the occasion would be special. All members of the diplomatic corp were invited. In anticipation of the event, Imelda had acquired some beach-front property at the town of Olot, and proceeded to claim she was born there. She had an "ancestral estate" constructed. Sullivan described it as "...a large, colonial-style house, with proper antique fixtures, a guest house, a swimming pool, a large coconut-log reception hall-cum-chapel, and a number of bamboo and coconut wood cabanas, all set among the palm trees. It was so new that the grass in front of the house was literally painted green. But members of Imelda's entourage, with tongue in cheek, sententiously spoke of it as 'The First Lady's birthplace.' "[10]

How Imelda probably obtained the money to build her new "ancestral estate" provides some insight into the darker side of her

---

* *Obbligato,* (New York: W.M. Norton & Company, 1984).

personality. In 1974 the Philippines hosted the Miss Universe
pageant. Imelda took the helm and decided that a new Folk Arts
Theatre was needed for the event. She solicited funds for the event
from private corporations and various government ministries.
Only many years later would it come to light that over ₱400
million ($57 million) of the budget and profits from the event
were missing.[11] Other more sinister plans were hinted at in an
interview that same year with *Newsweek*. Imelda had said: "I tell
him (President Marcos) what's the use of building up all those
billions of dollars in foreign exchange reserves if you can't spread
it among the people?"[12] At the time no one in their wildest dreams
could have known the depth of her commitment.

In 1975 *Cosmopolitan* listed her among the richest women in
the world. The article didn't mention how she came about her
wealth, but it did mention her international shopping sprees at
Dior, Bergdorf's and I. Magnin, and the large entourage that
usually travelled with her.[13] For most of her trips she used two
airplanes, either Boeing 747's or DC 10's, from the Philippine
Airlines fleet. On at least one occasion she used four. Herb Caen,
renowned *San Francisco Chronicle* columnist, attended the
coronation of King Birenda in Nepal in 1975. He wrote about the
event in his column back home, and mentioned Imelda had
attended "...with an entourage of 80...the Marcos group arrived
in four government jets, one of which flew back to Manila to pick
up food for her group."[14]

Imelda began her own political career that same year. After
ten years as First Lady, she decided she wanted something more.
Marcos appointed her governor of Metropolitan Manila (the new
name for the old province of Rizal), to "save the metropolis from
the fate of other suffering cities like New York."[15] Other
appointments quickly followed. In 1978 she was appointed
Minister of Human Settlements, which the *New York Times*
described as "a newly created post, whose functions she devises as
she carries them out."[16] The same year she ran against Ninoy
Aquino in the elections for representatives in the Interim National
Assembly and won by a landslide. The elections were a farce,
characterized by massive cheating. That November *Panorama*,
the Sunday magazine of the *Bulletin Today* newspaper, published

a poll of campus heroes. Marcos came in second, Aquino fifth, and Imelda sixth. As a result all 300,000 copies were confiscated. The fact that she out-polled Jesus Christ, who came in ninth, did not appease her.[17]

During this period she did not neglect the promise she had made in *Newsweek*. She continued in her efforts to spread the wealth among the people. Unfortunately it was not among her "poor and suffering" countrymen. She flew into Honolulu in 1977 under the escort of ten bodyguards and bought $40,000 worth of clothes without trying anything on.[18] In a jewelry store in the same city she had a reputation for paying for all her purchases in cash—suitcases of it brought in by her bodyguards. In July 1978 she flew into New York and purchased $1.43 million in Bulgari jewels, including a $1.15 million bracelet of emeralds and diamonds.[19] Where was the money coming from? The *New York Times* quoted a Cartier representative in Hong Kong, who said he believed Imelda had put together the world's largest collection of gems. He said this in 1978.[20] A less than gallant senior member of the church had already given her a new nickname—"Lady Bountiful."

In February 1979, Imelda was named chairman of the Cabinet Committee, composed of all the ministries, to launch the BLISS (Bagong Lipunan Site and Services) Program, an ambitious attempt to centralize control of all economic and social development in the Philippines.[21] Her Ministry of Human Settlements assumed responsibility for the "11 Needs of Man," providing water, power, food, clothing, work, medical services, education, culture, technology, ecological balance, sports and recreation, and shelter and mobility. The Cabinet Committee would oversee its implementation. The undertaking almost defied description. The "Ministry of Human Settlements Multi-Year Human Settlements Plan, 1978-2000," was geared toward the "improved quality of life, sustained economic growth, balanced ecology, and enhanced cultural heritage that underlie the formulation of the physical framework plan for the country." *The Far Eastern Economic Review* commented: "If the Ministry of Human Settlements (MHS) can achieve only one-tenth of the ambitious goals set for the BLISS project by Mrs. Imelda Marcos, it will represent a great leap forward socially and economically for the Philippines."[22]

It didn't. For all the lavish descriptions of her BLISS project, the only results it elicited were in purple prose. Her project managers would have been better off as fiction writers. Little they described was accomplished. The real reasons for such verbal obfuscation would only become known later. Because of BLISS, Imelda had considerable influence over the allocation of economic development funds. As a result she was regularly allowed to encroach on other ministries in the name of her basic needs program and take monies away from other, often more worthwhile, projects.[23]

In 1979 Imelda hosted the opening of the Marbella beach resort. Her usual coterie of European royalty and movie stars were flown in for the party. She didn't like the color of the beach so a plane was sent to Australia to get a load of white sand.[24] In May of the same year Ferdinand and Imelda celebrated their 25th wedding anniversary. There were 500 guests, including another planeload of European royalty. As usual the party was lavish. Imelda had purchased a silver carriage with eight white horses for the occasion, and trumpeters announced the arrival of each guest. *Life* did a several-page spread on the affair. That issue was banned in the Philippines and the party wasn't reported in the local media.[25]

The visit of the Pope was scheduled for February 1981. Imelda spent $31 million on a new statehouse made of coconut products, hoping he would stay there during his visit. It was a bit ostentatious so he politely declined. Later at a lavish dinner in Malacañang Palace he lectured Marcos on neglecting the needs of the poor.

In July, while the BLISS program was being undertaken, another equally-large program was initiated. Called the Kilusang Kabuhayan at Kaunlaran, or KKK, Imelda was appointed its head as Secretary-General. She called the program a movement of "national livelihood." Its aim was to give economic opportunities to the most disadvantaged people, and to help raise the standards of living of the country's poor. Why it was necessary to launch such a vast undertaking right on the heels of another vast undertaking, very similar in concept, and run by the same people, at a time when the government was accused of misutilization of its funds by the World Bank and the International Monetary Fund (IMF) was never explained. It was a huge venture costing billions of pesos and was launched publicly on national television.[26] Despite the public relations campaign and the philosophical explanations to the media by Imelda, the KKK concept was still considered fuzzy. The only thing clear about the KKK was that, like BLISS, there was a predominance of MHS officials at every bureaucratic level who had a reputation for bypassing normal channels of budgeting, auditing, and fund disbursement. Also, like BLISS, charges of favoritism and misuse of funds abounded. It was a known fact that, as much as possible, all monies controlled by the government were disbursed, not in accordance with economic necessity, but in accordance with political loyalty. Imelda's KKK was a prime example. Basic human needs had little to do with her guidelines. Also, like all her undertakings, there was no public accountability of funds.[27] Later on, a government commission would uncover some of the results of such procedures. A "ghost project" was discovered where fictitious contractors were paid ₱198 million (about $10 million).[28]

The same year she launched her KKK Imelda took trips to Kenya, Iraq, and New York that cost $1.5 million. Some of the monies for these trips were diverted from a government intelligence fund. Records show that Marcos authorized the disbursement of $200,000 from this fund "for expenses incurred in connection with the official trip of the First Lady to New York."[29] While in New York she spent another $4.5 million for the art, English antique furniture, and ceramics collected by philanthropist Leslie R. Samuels.[30]

Imelda's political clout continued to expand. In the period of six years she was appointed Governor of Metro Manila, Minister of Human Settlements, Chairman of the Cabinet Committee, Secretary General of the KKK, and was elected to the Interim National Assembly. In August 1982 Marcos, under criticism for not having a vice-president and in preparation for his state visit, set up an Executive Committee which, in the event of his death or incapacity, would run the country until a new president was elected. It was comprised of ten members, primarily cabinet ministers. Imelda was included. No one doubted she would dominate it and possibly emerge as president if anything happened to Marcos. This may have been the closest she ever came to realizing her greatest ambition.

In October, after the state visit, the Ministry of Human Settlements was appointed to implement the $200 million Economic Support Fund, which was part of the $500 million being paid by the U.S. for the rental of the bases for the period 1979-1984. Although the funds were made available as a grant from the U.S. Agency for International Development, and its counterpart was the Philippine National Economic and Development Authority, Marcos decided to create an inter-ministerial body to advise on all ESF projects. Imelda was appointed the chairperson.[31]

She had steadfastly acquired an awesome power base that made her the second most powerful person in the country. This power was exemplified that year when Marcos, still under pressure from the IMF, slashed all ministry budgets by 18 percent and announced a freeze on all government spending, which had ballooned from ₱1.1 billion ($114 million) in 1980 to ₱12.1 billion ($1.36 billion) in 1981. One can take a calculated guess as to who was to blame for the excess spending. So Marcos slashed all the budgets. All, that is, except Imelda's KKK program.[32] That proved to be a mistake. Despite the "freeze" government spending jumped to ₱14 billion ($1.6 billion) for 1982.[33]

In January 1983, Imelda hosted her pet project, the Manila International Film Festival. The first festival had been held the previous year. She had constructed a new film center at a cost of $21 million. Usually she could expect the government to assist her, but during the state visit the previous year World Bank officials had cautioned Marcos against wasting public money. They had specifically referred to Imelda's film center. Apart from its cost the bank complained that an estimated $4 million had been contributed by government ministries, agencies, and even the Central Bank, for the festival's operating costs which included giving a party for thousands, serving $100-a-bottle champagne, and flying in 300 of Imelda's jet-setters. This frivolous display of gaudiness in a country of abject poverty prompted World Bank officials to caution Marcos. He decided it would not be a good idea to go against their wishes at the time so Imelda was informed she would get no government assistance this time.

Left to her own resources, she allowed 13 soft-core pornographic films to be shown uncut at local theatres which generated huge profits and helped defray MIFF costs. Such films were in violation of the country's film censorship laws. The Catholic Church took notice. Cardinal Sin criticized the sex film showings in several speeches, reminding the government of its role in safeguarding the moral fabric of the people. Imelda, usually the epitome of morality, countered that such movies would contribute to the "process of maturity" of Filipino movie audiences. She added that, "If garbage affects us, then there must be something wrong with us."[34] Sin countered: "If the national leadership can suspend the operation of a law to achieve its ends—and this time it is to raise money to defray the prohibitive cost of mounting a festival—and if, as citizens, we are to accept it without protest, might not the same leadership be tempted to suspend some other laws safeguarding our basic rights, to accomplish an end that could be more sinister than just raising money?"[35]

The incident exemplified Imelda's frivolity, power, and adversary relationship with the Catholic Church in the Philippines. It also described a government with two sets of rules—one for those in power and one for the others. It allowed soft-core pornography into the theatres to make a few dollars. Yet talented movie directors were under constant attack by government critics for attempting to portray slum life as it really is. The message was obvious—in the Marcos government the portrayal of slum life had less redeeming social value than soft-core porn.

The rest of the year was remarkable even by Imelda's spending standards. She really outdid herself, spending $7 million in 90 days on a trip to Rome, Copenhagen, and New York, and another $10 million on the wedding of her youngest daughter. In what is known as the "Great Cheese Scandal," after taking off from Rome, Imelda discovered there was no cheese on board the plane so she ordered it to return to the airport for cheese.

In what some palace observers say was an overreaction to her being denied an invitation to the 1981 wedding of Prince Charles and Lady Dianne Spencer, Imelda decided her daughter's wedding would be a full-blown state occasion. The place was Sarrat, in Ilocos Norte—the hometown of Marcos and General Fabian Ver. This time, instead of just creating an "ancestral estate," she transformed an entire town. Ver's home and the homes of Marcos' relatives were taken apart and reconstructed to give the impression they came from the aristocracy. The town itself was made over to look like a seventeenth century Spanish colonial town. Native huts were replaced by European houses. Some were liveable; others were only a facade. The landscaping was enhanced by freshly planted flowering trees, from which paper mache "blossoms" bloomed. In addition, a new Spanish colonial-style hotel and new international airport were constructed for the occasion. An ocean liner was moored offshore to accommodate more guests. The cost of all this came to more than $10 million and was shared by the government.[36]

Imelda's propensity for enormous prestige projects, usually housed in luxurious and costly buildings and presented as benefits that she had bestowed on her people, was probably the main cause of the government's budget overruns. Critics called it her "edifice complex." In 1976 she spearheaded the building of 14 luxury hotels in preparation for the International Monetary Fund Conference held in Manila. Critics charged that the $300 million in foreign loans they required could have been better utilized to fight poverty. They were proved right. Most were bankrupt within a few years.[37] In addition to her "ancestral estate," the transformation of Marcos' home town, and the Coconut Palace, she built numerous private estates for Marcos, herself, and her children all over the country, and was the driving force behind the building of the Cultural Center, the National Arts Center, the Heart Center, the Kidney Center, the Nutrition Center, and the Eye Center.[38] She also spent $40 million on a "University of Life," a school with an ultra-modern campus but whose purpose was never made exactly clear.[39]

She raised money for a lot of the projects the same way she did with the Miss Universe Pageant and Folk Arts Theatre projects. In 1980, shortly after the World Travel Congress of the American Society of Travel Agents, which was held in Manila, she diverted ₱200 million ($20.6 million) from the Ministry of Tourism intended for improvement of certain tourist spots, and spent them instead on such things as a resthouse in the town of Tolosa for the Romualdez family and a mansion in Tacloban, Leyte.[40] Her particular fund-raising style earned her the nickname "The Iron Butterfly." She had a reputation for getting her way, telling one interviewer, "I'm like Robin Hood. I rob the rich to make these projects come alive...not really rob. It's done with a smile."[41] Smile or not, by the end of 1985, despite her fund-raising and money-grabbing from other ministries, her Metro Manila Commission had managed to accumulate ₱1.99 billion (approximately $150 million) in debts in its 10 years of existence.[42] It is unfortunate she never became interested in projects that included improving the telephone system, the road network, the water supply, or the electrical utilities.

Imelda had been known to use symbols, such as triangles, rectangles, circles, and hearts, when discussing her role in the development of her country. Such explanations, according to observers, tended to be somewhat hazy if not downright exasperating. She also truly believed that God had blessed her country. She knew this because of the "hole in the sky." In all seriousness she has shared with others on numerous occasions the belief that there was a hole in the sky directly over the Philippines from which God looks benevolently down on her people.

For the town fiesta in Tacloban, Leyte, in 1979, Imelda had a building constructed that was supposedly modeled after a palace in Versailles. Palatial in size and opulent in furnishings, it was a beautiful showcase for whatever its intended purpose. As one entered, the focal point was a huge mural of Imelda, larger than life, ascending into heaven as other smaller figures, resembling her family, look on. Perhaps this was her ultimate fantasy—the dream of a nine-year-old girl who achieved more fame and more wealth and rose higher than any Filipina ever before. That she did, but probably not in the way she wanted.

CHAPTER FIFTEEN

The Church

The Philippines is the only Christian country in Asia where religion has managed to suffuse life and culture. Eighty-five percent of the population are Catholic. During the Marcos reign the Catholic Church provided the only forum available to the poor farmers in denouncing the government whose laws seemed only for the protection of the wealthy. Marcos considered such involvement meddling. With each protest and criticism came an ever-widening rift between the church and government, and an adversary relationship with the military. The huge buildup in the size of the armed forces has already been noted. Many of these were used in a police rather than military capacity, assisting the wealthy landlords and Marcos cronies in enforcing their will on the people. It is no wonder the people gravitated away from the government and toward the church, and caused Cardinal Sin to comment, "When people lose faith in their leaders, fear the military, and don't trust the courts, the only person left for them to go to with their grievances is the parish priest...and he cannot just file away their complaints like everyone else and pretend they do not exist. He has to act to do something or he too will lose all hope."[1]

The Catholic clergy, almost exclusively Filipino, was a potent force although Marcos refused to believe it. In spite of enormous difficulties they continued to serve as advocates for the changes that were so desperately needed. The church's two major organizations were the Catholic Bishops Conference of the

Philippines, comprising 83 bishops, and the Association of Major Religious Superiors (AMRSP) of the Philippines, representing 2,500 priests and 7,000 nuns in religious orders. There was also an estimated 1,200 foreign missionaries throughout the country.[2]

Since the start of martial law the AMRSP had been receiving reports throughout the country of raids on churches and other religious institutions along with the harassment, arrest and torture of suspected "subversives" in the church. It became such a serious problem that at their next annual general meeting in January 1974 they organized the Task Force Detainees to monitor such military activities and to assist the victims whenever possible.[3] In addition, church-military liason committees were established in some areas the previous November. It had been agreed upon that the military authorities would not arrest any member of a religious order or community, or raid any religious institution without prior notification to the bishop or religious superior, but to no one's surprise it was soon violated. In mid-1974 several senior officials of the Protestant National Council of Churches of the Philippines were arrested and some were tortured. When questioned about the incident, the military authorities refused to discuss the arrests or the reason for them. The agreement continued to be disregarded. On December 5, 1974, the offices of the "Signs of the Times," the AMRSP news bulletin, were raided and closed down on charges of inciting to sedition. Church-military relations became strained even further as Marcos continued to tighten his grip on the country.[4]

In 1975 the Supreme Court, acting on Aquino's petition which asserted that the Marcos-appointed military tribunal didn't have the power to try him, affirmed in *Aquino, Jr. versus Comelec* that, based on Section 3(2) of the Transitory Provisions, Marcos was the sole legislative authority.[5]

We affirm the proposition that, as Commander-in-Chief and enforcer or administrator of martial law, the incumbent President of the Philippines can promulgate proclamations, orders, and decrees during the period of martial law esssential to the security and preservation of the Republic to the defense of the political and social liberties of the people and to the

institution of reforms to prevent the resurgence of rebellion
or insurrection or secession or the threat thereof as well as to
meet the impact of a worldwide recession, inflation or
economic crisis which presently threatens all nations including highly developed countries.

On September 22, 1976, Marcos issued Presidential Decree
1033, which proposed nine new amendments to his constitution.
They were ratified by plebiscite the following month. They
granted the Interim Batasang Pambansa (National Assembly) the
same powers given to the full National Assembly. However, such
cosmetic changes did nothing to limit Marcos' authority. He was
still empowered, under Amendments 2 and 5, to continue to
exercise legislative powers until martial law was lifted. Also
included in the nine was the now infamous Amendment 6, which
allowed him to continue, after martial law was lifted, exercising
his powers "whenever in my judgment...there exists a grave
emergency or threat or imminence thereof, or whenever the
Interim Batasang Pambansa or the regular National Assembly
fails or is unable to act adequately on any matter for any reason
that, in my judgment, requires immediate action."[6] The Supreme
Court was petitioned to stop the October 1976 plebiscite on the
grounds that Marcos had no power to propose amendments to the
constitution, that power being reserved exclusively for the Interim
National Assembly. As usual the petition was dismissed.

In November and December 1976 more than 70 church
workers in Davao were arrested, two Catholic radio stations in the
area closed down, two outspoken religious publications in Manila
padlocked, and two American priests who had been working in
Manila's slums—Father Eduardo Gerlock and Father Albert
Booms—were deported. This prompted a pastoral letter to be
prepared in early 1977 at the Catholic Bishop's Conference
meeting in Cebu, and read from pulpits throughout the country.
The letter complained that, in many cases, "This evangelising
work [of the church]...has been misunderstood [by the govern-
ment] and led to the arrests of priests, religious and lay workers,
and even the deportation of foreign missionaries."[7] Minister

Enrile, of course, denied that military action against some priests and lay leaders was an anti-clergy campaign.[8]

During the late seventies Marcos had lobbied for a visit to the Philippines by Pope John Paul II. He knew that such a visit would be interpreted as an indorsement of his regime and would be the ideal imprimatur for his Catholic country. However, the Pope let it be known that he would not visit a dictator. This called for some drastic action.

Thus the campaign began and the "return to normalcy" strategy contrived. With great fanfare, Marcos announced that martial law would end on January 17, 1981, and the people could choose their own leader in a free democratic election to be held the following June. He also announced the partial reinstatement of the writ of habeas corpus and the transfer of legislative powers to the Interim National Assembly. As usual in reality very little changed. The writ of habeas corpus was still denied in two secessionist Muslim regions in the south and in cases involving "national security," a well-worn euphemism for anything Marcos didn't like. Also, under Section 3(2) of the Transitory Provisions, all presidential proclamations, orders, decrees, instructions and acts were to remain in force after the lifting of martial law unless revoked by the president or the regular national assembly. The presidential orders and decrees were compiled in a National Security Code which was issued after the lifting of martial law. The Public Order Act was also issued at the same time. Derived from Amendment 6, it empowered Marcos to exercise emergency powers short of declaring a state of martial law which "included, but [was] not limited to, preventive detention."[9] Marcos was still very much in charge even without a declaration of martial law.

With martial law supposedly over, Pope John Paul II agreed to a visit and came to the Philippines in February 1981. Marcos must have been somewhat shocked when, during the visit, the Pope lectured him, right in Malacañang Palace, on the subject of human rights: "Even in exceptional situations that may at times arise, one can never justify any violation of the fundamental dignity of the human person or of the basic rights that safeguard this dignity. Legitimate concern for the security of a nation, as demanded by the common good, could lead to the temptation of subjugating to the state the human being and his or her dignity and rights. Any apparent conflict between the exigencies of security and the citizen's basic rights must be resolved according to the fundamental principle—upheld always by the church—that social organization exists only for the service of man for the protection of his dignity and that it cannot claim to serve the common good where human rights are not safeguarded."[10]

Marcos apologized to the Pope for what he called "petty and small" church-state differences: "Forgive us, Holy Father. Now that you are here we resolve we shall wipe out all conflicts and set up a society that is harmonious to attain the ends of God."[11] But his words rang hollow as the persecution of priests, nuns, and lay workers continued, and the human rights abuses escalated.

On April 22, 1982, Father Edicio de la Torre was arrested again. He had the distinction of being the longest detained Catholic priest (December 13, 1974, to April 18, 1980). He was charged with "conspiracy to commit rebellion" but never tried. He was granted a conditional release if he would leave the country and study abroad. He returned in 1981 and was reportedly carrying out fieldwork connected with his studies when he was arrested again.[12]

In June 1982 two nuns and three layworkers were arrested while returning to Manila after investigating human rights abuses in Lobo, Batangas. All were accused of subversion and multiple murder. The nuns were released the next day. On August 8, in Villaverde, Nueva Vizcaya, the Philippine Constabulary arrested two foreign priests and three lay workers. The priests were later released. On September 1, at the Pope Paul Action Center in Catbalogan, Samar, the Philippine Constabulary arrested a nun and two lay workers. The nun was released three days later.[13] In almost every instance the lay workers were detained longer than the priests and nuns, some up to six months or a year longer, although their purported charges were the same.[14]

While Marcos was on a state visit to the U.S. espousing his country's democratic principles and defending his human rights record, on the night of September 26, 1982, the convent of Father Anthony Schouten, a Dutch Jesuit priest serving in Bayug,

Zamboanga del Sur, was shot up by soldiers. Father Schouten narrowly escaped death and said that it was in retaliation for his complaints about the Air Force bombing of the village of Dimalinao, where innocent women and children were killed, and for later complaints about the military's torture and murder of two of his parishioners, one a 16-year-old boy.[15] On September 28, Father Brian Gore was arrested and began an ordeal that would last two years.

Persistent denials by Marcos that there was no persecution of the church led Sin to comment, "It would seem, however, from all the evidence at hand, that to believe the series of moves against the priests and nuns are a coincidence would be to strain the bounds of credibility."[16]

He and Archbishop Federico Limon, chairman of the Commission on Social Action of the Bishops Conference, announced that the government had begun a systematic campaign to discredit the Catholic Church in the Philippines, and provided some examples, citing incidents between January and September 1982 where at least 30 priests had been arrested. The government once again steadfastly denied that its war against a handful of militant priests and nuns was a war against the church. However, there were too many raids on convents and presbyteries, and too many church social activities which the military labelled "subversive," and too many priests, nuns, and lay workers arrested as "subversives" without justification.

Faced with the evidence, the military admitted there was a clampdown, but, they claimed, it was only connected with the subversive activities of the "Christian Left," a term which supposedly applied only to communist sympathizers or supporters. In reality it was used by the government to describe anyone connected with the church who was critical of martial law. Of the 14,000 priests and nuns in the country it wasn't known how many actually supported the communist insurgents, but Sin stated that if priests and nuns were picking up guns, then the blame rested squarely on the shoulders of Marcos.[17]

Less than five were thought to be actually fighting alongside the rebels. For them rebellion was the only way to right the injustices and inequalities affecting the poor. Some were quite well known. Father Conrado Balweg was a parish priest and high school principal from Abra province. He had reportedly been identified as the leader of a New People's Army unit that killed seven government troops in a September 1980 attack. He was once photographed with a bandolier of bullets across his chest with a rifle cradled in his arms. There was a ₱200,000 ($23,000) dead-or-alive reward posted on him.[18] Another priest, Father Zacarias Agatep, of the archdiocese of Vigan, who had alledgedly joined the communist guerrillas, was shot dead by government troops in October 1982, the day after the government announced a ₱260,000 ($29,885) dead-or-alive reward for him. The church called it murder. He was killed in a gun battle with soldiers intent on taking over land for a government dam. The land was sacred to his parishioners, who believed that the wrath of God would descend upon them if the graves of their ancestors were disturbed.[19]

Two months after Marcos had returned from his state visit to Washington, on November 29, 1982, members of the Catholic Bishops Conference of the Philippines met with Enrile to try and resolve their differences once again. It had been a year since Amnesty International had visited the Philippines. Enrile had refused to see them to discuss the numerous charges of human rights abuses. His attitude at the bishop's meeting seemed to be about the same. Diplomatic observers noted that the church lay leaders presented strong evidence of military abuses but to no avail. Enrile was somewhat blunt in his refusal to grant any of their demands.[20] A week later the confession of Father Edgardo Kangleon, a priest from Samar, was made public. He had been arrested on September 12 and held incommunicado until then. He confessed to having links with the communist New People's Army and implicated other religious and lay leaders.[21] This did not bode well for the bishops. Further meetings were held in December and January between the military and the Bishops Conference. Finally, on January 25, 1983, the bishops announced they were no longer willing to continue the dialogue with the military which one bishop described as "an exercise in frustation."[22]

The case of Brian Gore and the events surrounding it serve as an example of the church and its difficulties with the government. Gore, an Australian priest of the Columban Order, was sent by his mission to Oringaoh, near the town of Kabankalan in Southern Negros Occidental, the heart of the sugar country, in 1969.

Since the mid-70's the Roman Catholic Church actively promoted lay leadership of social communities in a program to establish Basic Christian Communities. Following in some respects the "Liberation Theology" associated with the church in Latin America, their idea was for the evolution of a "people's church" concerned with Christian worship and also human rights and social justice.[23] In 1975 Gore and a Columban colleague assigned to a neighboring parish, Father Niall O'Brien of Dublin, Ireland, began to organize these communities, called Katipunan ng Kristianong Katilingban (KKK) locally. (This should not be confused with Imelda's Kilusang Kabuhayan at Kaunlaran.) Gore set up about 40 KKK's for 3,000 ready parishioners and O'Brien set up about 30, taking in some 8,000.[24]

The local priest, Monsignor Antonio Y. Fortich, Bishop of Bacolod, noted: "Those priests have taught the people about justice, the minimum wage, the dignity of labor, and to denounce the atrocities of the military and land-grabbers' abusing small men."[25] Unfortunately, some of their teachings ran counter to the beliefs of the sugar barons and landlords. Almost from the start of the KKK's, the military had labelled them as "communistic" and had harassed their members. On March 29, 1980, eight farmers were abducted from a party in Barrio Marcopa, Kabankalan. Only one returned.[26]

In June, 1980, a petition initiated by Mayor Pablo Sola of Kabankalan was circulated. Addressed to the Pope, it asked for the removal of Gore because his activities led people "to suspect that he has communist learnings and under the guise of his office as a priest is sowing the seeds of discontent, confusion, and chaos among the people, therefore preparing the group for the seeding of communist ideas." The petition also stated Gore's alleged opposition to the "realization of government projects designed to alleviate the living conditions of the poor."[27] Bishop Fortich, hearing of the petition, denounced it and defended Gore during this campaign.

On September 16, 1980, five and one-half months after their disppearance, the bodies of the seven abducted farmers were discovered buried in a canefield 150 meters from Mayor Sola's house.[28] Fourteen people, including Mayor Sola and members of the Philippine Constabulary, were subsequently arrested and charged with murder.[29] Sola's petition did not fare too well either. The following February, Pope John Paul II visited the island during his tour of the Philippines. He told the impoverished sugar cane workers of Negros that they should unionize to resist exploitation by their employers.[30] On viewing firsthand the poverty of the sugar workers who earned as little as ₱3 (25 U.S. cents) a day, the Pope spoke about the widening inequality of wealth: "Injustice reigns when the laws of economic growth and even greater prosperity determine social relations, leaving in poverty and destitution those who have only their hands to offer."[31] The Pope made no mention of recalling Father Gore. A year later, on March 10, 1982, Sola, out on bail while his trial was continuing, was ambushed and killed along with two policemen, his driver, and the overseer of his plantation.[32] The military investigated and credited the New People's Army with the ambush.[33]

While Marcos was on his state visit, Gore's presbytery was raided by members of the Philippine Constabulary on September 23, 1982. They claimed to have found a grenade, some 45-caliber ammunition, and subversive documents. Gore appeared in court on September 28, and was charged, along with six others, for violation of the anti-subversion law and illegal possession of explosives and ammunition. They were released on bail. On October 12, an additional count of inciting to rebellion was lodged after affidavits were filed alleging that Gore and his associates had, over the last several years, incited the people of Oringao to rise up against the government.[34] On October 18, all seven were rearrested and jailed. The next day 6,000 supporters attended a prayer rally and several hundred of them maintained a constant vigil outside the prison until they were released on bail on October 21.[35]

On February 25, 1983, a further set of charges were filed against Gore and his associates. This time O'Brien and Vicente Dangan, a Diocesan priest under Bishop Fortich, were included. All were accused of being "principals by inducement" in the killing of Mayor Sola and his aides.[36] This came as a surprise since the Philippine Constabulary had already admitted that the New People's Army were responsible for those killings. The six lay leaders languished in jail for a year. In January 1984, Gore, O'Brien, and Dangan, who had been under house arrest, decided to join their associates in jail. Fearing repercussions at having three priests in jail, the government decided it was time for a trial. The court case opened on February 23. Enrile, who was a Harvard-trained lawyer, stated at that time that the evidence was "strong enough for conviction."[37]

Present in the courtroom were Bishop Fortich, Australian and Irish diplomats, representatives of the International Commission of Jurists, the Law Council of Australia, the Australian Bishops Conference, and numerous Western newsmen and television crews.[38] Marcos had offered to deport Gore and O'Brien and have the charges dropped, but the two priests demanded that the charges be dropped for all the accused. Their demands were not met. The trial continued.

After all the buildup the "evidence" for the case was not that strong. In reality there was no evidence. The Philippine Constabulary investigators had collected 90 shell casings from the ambush site but no forensic evidence, fingerprints, or ballistics testing were presented to link any of the accused to the ambush. When pressed to produce the notes of his investigation, the investigating officer claimed they had been lost. In a remarkable coincidence the officer who had preceded him as chief investigator of the case also claimed that his notes and photographs had been lost. All the witnesses for the prosecution turned out to be on the payroll of the Philippine Constabulary, and gave testimony that was riven with obvious lies, contradictions, and factual errors. The government prosecutor finally conceded that the evidence presented by the defense overwhelmingly showed the innocence of the nine. The charges were dropped, but Gore and

O'Brien were ordered to leave the country within 30 days. Before they left they celebrated mass and forgave all those who had made their lives so difficult.[39]

The church had won a victory, but sadly very little changed. Conditions on Negros remained the same. The landlords still ruled; the military still protected them; and the poor remained oppressed. A month before the charges were dropped, on the previous May 16, the bodies of nine men, all residents of Inayauan, Cauayan, on the island of Negros, were found. They had been tortured and murdered. Eight days later Melecio Villanueva executed an affidavit charging two officers and 21 enlisted men of the local Philippine Constabulary detachment with the massacre on May 14, parliamentary election day. Those charged claimed the nine men had been ambushed while on their way to raid the detachment headquarters. However, witnesses disagreed. They said that eleven men, one of them Villanueva, were arrested, beaten up, tied together, and paraded through town to the detachment. Villanueva and one other person had managed to escape the massacre and reported the incident to Bishop Fortich who demanded an investigation. The local authorities then filed an amendment to a murder charge, which had been filed on January 31, 1983 — 16 months earlier — charging Villanueva and the nine massacre victims with that murder. General Fidel Ramos, head of the Philippine Constabulary, then stepped in. He stated that filing a murder case against dead persons just showed ignorance of the law and guaranteed there would be no coverup in the investigation.[40]

As the human rights abuses became a bigger and bigger embarrassment, the church became a bigger and bigger problem for Marcos. He could jail his political opponents and stifle the press, but he couldn't control the church. Thus he began to carry out, through the military, a concerted, all-out campaign to discredit them: harass the priests and nuns; raid the churches; and imprison the layworkers. However, with every raid, include a denial that there is a campaign against the church; and with every arrest produce the required "subversive" documents. Create the illusion. Confuse the people. The incidents involving Gerlock,

Booms, de la Torre, Schouten, and Gore are but a few examples
of this campaign. Incidents of arrest without charges, torture,
murder, and disappearance were documented in the thousands by
Amnesty International and other church and civil rights groups,
but the more the evidence presented, the more the denials, and the
more the raids and arrests.

CHAPTER SIXTEEN

The Military

When Marcos declared martial law, he ordered all private armies to turn over their weapons and disband. He pointedly emphasized that it was not a military takeover of the civilian government, but he immediately expanded their size from about 60,000 to about 155,000. (It would grow to 200,000 over the next 10 years.) This rapid expansion created problems of organization and discipline. A larger force required more officers, which meant rapid promotions for the officers who now owed their careers and loyalty to him. He allowed some generals due for retirement to overstay. The recruitment of so many enlisted men caused the standards to fall. The results were not surprising.

More and more incidents were reported of troops accused of looting, raping, torture, and killing.[1] The rapid promotion of some junior officers not accustomed to the rank and responsibilities occasionally resulted in some ugly incidents. The young undisciplined, non-professional soldiers hurt the professional reputation of the non-commissioned officers and officers alike. Heretofore the Philippine Armed Forces had been the very model of a Western army. General Douglas MacArthur played a very large role in this. Most senior officers had fought with the Americans in World War II and attended U.S. military institutions. Now these unprofessional so-called soldiers discredited what had been a proud military tradition. That tradition became one of the first casualties of martial law.

On September 21, 1975, to dramatize the third anniversary of

martial law, Marcos announced a purge of the defense establishment to weed out so-called undesirables because of reports of
wide-ranging corruption in the military. The idea backfired.
Ranking military commanders, led by Minister Enrile, submitted
their resignations en masse. Marcos backed down. While Enrile
owed his loyalty to Marcos, his decision to back his soldiers
indicates that perhaps Marcos was using the purge to improve the
positions of commanders loyal to him to the detriment of others.
Enrile's stance may have been a factor in General Ver's
increasingly prominent role in the military establishment.[2]

Military spending increased over twenty-fold during Marcos'
reign, from ₱317 million in 1965 to ₱7.4 billion in 1983. This did
not include military aid provided by the U.S. which totalled $674.8
million from 1962 to 1981; nor did it include military aid provided
by the bases agreements, which was $50 million a year from 1979
to 1984, and $85 million a year beginning in 1985. (The new
agreement actually provided $180 million in annual rents, of
which $85 million was allocated for military aid.)

A 1984 report, prepared for the U.S. Senate Committee on
Foreign Relations,* noted that Philippine defense ministry
officials, in discussing their desperate need to modernize their
armed forces, had indicated that top priorities included replacing
their older aircraft with modern jets, acquiring new surface-to-air
missiles, and expanding their navy. The report commented that
these priorities were "radically out of touch with the realities of
the current and anticipated challenge posed by the New People's
Army." Many military units even lacked such basic supplies as
military uniforms and boots. Further discussions with the defense
ministry officials convinced them to adjust their priorities to
reflect the internal threat and procure vehicles, weapons,
communications systems, and other support equipment suitable
for operations against the NPA. With one notable exception.

In the case of helicopters, the report remarked, "President
Marcos chose to purchase state-of-the-art technology, which
involved paying state-of-the-art prices." He did this despite strong

---

* "The Situation in the Philippines," A Staff Report, prepared for the
U.S. Senate Committee on Foreign Relations, October 1984.

recommendations to purchase older models in large numbers that would fit in with the established maintenance and logistics systems. Moreover, he purchased mostly civilian versions, acquiring two Sikorsky Blackhawks as personal transport, at a cost of about $4 million each.

Although it wasn't mentioned in the report, there was another reason for the defense ministry officials' desire to purchase missiles and jets and modernize their navy. There was big money to be made in the procurement of such items. The bigger the price tag, the bigger the kickback. This would later be confirmed when a colonel in the J-4 (Procurement) section of the Armed Forces of the Philippines became fed up with the practice. He retired, moved to the states, and, finally, in early 1986, decided to tell what he knew about such matters. In one instance all members of a contract committee, formed to handle the purchase of helicopters, were dismissed, including the colonel, because they refused to allow a $1 million kickback. Such kickbacks were potentially a very large source of income.

The excuse given for the rapid expansion of the military was "the communists." Even before he was president, Marcos had used the term rather broadly, calling just about everyone who was against him a communist. He appeared to be somewhat contradictory when, on the one hand he would belittle the New People's Army as a small, ill-trained, and poorly-armed bunch of bandits, but on the other hand every increase in the size of the armed forces, and correspondingly the defense budget, was justified by the "ever-threatening spread of communism."

The New People's Army (NPA) is the fighting arm of the Communist Party of the Philippines (CPP). It began with only a few hundred fighters in 1969. With the imposition of martial law its numbers grew quickly. Estimated strength in 1972 was 950 to 1,300 armed men.[3] In 1983 their strength was estimated by Western analysts to be 7 to 12,000. Defense Ministry officials claimed that estimation was an exaggeration, that the number was only 4 to 6,000, with about 2,500 armed.[4] The CPP claimed the number was 20,000. Regardless of actual size, the NPA did continue to grow and expand, operating in 63 of the Philippines'

73 provinces.[5]

The reasons for its growth were classic. Military abuses, chronic neglect of rural areas by the government, hard economic times, and an ineffective land reform program all played into the hands of the CPP. They emphasized the lack of government concern for the hardships of the peasants, and expressed their sympathy by terrorizing abusive landlords who treated them harshly. All this made recruiting easy, and membership in the CPP and the NPA grew. Most recruits were not communists in the Marxist sense. Most were Catholic in a devoutly religious country. Their motives for joining were related more to injustice than to ideology.

The original communist movement, which began in the 1920's and 1930's, had been aligned with Moscow and helped form the Huk movement. They were crushed in the early 50's and were all but extinct by the early 60's. Then a new generation of leaders emerged. They came from the ranks of students, teachers, and intellectuals, and looked to China and Mao Tse Tung's experience with agrarian revolution for their inspiration and guidance. Although influenced by China, the CPP did not appear to have any outside association or receive any outside support. The insurgency appeared to be an internal revolution.[6]

Throughout the 70's and into the 80's Marcos continued to belittle the effectiveness of the CPP and the NPA, but he was unable to eradicate them. In fact, the CPP stepped up its NPA operations. In addition to classic guerrilla tactics of highly selective terrorism, assassinations, and army patrol ambushes, the NPA began to confront the enemy in company-size (60 to 100 men) and even battalion-size (200 to 300 men) strength.[7] Some military units became more and more frustrated. The arbitrary arrest, detention, torture and killing of "suspected" NPA guerrillas increased, and only led to an even larger network of supporters in the countryside. The appalling brutality of units such as the 60th Battalion of the Philippine Constabulary in the Chico Dam area serves as an example.

In the early 70's the government began construction on a vast hydro-electric dam in the mountains of northern Luzon. When completed it would flood thousands of acres of mountains and forests, including the rice terraces and ancestral burial grounds of many of the mountain people. More than 40,000 people were threatened with resettlement. They objected and began to fight back. Many joined the NPA. The 60th Battalion was called in and brutally suppressed the uprising. The incident only confirmed the people's belief of an uncaring and repressive government.[8]

The National Democratic Front was also a part of the CPP, serving as its quasi-legal and propaganda arm. Formed in 1973, the NDF served as a coordinating committee for protest activities with other sectors of society, including doctors, lawyers, teachers, and students.[9] Most protest groups have acknowledged that the NDF was the best organized, best funded and most militant. Because of this they were able to blend in with the overall opposition effort and even infiltrate some of the non-communist protest groups. They played a large part in the anti-Marcos rallies and demonstrations that proved to be very successful.[10]

The Moro National Liberation Front (MNLF) was the only other organized guerrilla force in the Philippines. The hardy, proud Muslim minority's conflict with the government in Mindanao and the Sulu Archipelago was the result of inequities and misunderstandings going back more than 400 years. It stemmed from competition with the Christians for traditional lands and the Muslim's desire to preserve their cultural identity.[11]

The guerrilla struggle for autonomy can be traced back to 1968. The military had recruited Filipino-Muslims and trained them on the island of Corregidor. When they found out their mission, code-named "Jabidah," was for sabotage and insurgency in Sabah, they rebelled and 68 were massacred. Only one survived. The officer in charge of the creation of the Jabidah force was Romeo Espino, Commanding General of the Philippine Army, who would later become Armed Forces Chief of Staff. He was also responsible in 1972 for the takeover and management of the Jacinto group of companies.

Actual armed conflict between the Muslims and the military began on June 19, 1969, the birthday of Philippine national hero Jose Rizal, after another military massacre of 67 Muslims inside a mosque in Manili, Cotabato.[12] Initially they called themselves the Mindanao National Liberation Front. In 1971 the name was changed to Muslim National Liberation Front, and finally to Moro National Liberation Front in 1973.[13] When martial law was declared and more government troops were sent down to quash them, the fighting flared up into what many described as full-scale war. At its height in the mid-70's the Muslim rebellion tied down 70 to 80 percent of the armed forces. The MNLF was once a sophisticated organization with a central committee, political bureau, propaganda intelligence bureau, and a regular army, the Bangsa Moro (Muslim Nation) Army, whose estimated strenth was about 20,000.

There was a ceasefire declared in 1976 when the government and the Moros met in Libya and signed the Tripoli Agreement in December. The agreement was supposed to grant autonomy to 13 provinces in Mindanao, Sulu, and Palawan. Marcos reneged on the agreement, however, and granted autonomy to only two in 1977. The MNLF resumed the fighting but on a smaller scale. They had become less effective because, during the ceasefire, they made the mistake of having faith in the government by allowing them to pinpoint the MNLF areas of operation.[14] The government continued to offer inducements to those who would lay down their arms. Those who surrendered were offered rehabilitation and given special treatment in helping them to acquire land and received scholaiships to make up for their lost education. Some were offered administrative positions in the new "autonomous" government. There are still a few MNLF strongholds but most have gone back to farming. Only 6 to 7,000 still remain in the hills.[15]

The police powers of the military, which were becoming increasingly more and more abusive, began to attract the attention and criticism of human rights organizations and international jurists. Thus in June 1977, Marcos issued a new General Order 60, which stated that the Arrest, Search and Seizure Orders (ASSO's) of the Ministry of Defense should be limited to those offenses in the new General Order 59 which was amending General Order 2. This appeared on its face to limit the powers of the military. However, it wasn't so. It actually broadened them. While the new list of the offenses was much smaller, the General Order had a qualification tacked on at the end: ASSO's could be issued by the Minister of National Defense "for crimes which, although not cognizable by the military tribunals, likewise have the effect of undermining national security or public order as determined by him."[16]

Marcos wasn't about to give up his ASSO's. They were just one more weapon in his private arsenal of intimidation and terror. And there was "Operation Mad Dog." Officially it didn't exist, but it did. The plan was simple. If any of the Marcos children were ever kidnapped or killed, then justice would be swift. There would be no trial, just executions. Different ratios were bandied about, from "ten for one," to "the entire family, or families, of the perpetrator(s)." Whether or not such an operation was real is academic. Everyone knew Marcos was quite capable of such measures. Just the idea undoubtedly protected the members of his family and his friends' families as well.

Such was the setting for the 1978 elections—more powerful ASSO's and an obedient public. Of course, all of the KBL (Marcos'political party—Kilusang Bagong Lipunan) candidates won, including Imelda, who ran against Ninoy Aquino, who was still in prison but allowed to run for office. In fact, all ballots were counted and the winners declared within a few hours after the election, an amazing feat of bureaucratic organization. (Fox Butterfield, of the *New York Times*, was in Manila covering this event. He walked in on some surprised members of the Commission on Elections who were actively engaged in a vote-tampering session and was seized by government guards and unceremoniously thrown down the stairs.)

The Interim National Assembly was convened shortly afterward, but its authority was limited and its legislative powers heavily circumscribed. No bill of general application could be placed before the assembly without the prior recommendation of the Cabinet, and Amendment 3 of the 1976 amendments allowed Marcos to appoint and remove Cabinet members at his discretion. He continued to issue legislative acts after the National Assembly was convened. The overwhelming majority of the bills passed by the Assembly were only of local application.[17]

The most memorable thing about that election was the huge

election eve noise barrage that Aquino had asked for. At a predetermined time almost every street corner in Metro Manila overflowed with people beating on cans and frying pans, shouting "LABAN! LABAN! LABAN!" (the name of his political party). The date was April 6, 1978.

Out of that night and that rigged election was born the April 6 Liberation Movement. Before this date the moderate opposition had only sought peaceful means to resolve the country's problems. Now they realized that the government would not even allow an honest election; now they realized that the military would go on with its police powers and continue with its government sanctioned arrest, torture, and killing (the soldiers had even coined a catchy term for this part of their work — salvaging — borrowed from the latest John Le Carre spy novel); and they finally realized that there was only one alternative left — to fight fire with fire...literally.

By early 1979, a group had organized and called itself the "Light-A-Fire Movement." In an attempt to destabilize the government, several government buildings and hotels were set afire. The floating casino, one of the gambling operations owned by Imelda's brother, was destroyed. On Christmas Day 1979, Eduardo Olaguer was arrested, along with about 20 others, and tagged as the head of the movement. He was 47 years old at the time, a Harvard MBA, and a newspaper executive. The "urban guerrilla" had materialized — out of fear, out of frustration, and out of need.

Despite Olaguer's arrest and imprisonment the resistance continued. Gaston Ortigas, one of the leaders of the movement, managed to flee before his arrest (he was warned by a former student of his at the Asian Institute of Management who was a lieutenant colonel in the Philippine Constabulary) and made it to San Francisco where he joined the "Movement For a Free Philippines." In Manila the April 6 Liberation Movement emerged and took over where the Light-A-Fire Movement left off. Victor Burns Lovely, a Filipino-American from Los Angeles, was captured in Manila when the bomb he was attempting to rig exploded, blowing off his right hand.[18] Lovely turned state's evidence and implicated several others from the U.S., including

Ninoy Aquino and businessman Steve Psinakis of San Francisco, the husband of Presy Lopez, whose uncle was the former vice-president of Marcos. Psinakis had master-minded the dramatic escape in October 1977 of the vice-president's nephew, Eugenio Lopez, Jr., and Sergio Osmeña III. Psinakis was repeatedly accused of being the head of all terrorist activities in the Philippines.

In October 1980 a bomb exploded at the American Society of Travel Agents convention in Manila, just minutes after Marcos had delivered the welcoming address. As a result the scheduled week-long conference, attended by more than 4,000 delegates from the U.S. and other countries, was cancelled.[19] Doris Baffrey, a Filipina residing in New York and attending the convention, was arrested. She confessed to the crime, was convicted, and sentenced to six months in prison. That was in 1980. After completing her sentence the military refused to release her despite a court order granting her freedom. She was held until February 18, 1985, and finally released.[20]

The powers of the military were further broadened in November 1980 by General Order 68, which was promulgated in preparing for the termination of martial law. Added to the already extensive list were the crimes of cattle rustling, illegal telephone, water and electrical connections, violation of immigration laws, squatting on public and private property, fraud in relation to government, professional, and civil service examinations, and "not only those crimes directly affecting national security or public order but also those that are pernicious and inimical to social and economic stability."[21] The ambiguity of such orders allowed just about anyone crossing the government to be detained. This coverall general order remained in force after martial law. The general order which granted jurisdiction over martial law offenses to military tribunals was revoked at the end of martial law. However, some cases were retained by the military courts. The exceptions were "[those cases] which may not be transferred to the civil courts without irreparable prejudice to the state in view of the rules of double jeopardy, or other circumstances which remedy further prosecution of the cases difficult if not impossible."[22] Amnesty International complained

that the exceptions included a significant number of cases of
arrest and detention "for political reasons," and that these cases
had never been referred to the appropriate court.[23] Once again the
ambiguity of such rules allowed Marcos exceptionally broad
control even after martial law. The military's role expanded even
further.

Military expansion included the formation of the Irregular
Civilian Home Defense Force (ICHDF). The ICHDF were local
militia and numbered about 75,000 throughout the country in
1979. A U.S. Senate report noted that they were comprised mostly
of town toughs and petty criminals who used their weapons to
exploit the local people more than to fight the NPA.[24] Under the
command of the Philippine Constabulary, their responsibilities
included, at one time or another, spying on residents, getting out
the vote during elections, and breaking up local anti-government
meetings. Amnesty International received persistent reports of
their abuses, both acting alone and in conjunction with the
military.

In 1981 the 125th Airborne Company was assigned to
Pagadian City in Zamboanga del Norte, Mindanao, shortly
before the presidential election to be held on June 16. The
movement to boycott the election had gained considerable
support, and most eligible voters in the area abstained from
voting. The 125th began recruiting members of a local religious
sect called Rock Christ into the local ICHDH. Rock Christ
members wear amulets which they believe render them invulner-
able, and their high priests are said to have healing powers.
Between the first week of July and the end of October 1981 at
least 16 people were killed in various incidents in this area, and
others were beaten, abducted, or simply disappeared. All victims
had organized or participated in the boycott.

Another group which operated with official approval was the
Lost Command, under the infamous Lieutenant Colonel Carlos
Lademora. Lademora was the recipient of many awards for
heroism in the Mindanao secessionist campaign in the 70's, and
had even been featured in the *Soldier of Fortune* magazine. Based
in Tambis, in the Dimata mountain range in Agusan del Sur,
Mindanao, the strength of the Lost Command was reported to be

about 250, of which 15 were regular Philippine Constabulary officers and men, and the rest convicted military and civilian criminals and deserters. They ran protection rackets and acted as security guards to agricultural corporations in addition to fighting the NPA. The Philippine government supplied weapons to private guard forces such as Lademora's, hired by the wealthy crony plantation and factory owners.[25] They were the law in the area. Numerous abuses were reported. Church sources reported that more than 80 people were killed in the area in 1980 and 1981. In one incident, on September 15, 1981, some of the members of the Lost Command are alleged to have massacred 45 men, women, and children in northern Samar because they were suspected of supporting the NPA.

In 1981 General Romeo Espino retired as Armed Forces Chief of Staff. On his retirement General Fabian Ver became the new Chief of Staff. This was part of Marcos' overall strategy to strengthen, rather than loosen, his grip on the country. Ver was from Ilocos Norte, Marcos' home province. They were townmates and cousins. Ver finished the advanced ROTC training program at the University of the Philippines in 1941, but there is no record of his ever graduating or receiving a degree. It isn't known what he did in 1942 and 1943 during the war. He was listed on one of Marcos' Maharlika rosters, in Major Valdez' unit, as a third lieutenant with service in the U.S. Army beginning March 12, 1944. That is all. There is no other record or biography of his service for that period. He was commissioned in the Philippine Constabulary in 1945. In 1963, Captain Ver was assigned to Marcos, who was then president of the Senate. He stayed with Marcos, rising in rank and prestige. He became head of the 15,000 man Presidential Security Command and was director general of the National Intelligence and Security Authority (NISA), the largest intelligence organization in the country. During martial law there was a proliferation of intelligence and security units created and empowered to arrest and detain people suspected of offenses related to national security. NISA was the chief coordinating body. It had authority over all intelligence bodies, including the Civil Intelligence and Security Agency (CISA). These intelligence units were effectively not subject to any of the standard rules regarding arrest, detention, and the treatment of prisoners. Ver gradually eclipsed the power of Minister Enrile. By the time he became Chief of Staff he was the only person besides Marcos who could initiate troop movements and appoint officers.[26] He was also appointed to the Executive Committee by Marcos in 1982.

The Vice-Chief of Staff of the Armed Forces was Lieutenant General Fidel Ramos. He headed the Philippine Constabulary and the Integrated National Police. He was a first cousin of Marcos, from Pangasinan province. Ramos graduated from West Point, fought in Korea, and served in Vietnam with the Philippine Civic Action Group. He had also trained at the John F. Kennedy Center for Special Warfare in Fort Bragg, North Carolina, home of the Green Berets. A dour man who never seemed to smile, Ramos was praised by Marcos loyalists and oppositionists alike for his professionalism and was reportedly incorruptible. His only caprice seemed to be his trademark cigar. On the face of it he was eminently more qualified than Ver for the top job in the armed forces, but not being corrupt surely played a large, and detrimental, part in his military career in the Marcos government.[27]

In 1975 the Philippines was a sponsor of the Declaration Against Torture adopted by the United Nations General Assembly. In 1979 it was among the few governments to make the so-called Unilateral Declaration, stating its intention to implement the provisions through national legislation and other measures. In 1980, during the 35th session of the United Nations General Assembly, it was a sponsor of Resolution 35/178 on Torture and Other Cruel, Inhuman or Degrading Treatment or Punishment, and of Resolution 35/170 on a Code of Conduct for Law Enforcement Officials.[28] All this was an ongoing and impressive show of support for human rights, but that is all it was—a show. When Amnesty International visited the country in 1975, it found that 71 of the 107 prisoners interviewed had been tortured and an estimated 6,000 people still detained for political reasons.[29] In January 1977, in a speech to the University of the Philippines Law Association, Marcos said, "I would like to state that if by political prisoners we accept the original connotation of the word in international law, which means those who have been detained without proper criminal cases filed against them, we have no political prisoners in the Philippines."[30] This was debatable. In 1983, the Defense Ministry admitted it was holding more than 500 "public order violators," which included those imprisoned for national security crimes, such as subversion, insurrection, rebellion, and illegal possession of subversive documents or firearms.[31] Also, as of 1983, the Manila-based Task Force Detainees estimated the number of political detainees at 963.[32]

In 1980 the U.N. sent information to the Philippine government of more than 200 cases of "disappearances" which were reported to its Working Group on Enforced or Involuntary Disappearances. Instead of investigating the Philippine government dismissed the charges with a curt reply: "Though we share a deep concern for missing persons in the Philippines we believe...these persistent reports...to be misleading and may be again part of the overall propaganda effort of the underground to discredit the government."[33]

Amnesty International visited again in 1981, after martial law was supposedly over, because of more reports of human rights violations, including disappearances and extrajudicial executions. While there Amnesty requested a meeting with Enrile to discuss the issue. He was too occupied with other business at the time and refused to see them.[34]

Amnesty International reported that "the lifting of martial law has not curtailed the incidence of those grave violations which occur in disregard of the most fundamental human rights regarded as inalienable in all circumstances." They also complained that at least ten presidential decrees had been made public after January 17, 1981, although they were dated January 16.[35] Chief among these were the so-called "Death Decrees." PD 1834 increased the penalty to life imprisonment or death for both leaders and followers of a rebellion, and included in this category editors and publishers who used or allowed their facilities to be used to print or broadcast propaganda or to plot "any of the acts which constitute rebellion or insurrection or sedition." These

crimes were previously punishable by six months in jail. The
other, PD 1835, authorized the trial in absentia of anyone accused
of subversion and "confiscation of his properties in the Philippines."[36] A number of Marcos' decrees did not have consecutive
numbers. They were obviously antedated, which violated the Bill
of Rights ex post facto laws.

The violations discovered by Amnesty International were
numerous and varied: arrests were commonly made without a
warrant; the arrests often involved undue force, including
beatings; detainees were held for long periods without being
charged and without access to relatives, lawyers, or medical
examinations; detainees were ill-treated and tortured while in
detention; detainees were commonly coerced into signing waivers
of detention, waiving their right of delivery to the proper judicial
authority, and signing statements asserting they had not been
ill-treated while in detention; and the refusal of military personnel
to submit to the ruling of civil courts.[37] Amnesty International
charged that it was during this process of detention that so-called
"tactical interrogation" was used, which often included torture
and other forms of mistreatment to extract confessions from
detainees.[38] Another finding was that a large number of those with
grievances were afraid to complain to the authorities because of
open threats of reprisal and a fear of being killed when taken into
custody.[39]

Most of the victims of the reported abuses were people
suspected by the authorities of being opposed to the government
although they had not taken up arms and were not engaged in
armed combat. For most their only crime was being a suspect.
There is convincing evidence that these victims of abuses who
were alleged to be subversive were either selected arbitrarily or at
random because they were engaged in non-violent activities such
as organizing unions, participating in a boycott of the presidential
election, or membership in church-sponsored social action
groups. They would be arrested without a warrant, taken to a
"safe house" and held incommunicado, and tortured until a
confession was extracted, or "salvaged," thus ending the need for
a confession.[40]

It also found that investigations involving abuses of military personnel were not shown impartiality. To the contrary, agents of the government, primarily members of the armed forces, enjoyed de facto immunity from accountability to the civil court system and even disregarded rulings made by the civil courts.[41]

Claudio Teehankee was the only associate justice in the Supreme Court who persistently questioned the validity and legality of Marcos' martial law regime. He was rewarded by being twice passed over for chief justice although he was the senior associate justice at the time. Marcos' political allies tried to have him impeached in 1983, and his citizenship was questioned in 1984 (Teehankee, a natural-born citizen, is of Chinese descent), but his integrity and honor could not be questioned. He survived the political intrigues and continued his uncompromising stand in protecting the victims of abuse and injustice. The irony is that he and Marcos had been allies at one time. He was the bar top-notcher in 1940; Marcos had registered the same achievement the year before. After Marcos was first elected president he appointed Teehankee to his Cabinet as Secretary of Justice in 1967. He served loyally and was appointed to the Supreme Court in December 1968. Then, in 1971, the Plaza Miranda bombing occurred. Doubts were raised about Marcos. There was no doubt, however, about the law and its constitutional guarantees of human rights. From then on Teehankee consistently dissented in his opinions against the Marcos government.

The Constitution and Bill of Rights notwithstanding, Marcos still had absolute powers when it came to arresting or detaining people. And Teehankee, called "the lone voice in the wilderness" for obvious reasons, in one of his many dissenting opinions under Marcos, stated: "These rights are immutable, inflexible, yielding to no pressure of convenience, expediency, or so-called judicial statesmanship."[42] He was dissenting in the 1983 ruling which reaffirmed Marcos' absolute arrest, detention, and release powers. The ruling superseded the Lansing Doctrine of December 1971. Respected by jurors and scholars alike, the doctrine authorized the courts to look into the factual basis of detention. Such judicial interference was held to be permissible, not necessarily to test whether the president had acted correctly, but whether he acted arbitrarily. However, with this new ruling, there was no longer any test for arbitrary detention.

Under the so-called Presidential Commitment Orders (PCO's), which had replaced the dreaded Arrest, Search and Seizure Orders (ASSO's) used during martial law, Marcos still had the power to arrest people suspected of crimes relating to "national security." All persons arrested under a PCO were denied the right to bail and the right to petition for a writ of habeas corpus. Even Chief Justice Enrique Fernando, a known Marcos ally, argued, along with Teehankee, that the right to bail cannot be infringed upon, even when the writ of habeas corpus is suspended. Teehankee stated: "If the Bill of Rights is incompatible with a stable government and a menace to the nation, let the Constitution be amended or abolished."[43]

After the ruling on the Presidential Commitments Orders, the bishops decided to prepare a message to be read in churches throughout the country on August 7, 1983, stating "The PCO and its implementation is immoral." Marcos, upon hearing of their intention, announced the abolition of the PCO on August 5. The bishops called off the reading. Then, by decree, he replaced it with the equally powerful Preventive Detention Action (PDA). Whatever the name, Marcos and his military could still arrest and detain at will without justification.[44]

Such underhanded treatment of the church was commonplace and it set the stage for the start of the final confrontation between what Cardinal Sin called "the forces of good and evil." Regrettably, the United States was still officially backing the evil forces. On June 25, 1983, Secretary of State George Shultz arrived in Manila and praised Marcos' democracy and the "very special" ties with the U.S.[45] His timing was bad. Human rights abuses were getting worse and Schultz' praise only seemed to endorse such acts. In less than two months the U.S. would see how awfully wrong such support was. Ninoy Aquino had already started planning his return. The countdown to August 21 had begun.

CHAPTER SEVENTEEN

Expression

During martial law there was no debate on public issues and no creative exchange of ideas. It was not allowed. All decisions regarding the people were decided for them. Marcos attempted to control all information which the publc received. There were children in the Philippines who had known no other president. By the time they entered school they didn't know what it was to have a free exchange of ideas. Textbooks were full of propaganda hailing the "Hero from the North" in blatant or subtle ways.

Parents of these students had perfected the art of being let alone, of first thinking what was safe to say before saying anything. Marcos wanted to think for the people, and decided what the people were allowed to read and see and hear. If a *Time* or *Newsweek* carried a derogatory story, then it was banned. This was not a novel concept. It had been done in Nazi Germany, and was being done in Russia, Cuba, and Iran. The *Far Eastern Economic Review* in Hong Kong summed it up in November 1972: "The Philippine mass media, once considered the freest in Asia, have been suppressed to the point of death; the most well-known and established among them have no chance of reappearance, and this country of 39 million people is being fed only propaganda bulletins, which are financed and operated by President Marcos' own friends and subordinates."[1]

It wasn't just the media. All forms of expression came under the watchful eye of Marcos and particularly Imelda. The artist that painted pictures of slums or peasants could not expect to be patronized by Imelda and her followers. Nor could they expect any commissions from them or exhibitions at official galleries. Only those painters whose subjects were considered "pleasant" and "pretty" or "nice" were acceptable. Manansala, Legaspi, and Bencab were in. Egay Fernandez, Neil Doloricon, Biboy Delotavo, Adi Baens, and others who painted pictures of the urban poor, hungry farmers, or other such "ugly" scenes were out. Movies like Lino Brocka's "My Country" were banned because they depicted unpleasant social situations. In this case the movie portrayed a worker driven to robbery because of oppressive labor conditions.

Theatre groups were also under the gun. Doreen Fernandez of Ateneo University noted that, "Just like the journalist, their plays have to touch reality only gently, obliquely, so as to keep the arrests at bay." Groups like PETA, a semi-professional troup in Metro Manila who were oriented to contemporary issues, and Peryante, composed of University of the Philippines students, who presented their plays at rallies and demonstrations and liked to spoof those in power, were constantly taking risks in order to present theatre that dealt with reality, a subject not favored by the Marcos regime. Needless to say, no one, not even the truly gifted of their craft, ever got rich during martial law going against the wishes of Imelda.

The teachers, poets, and writers who decided to remain apolitical were left in an intellectual void. Father John Doherty of Ateneo was deported for his work on the economy. Noel Soriano, former president of the University of the Philippines, was told by one of the regents, "You're dead," when he went against the wishes of Marcos and allowed student council elections to be held in September 1980. Student councils were not allowed during martial law. Mahar Mangahas was forced to resign from the Development Academy of the Philippines after he published some negative findings on Imelda's social projects.

However, if one chose to offer his services to those in favor, there were rewards—good positions, high salaries, political favors, government contracts, and other perks. Examples of such jobs were those assigned to the Presidential Center for Special Studies, a think tank for Marcos, and those historians who were assigned to write the new history of the Philippines.

There were also rewards for journalists who toed the line. Reporters at every newspaper were paid by the government to embellish its viewpoint and inform on those who would not. Some were wined and dined and given expensive gifts. Life could be good if you were in favor.

Before martial law no government permit or license was necessary, but on its declaration the Mass Media Council was set up. Headed by Minister Enrile and Minister of Public Information Francisco Tatad, its duties included media censorship and licensing. Opportunities for enrichment were always available under such a setup. So much so that feuding broke out between the Enrile and Tatad factions almost immediately. Within six months Marcos did away with the MMC. In May 1973 he created the Media Advisory Council headed by Primitivo Mijares.[2] This set-up lasted until November 9, 1974, when he abolished the MAC and created the Print Media Council for newspapers, magazines, periodicals, journals, and publications, and the Broadcast Media Council for radio and television broadcasting.[3] The apparent reason for this change was Marcos' appearance on the "Today" show on U.S. television on September 20, 1974. He had claimed that the media was no longer controlled by the government, stating that it was now an independant entity and "supervised by its own policemen—the publishers, the owners of the radio and television stations. There is no censorship at present."[4] Apparently he wasn't convincing enough. In May 1975 the International Press Institute, at its convention in Zurich, withdrew recognition of the Philippines on the grounds that a free press no longer existed.[5]

By then all the owners and publishers were personal friends and relatives of Marcos. The *Daily Express* newspaper, owned by Roberto Benedicto, was allowed to open the day after martial law was declared, as was his television station, Channel 9, and the two radio stations of his Kanlaon Broadcasting System. Benedicto later took over the radio and television network owned by Vice-President Fernando Lopez.[6] His brother, Eugenio, Sr., owned the *Manila Chronicle,* which was closed down on September 23. Kokoy Romualdez, Imelda's brother, took over these facilities to publish his own newspaper, the *Times-Journal*.[7] The former *Manila Daily Bulletin* was allowed to reopen as the *Bulletin Today*. Its owner, the late Hans Menzi, was a retired brigadier general and former aide-de-camp to Marcos. He was appointed head of the Print Media Council in 1974, and, in June 1976, had announced that criticism of Marcos and Imelda would not be allowed in newspapers and magazines. Benedicto, Menzi, and Romualdez, along with a few other friends, also published some small-circulation dailies.[8]

Other newspapers were not so lucky. The *Philippine Herald* was never allowed to reopen. Another, the *Manila Times*, one of the most influential newspapers, was never allowed to reopen. Its war correspondent in Korea in 1950 was Ninoy Aquino, age 18. Its publisher, Joachin "Chino" Roces, had been arrested on the Friday night before Marcos announced martial law. One of the most respected men in his profession, recognition by "Chino," or the lack thereof could make or break a congressman or senator, or even a president.

In February 1975, while on a trip to the United States, Primitivo Mijares, former head of the Print Media Council, defected. In the states he wrote a book, *The Conjugal Dictatorship*, which chronicled the corruption and oppression of the Marcos regime. He also testified before the Congressional House International Relations subcommittee in June 1975. He was offered a $50,000 bribe by the Philippine consul general not to testify, but he declined. After testifying, he was offered $100,000 to recant his testimony, refute Anderson's story (Jack Anderson had chronicled the story in his nationwide column), and retire to Australia. He refused again.[9] Then he disappeared. He was last seen alive in the states on January 7, 1977, at San Francisco International Airport, in the company of an intelligence agent of the Philippine government assigned to the Philippine consulate in San Francisco.[10] He mailed a letter from Honolulu to Colonel Narciso Manzano in San Francisco, who had financed the publishing of his book, and said he was going on a secret and "daring foray" back to Manila and should return by January 13. He did not make it back, and was last seen alive on the U.S. protectorate of Guam on January 23. Five months later, Mijares'

15-year old son disappeared in Manila, and was later found murdered.[11]

The 70's could be labelled the "dark ages" for the Philippine media. No friend or relative of Marcos or Imelda could be criticized. Other forbidden topics included Marcos' health and Imelda's extravagance. Only government accounts of political and economic news could be reported, and these accounts were usually so self-serving, or so out of sync with international press reporting, that they were unbelievable. Military encounters, especially those in the south with the MNLF, were so heavily censored, or so highly fictionalized, that it was impossible to determine what was happening. Magazines such as *Time*, *Newsweek*, *Asiaweek*, and the *Far Eastern Economic Review* were occasionally banned when the government felt their version of events did not coincide with, or support, the government's version. On one occasion a 1978 issue of *Life* was banned because it featured the lavish celebration of the Marcoses' 25th wedding anniversary. Even college newspapers like the University of the Philippines' *Philippine Collegian* and the Ateneo University's *Matanglawin*, forums where criticism of the government was almost routine and tolerated, were occasionally banned. The industry was rigidly controlled. "Xerox" journalism was very much in vogue then. Anything that was newsworthy but not allowed in the local papers, which included anything critical of the government, was photocopied and passed around secretly from hand to hand. It just didn't pay to be critical at that time. Saturnino Ocampo, former business editor of the *Manila Times* newspaper and vice-president of the National Press Club, was arrested on January 14, 1976, on suspicion of being an officer in the Communist Party of the Philippines. He had published articles critical of the Marcos regime. Such was the reward for honesty. You could be fired from your job, or jailed, or sued for libel, or murdered. In fact, the killing of newsmen not only continued but got worse after martial law. A Committee to Protect Journalists was formed to document the crimes. They noted: "Against this climate of violence, it is remarkable that Philippine journalists continue to pursue stories about official corruption and human rights abuses...but the journalists have not

been silenced, and they continue to be killed." (Ocampo, one of
the longest imprisoned political prisoners, finally managed to
escape on May 5, 1985.)

There was a separate standard for the foreign press in the
Philippines. They were tolerated most of the time. However, on
two occasions the government got really angry. The first incident
occurred in 1976. Arnold Zeitlin, Manila bureau chief for the
Associated Press, was barred from reentering the Philippines.
According to the government, he had carried out activities which
endangered national security and public order. He had also
worked for a sinister "foreign organization, or organizations
other than the legitimate media organization he works for."[12] At
the time everyone believed that the government had just finally
become fed up with Zeitlin's critical stories about the Marcos
regime, particularly relating to its unsuccessful attempts to quell
the Muslim secessionist rebellion in the south. However, it was
much bigger than that. Zeitlin didn't know it at the time but he
had stumbled on one of the biggest stories in the Philippines since
Marcos became president. He had caught Marcos perpetrating
one of his hoaxes.

There had been a front page story, replete with pictures, in all
the Manila newspapers about how Marcos had flown into
forbidden, and extremely dangerous, rebel territory in Luuk,
Jolo, and negotiated with the Muslim rebel leader, Maas Bawang,
and his band, and convinced them to abandon their jungle
hideaway, leave the rebellion, and cooperate with him in
pacifying Mindanao. This was indeed a brave feat reminiscent of
Marcos' war exploits. Unfortunately it never happened. Marcos
never went to Jolo. Instead he authorized a former congressman,
Antonio Raquiza, the former friend of Maas Bawang, to contact
the rebel leader and ask him and his followers to come to Manila
to meet with Marcos. Certain financial inducements were offered
and his safety assured. The meeting took place at Fort Bonifacio
in Metro Manila, not Luuk. The pictures were taken near the
Malacañang golf course.[13] Shortly afterward Zeitlin filed a story
for the Associated Press, stating that this much-publicized
meeting could not have taken place "in any spot within the area of
Jolo Island on the date officially reported by the Department of

Public Information and released through the Manila newspapers."[14] That was enough to seal his fate as a reporter in the Philippines. He was not allowed to reenter. A few months later Maas Bawang and members of his family were killed in an ambush. The Muslim insurgency continued.

Another incident occurred in February 1977 a few months after Zeitlin departed. After dealing successfully with one foreign media problem the government decided to try it again. Bernard Wideman, Manila correspondent to the *Washington Post* and American Broadcasting Company, was informed in February that his visa would not be renewed. His request for an extension had been denied on the grounds that he was an "undesirable alien" and a security risk. The real reason was that he had written some critical articles about Roberto Benedicto. Apparently Wideman was not aware that the friends of Marcos were not to be criticized. The government decided to make an example of him. However, it didn't turn out that way. The U.S. State Department inquired about the matter and, as a result, Wideman was given a public hearing. At the hearing Filipino intelligence agents reported that he "helped to instigate, and took part in, anti-government demonstrations, and that he was in contact with a man connected with the outlawed Communist Party of the Philippines and the New People's Army." Wideman, in turn, produced witnesses proving he was just doing his job as a correspondent. The charges were subsequently dismissed and he was allowed to remain, but he was warned that he should pursue his profession "without injury to private reputations or unfair accusations against any public official or public office."[15]

A year after martial law had ended, the U.S. State Department, in its "Country Reports on Human Rights Practices for 1981," reported that "While there is no formal censorship, the media exercise restraint in criticism of government policies. Government information officers sometime seek to influence or pressure editors on coverage of various topics. One newspaper editor was forced to resign after the government reacted sharply to an article she wrote criticizing President Marcos. The largest newspapers and broadcast facilities are all owned by persons sympathetic to the government."[16]

On September 7, 1982, Marcos spoke at a convention of Filipino publishers. He proclaimed that there had been no restrictions on the right of any publication to print in the Philippines since martial law was lifted and wondered aloud at the sad state of the local media. He chided them for relying too much on government press releases, and criticized publications that only praised his administration as well as those that only criticized it.[17] Everyone there wondered what he was up to. They knew the potential penalties for doing exactly what Marcos was complaining about. At least one journalist in attendance probably didn't believe what she was hearing. Letty Magsanoc, of *Panorama* magazine, had been forced to resign by her boss, Hans Menzi, for calling Marcos "the country's number one problem" in its July 12, 1981, issue, six months after martial law ended.[18]

There were hopes that Marcos' speech might mean a new government stance regarding the media but they were only fleeting. The real reason for the speech was to try and offset the negative effects of that State Department report which put the Philippine media in such a bad light. Not only that, Marcos was to leave a week later for his state visit to the U.S. There he would encounter one of his most persistent critics — the foreign media — and his speech was just one bit in the overall public relations campaign to promote himself and his country as a bastion of democracy. His task was difficult if not impossible.

Another journalist decided that, since Marcos had proclaimed freedom of the press, it was time for an article on just that subject. While Marcos was on his state visit, Arlene Babst, columnist for the *Bulletin Today*, wrote that there could only be press freedom "if reporters could do investigative reporting on the financial statements of top government officials; if it could have reported comprehensively on the Anido case, the Manotoc case, and the Pelaez case;* if it could act as the public's watchdog in the

---

* Anido, an actor, supposedly committed suicide after an argument with the daughter of Minister Enrile. Manotoc was supposedly kidnapped by the New People's Army after he married Marcos' daughter. He was later "rescued." Pelaez was ambushed after he criticized the questionable practices of UNICOM, the coconut monopoly. Media coverage of these events could best be described as sketchy.

handling of government contracts, especially when the firms involved are known to be particularly close to those in power; if it could print differing views than those expressed by the First Lady; if more Filipinos shared in the ownership of the newspaper, radio, and television facilities; if press conferences are not treated as royal audiences, that the press is equal in stature to any official, no matter what rank, because they are supposed to represent the people; if more Filipinos realized that the fight for press freedom is not merely the concern of those in the press, because a muzzled press is tantamount to a muzzled general public."[19] Unfortunately Babst found out that it wasn't the time for such an article. Hans Menzi, her boss, asked her to tone down her writing. She didn't. In July 1983, she was informed she no longer had a column.

After Marcos returned from his state visit with an affirmation of support from President Reagan, it was no longer necessary to carry on any pretense of press freedom. The crackdown began anew. On October 13, Ninez Cacho-Olivarez was relieved as a newscaster on Channel 9 because her columns in the *Bulletin Today* newspaper criticized the government.[20] A few weeks later soldiers raided the offices of the *We Forum*, the largest circulation opposition newspaper, and closed it down. Publisher Jose G. Burgos was arrested, along with Dean Armando Malay, Francisco "Soc" Rodrigo, and other columnists and staff members.* They were charged with "subversion and conspiracy to overthrow the government through political propaganda, agitation, and advocacy of violence."[21] Burgos, Malay and Rodrigo were detained for seven days. Burgos was also linked to the Light-A-Fire urban guerrilla movement. It seems two of the defendants in the three-year-old case suddenly remembered that he was part of that movement.[22] As usual the real motive for the closure was ulterior. Of the 19 court exhibits eight dealt with the paper's series of articles written by Bonifacio Gillego, which questioned the facts regarding the awarding of medals of bravery for Marcos' war exploits.[23] A ₱40 million libel suit was also filed

---

* Others arrested were columnists Salvador Roxas Gonzales, Ernesto Rodriguez, Raul Gonzales, and Joaquin Roces; and staff members Crispin Martinez, Teddy Cecilio, Eduardo Burgos, and Angel Tronqued.

against Burgos and Gillego by some of Marcos' men. It was a harbinger of more bad things to come. The government was adding a new weapon to its arsenal in its fight against the journalists. More libel suits followed. *Mr. & Ms.* editor, Eugenia D. Apostol, was sued for reporting on the tampering of election returns by the Commission on Audit in Palo, Leyte. *Bulletin Today* columnist, Isidoro Chammag, was sued for an article about terrorism in Abra. The list would grow.[24]

About the same time, in December 1982, eight women journalists* were "invited" by the National Intelligence Board, comprised of military officers, for questioning. They were questioned for several hours about their personal lives, religious beliefs, and their income ["You go to all that trouble for ₱250?"]. They were asked if they belonged to the Communist Party of the Philippines and if they understood the meaning of "national security." They were warned that their activities could be labelled "subversive." Several of them sought an injunction against the board, stating that it was unconstitutional for the military to question them. When the Solicitor General finally got around to replying, he announced that the injunction was "moot and academic" since the board had been dissolved by then. The journalists then petitioned the Supreme Court, asking that the Minister of Defense and the Armed Forces Chief of Staff refrain from creating any other commission to interrogate journalists. The court never ruled on this matter.[25]

Four months later journalist Antonio Nieva was arrested. He worked for the *Bulletin Today* and occasionally for the *Malaya*, an opposition newspaper, and was very vocal in his criticism of the government. As head of the *Bulletin Today*'s labor union he was linked to the Kilusang Mayo Uno (the KMU or May 1st Movement, an opposition trade union movement) and accused of being its propaganda arm.[26]

The government decided it needed some justification for this new crackdown. In December, Minister Enrile made public

---

* Those called in for questioning were Arlene Babst, Ninez Cacho-Olivarez, Ceres Doyo, Jo-An Maglipon, Domini Suarez, Lorna Tirol, Eugenia Apostol, and Doris Nuyda.

"recently captured documents" showing that the Communist Party of the Philippines and New People's Army were using the media to create a revolutionary atmosphere in order to overthrow the government. He quoted from the documents: "Propaganda is a powerful weapon to unite and educate the people, to attack and isolate the enemy (government and people running it), and to help the people fight the enemy with one heart and one mind. Propaganda prepares the ground ideologically for revolution. It constitutes an important and essential fighting front absolutely indispensable for uniting our ranks and defeating the enemy."[27]

The world press didn't buy the "communist conspiracy" theory. They voiced the opinion that the main concern of the Philippine government was to stifle dissent. The *Washington Post*'s reaction to the closing of the *We Forum* was typical: "A trend toward more press freedom has been arrested." Although the Philippine Constitution has the same First Amendment as the U.S. regarding press freedom, the paper noted, Marcos still had the power to close "subversive publications" and order "preventive detention."[28]

As usual, Marcos continued to vigorously deny there was a lack of press freedom. He needn't have bothered. Soon enough events would give the lie to his histrionics.

CHAPTER EIGHTEEN

The Grand Coalition

The Marcos style of dictatorship was unique in several ways. Even during martial law, and especially afterward, he constantly professed that his government was a bastion of democracy. When reminded that he still controlled the government after martial law through Amendment 6, he would dismiss his critics by stating that it was only a safeguard to be used to speed things along in case of an emergency.

He was also reminded that he controlled the military, the judiciary, and the media. When asked why it was really necessary to have such complete control, the official answer was that it was necessary to improve the economy, stabilize the country, and eliminate the "communist threat." That so-called threat became the standard government line as he arrested those who protested and imprisoned his enemies. Gradually he tightened his grip on the country and expanded his powers, all the while espousing democracy and its ideals. However, it would soon become apparent that he was perpetrating an elaborate hoax, paying lip service to his critics in order to be able to borrow more and more dollars as he took control. And gradually the truth dawned. Marcos was no more a statesman than he was a soldier. He was a greedy politician turned dictator.

Such control was only necessary if he had greater designs on the country than he cared to admit. Marcos knew that a tight grip on the economy would enhance his political power. Not only could he improve his position financially, he could reward his friends with desirable "opportunities" in business and government. This he would do on a grand scale. There would be few complaints and few interruptions. If there were, they would not be publicized; if they were publicized, the police would "investigate"; and if a trial were necessary, the judiciary would handle it.

Such control was not possible without a loyal group of friends capable of administering his policies. This group consisted of military officers; cabinet members; technocrats and their bureaucracies; appointed and elected local officials; persons close to Marcos or Imelda, whether relatives or friends and former politicians; and several big businessmen. They were finally given a name in the mid-70's—The Grand Coalition.* Their qualifications were varied and, at times, questionable, but they all shared one common trait—total devotion and unflinching loyalty to Marcos. In exchange they were given almost total and absolute immunity from the law.

In the Philippines under Marcos the law had little to do with the constitution or democracy. Marcos controlled it just as he controlled all aspects of government. There were different standards of justice for different people. Only in cases where Marcos, Imelda, or the Grand Coalition had no political or pecuniary interest was impartial justice dispensed by the courts without fear or favor. There was one standard of justice for those in power and another for the disloyal or anyone unlucky enough to be tagged an enemy. Political oppositionists, multinational corporations, priests, layworkers, and even local and foreign journalists experienced varying degrees of this justice. Of all the crimes disloyalty was the worst. Somewhere along the way values became convoluted. Allegiance to Marcos became more important than loyalty to one's country. The latter meant nothing without the former.

If there were a creed adopted by the Grand Coalition it would have something to do with money and the high social value placed on wealth. By now it is apparent that self-enrichment was the first

---

* Father Joachin G. Bernas, priest, lawyer, and president of the Ateneo de Manila University in the Philippines, coined this very descriptive term.

priority with all of them. They were corrupt, selfish, and fit the classic mold of the oligarch, lording it over the poor and oppressed. Oligarchy was nothing new to the Philippines, but the Marcos version was obscene in its kingly opulence and excesses.

Knowing how he operated, it should come as no surprise that he was extremely critical of the oligarchs before martial law. In a speech in 1971, he expressed concern about such a status when he said, "Ours tends to be an oligarchic society. This simply means that the economic gap between rich and poor provides the wealthy few the opportunity of exercising undue influence on the political authority."[1] And he recommended: "The fundamental task of drastic political reform is to democratize the entire political system."[2]

There was that word "democracy" again, along with "drastic political reform." Well, he did get to reform the system, but there was nothing democratic about it. He merely replaced one oligarchy with another. The only difference between the new and the old, besides the players, was that the greed of the Grand Coalition was so much larger than anything heretofore experienced.

By now their incredible greed is well known. Marcos' real estate holdings—200 deeds to properties in the Philippines, real estate in Texas, California, London, New Jersey, and New York; and his Swiss bank accounts with hundreds of millions of dollars deposited (his first account in Switzerland was supposedly opened in 1968 using the name "William Saunders," a fake name he used back in his guerrilla days when he was trying to wangle money out of the Americans); and the millions of dollars in kickbacks from various foreign corporations, mostly Japanese—all that is fairly common knowledge now. The big surprise to those who considered themselves somewhat knowledgable on the greed of the Grand Coalition was that Marcos himself proved to be so excessive in his lust for riches.

Between Marcos and Imelda a sizeable fortune that is estimated at $10 billion was stolen from the people of the Philippines and taken out of the country illegally. This does not count the billions of pesos that Imelda lost in the Philippines through bad management of her so-called social projects; nor does it take into consideration the monies she lavished locally on her "edifice complex"—construction projects that had little value except to appease her ego. In addition, there was at least $3 billion lost in bail-out funds, most of it going to prop up crony corporations; a billion dollars unaccounted for in the coconut levy; and an estimated $1.1 billion loss to the sugar farmers. Such vast sums of money, combined with little accountability, was invariably linked to the Grand Coalition.

There were other bit players who were rewarded for their loyalty whose crimes don't seem quite so bad, but they were crimes just the same. It was quite a plan with self-enrichment on a scale difficult to imagine. The apparent motive was the perpetuation of a Marcos dynasty. Not since the Soongs perpetuated their dynasty in China in the 30's and 40's, with the help of Chiang Kai Shek, has any family exploited the U.S. government the way Marcos and Imelda did. The Soong family used a similar modus operandi, shouting "communist" everytime they wanted to borrow dollars. They got an estimated $2 billion before Chiang and his army was forced off the mainland.

A part of Marcos' true character begins to be understood when his economic structures are examined, for they were just an extension of his social network with a few personal touches. He took his patron and compadre systems a step further than most. They were the crux of the issue and lay at the heart of cronyism and state capitalism. The more the loyalty, the bigger the reward. The favors he bestowed still carried with it "utang na loob," but such ties and such obligations seemed to go deeper with him. Those that understood this seemed to profit more than the others. Marcos appointed Benedicto the head of the sugar monopoly, but in reality Marcos "owned" the monopoly with Benedicto as its manager. It was the same with coconut and all government owned or controlled corporations. Those he did not own he expected homage to be paid in some form or other, preferably money. The Japanese recognized this and rewarded him handsomely. The Americans were more difficult in this respect, but Marcos was deferential to them because of their World Bank and other associations.

He allowed the Grand Coalition to take over vast sections of commerce and industry through favorable legislation and unlimited access to capital and credit. Some abused this privelege more than others. Others, more powerful, even resorted to extortion to amass their ill-gotten gains. State capitalism as well as crony capitalism* abounded. The agricultural monopolies were examples of government control at its best and efficiency at its worst. The Grand Coalition deliberately and systematically raped, robbed, and plundered the entire country but refused to accept any responsibility for what happened. When such practices began to affect the economy, Marcos seemed unfazed and continued to deny their existence until the very end. Such denials were commonplace with him and were alsc a part of his true character.

During martial law Marcos warned in a speech, "Man is driven to rebellion, not because of hunger or inadequate income, but, more often, because of injustices that deprive him of his dignity."[3] He said this as he amassed more wealth and power, and practiced less democracy, and heaped more injustice on his people than any Filipino leader in its history. Like Marcos' role as a statesman, justice was only an illusion. It never was what it seemed to be. How he amassed his wealth is a study in greed beyond comparison. Why he did it may be a little more difficult to explain but by now it is obvious that Marcos wasn't just your average corrupt politician.

---

* Bernie Villegas, PhD Economics, Harvard University, of the Center for Research and Communications, a privately funded think-tank and school of economics in the Philippines, coined the term to explain the phenomenon of so much of the economy being taken over by friends and relatives of Marcos and Imelda.

PART III
Shaman

CHAPTER NINETEEN

Introduction

In the mid-1970's some of the country's leading historians were approached by a Marcos emissary with a very attractive offer. Marcos wanted to write a history of the Philippines and would they be of assistance? They would be paid handsomely and could travel anywhere in the world to gather research material. All expenses would be paid. There was only one catch. Their names wouldn't show up on their work. Titled *Tadhana* (Fate), it was quite an ambitious project. There were supposed to be 4 volumes, starting from the beginning of Philippine history and ending with Marcos' New Society. Only two or three volumes were finished before he was overthrown.

In January 1986, when the *New York Times* broke the story of his World War II guerrilla unit being fraudulent, one of Marcos' comments in defense of his record was that he might write his own history of his guerrilla record to prevent the story from being "mangled."[1] No one bothered to remind him he had already tried that.

Marcos' use of propaganda is interesting. He knew he was better than most and was willing to rewrite history to prove it. He had rewritten part of World War II in an attempt to become its greatest hero; he had rewritten his country's system of government; and he was in the process of rewriting his country's history to insure that he was remembered fondly, or perhaps, in the Marcos style, to insure that he was remembered as the country's greatest statesman. This shameless attempt at immortality was also exemplified in other ways. Streets, rivers, and towns bore the Marcos moniker but that didn't seem to satisfy him. Thus one of the most grandiose schemes of his career was initiated.

Alongside the Marcos Highway leading to the little farming community of Pugo, in La Union province, 120 miles north of Manila, a 300-hectare (741 acres) Marcos Park had been constructed. It included an 18-hole golf course, a swimming pool, tennis courts, an area for horseback riding, guest lodging, and a conference center. In June 1985, a typhoon roared through the area and knocked down the scaffolding that had been protecting, and hiding, some construction on the side of a hill overlooking the park. The local farmers' curiousity had already been aroused because of the armed soldiers who had been guarding this particular site for years, but nothing prepared them for what the winds uncovered that day. There, gazing sphinx-like out over the park, was a huge concrete bust of Marcos, rising more than thirty meters into the air. News of the surprising discovery spread quickly. The government was quick to explain that the project was begun in 1981 and had only recently been completed. The purpose of the monument, they explained, "is to make Filipinos proud of their history and culture,"[2] but everyone knew that it was just another extension of Marcos' immortality complex.

The various Asian cultures have always had a healthy respect for superstition with their fortune tellers and astrologers. Even Imelda alluded to the notion that Marcos had certain "powers." Testifying before the Agrava Commission investigating the assassination, she admitted that she had warned Ninoy Aquino about coming to the Philippines, and had told him, "...the president is sort of a clairvoyant."[3]

Marcos is a very superstitious man who has admitted that he sometimes heard "voices" and believed in the supernatural. He tried to cure his kidney problems by "psychic surgery," in which a faith healer supposedly enters a patient's body with his bare hands and removes diseased organs. He recently embraced a quasi-religion which advertised claims that it could improve health, athletic ability, and business performance, "create a problem-free life," and "reverse" the biological aging process.[4] One of the items found on Marcos' desk after he left was a note from a member of a religious cult predicting that Marcos would be the vehicle for the second coming of Christ.[5]

Marcos also publicized the anting anting (amulet) he received from Gregorio Aglipay, a legendary Catholic priest who joined the revolution of 1892 against Spain, resisted the American occupation, and later founded his own church. Aglipay was a friend of the Marcos family and, just before young Ferdinand went off to war, reportedly gave him a talisman for protection. It was a sliver of magical wood bequeathed down through the ages and supposedly gave the owner magical powers. Marcos claims that Aglipay allegedly inserted the amulet in his back with an incision made by his own hands.[6] Amulets and magical powers may sound strange to a foreigner but Filipino provincials have always had a healthy respect for such things and have practiced animism in one form or another for centuries.

Such beliefs and practices make the Marcos character that much more difficult to understand. As a dictator he single-handedly controlled his country and also tried to control most of its events. He never tried to hide the fact that he thought himself "gifted"—some think "touched" is a better choice of words—and professed to have a mystical power to control events and manipulate nature through supernatural or mediumistic means. Did he really believe this, or did he just want the people to believe he had this communion with the spirit world?

There are other dimensions to Marcos' personality worthy of consideration. Not once in his entire career did Marcos ever admit that he was wrong about anything. If he were always right there would be no problem. In that case he would probably qualify as some sort of political deity. However, this isn't the case. In so many instances Marcos persistently denied any wrongdoing despite overwhelming evidence to the contrary. This could reflect some sort of behavioral disorder.

A person who matures normally would have a super-ego, or conscience, which transmits commands and admonitions to the ego. Lacking such a governor on his actions he would feel little or no guilt or remorse. Hence the absence of guilt and the denial of wrongdoing no matter what the crime. Despite this emotional instability, reality is usually clearly perceived. He knows the difference between right and wrong but doesn't care. Such abnormal ideas and behavior patterns are the characteristics of a psychopathic personality. A psychopath may be quite intelligent. He just hasn't grown emotionally. To quote one medical encyclopedia, "Free of worry or concern for the present or the future, the psychopath may lie, cheat, steal, and swindle. He may physically harm others or even commit murder."[7]

There is no doubt that Marcos was a smart man. He was also cunning, clever, and ruthless—attributes which enabled him to thrive in his social and political milieu. With those thoughts in mind try to imagine the leader of a country devoid of a conscience, a profound belief in the supernatural, and attempting to achieve immortality. Then review Marcos actions of the past 50 years.

The biography of Marcos, written by Hartzell Spence and later copyrighted by Marcos, is remarkable, not because of the man's life story but because Marcos expected everyone to believe it. The book can only be described as a fantasy. It was probably intended to be left behind as some sort of proof that such an epic hero lived, another building block, along with the *Tadhana*, that would serve as confirmation of his immortality. His war claims, trumpeted throughout the book, serve as an example. He couldn't be just another hero. He had to be the greatest of all. Wanting to be the best is acceptable behavior. Rewriting his role in the history of World War II in the Philippines in order to be the best is not acceptable behavior. In fact, it is irrational.

Marcos wasn't the epic hero that he yearned with all the fibre of his heart and soul to be. But he expected everyone to believe he was. The real Marcos was a corrupt tyrant—a frustrated soldier, phony statesman, and a shaman, a mysterious being who tried to exercise total control over his world and his immortality. It is in this third role, as shaman, that his true character seems to emerge. Marcos' participation in the Aquino assassination is yet to be proven but a murder in broad daylight at a busy airport in front of 1,200 soldiers somehow doesn't seem that incomprehensible when viewed in this light.

Buried somewhere in this complex character is an insatiable lust for power and riches. Marcos was the supreme capitalist, an oligarch of the highest order. If he did indeed steal more than a billion dollars, how was he able to get away with it?

CHAPTER TWENTY

Cronyism

The friends and relatives of Marcos and Imelda were allowed access to capital and credit based not on their ability to borrow but on their closeness to the first family. This financial leverage, coupled with political power, enabled them to take over major segments of commerce and industry. In effect, they controlled the economy. There was little competition and virtually no free enterprise.

Father John F. Doherty holds a PhD in Sociology from Fordham and had taught sociology at the prestigious Ateneo de Manila University for ten years. His study of 453 Philippine companies in 1980 showed that there were 1,132 interlocking directorates with 32 government and commercial banks. In effect, the country's major banks controlled the corporations and ultimately the economy. Another finding was that about 60 families controlled the finance and commerce of the country. Of the 60, about 40 could be called crony capitalists.[1] In 1980, while Doherty was on a visit to the United States, a copy of his study, as yet unpublished, was leaked to the government. It was considered subversive. Because of his reputation as priest and scholar he was not jailed on his return to the Philippines, but he was not allowed to reenter the country.

Charity does begin at home. The Marcos family enjoyed considerable success in just about every form of business in the Philippines, as did the Romualdez family. However, just as Marcos and Imelda operated as separate political entities dealing with separate groups of people, their business connections were also separate and distinct.

Doctor Pacifico Marcos, the younger brother, had his own conglomerate, owning or controlling about 20 corporations engaged in gold and copper mining, petroleum products, coconut products, banking, insurance, real estate, farming, chemicals, minerals, publishing, and travel. His son was involved in amusement services, records, janitorial services, and manufacturing.[2] Mrs. Fortuna Marcos Barba, a sister, was involved in the real estate, travel, and shipping businesses.[3] The mother, Doña Josepha, was also quite active, despite her age. Shipping, timber, wood processing, and the wholesaling of food, beverage, and tobacco products were her lines.[4]

Judge Pio Marcos, an uncle, was involved in sugar milling, copper and gold mining, and a memorial park. He is most remembered for the Golden Buddha scandal. In 1971 treasure hunters found a three-foot tall statue of Buddha in a tunnel in Mountain Province, near Baguio, which the Japanese had used during the war. It was pure gold, weighed over a ton, and valued at more than $5 million. Pio, a judge in Baguio City, ordered the statue confiscated. It was never seen again.

Another uncle, Simeon Marcos-Valdez, who served in the war with Marcos, was in the furniture, cement, office equipment, iron and steel products, and paper products businesses.[5]

Besides Imelda, her brother, Benjamin "Kokoy" Romualdez, was the most well-known. Before rising to prominence because of Imelda, he was not known for his managerial or diplomatic talents and had no connection to any particular business or other interests. He was governor of the province of Leyte, and then ambassador to Peking. He was the ambassador to the United States at the time of Marcos' sudden departure. Even then he spent more time around the coffee shops of Makati than attending to his diplomatic chores. His business interests gradually expanded to include banking, insurance, engineering, and construction. He also took over the *Times Journal* newspaper without paying for it.[6] His holding company. First Philippine Holdings, managed by Cesar Zalamea, was the front for many of his business interests. He also handled the so-called "sale" of

Meralco in 1974.

Fernando Lopez served as Marcos' vice-president for two terms. His family was one of the traditional elite and was very wealthy. After martial law was declared, the vice-president's nephew, Eugenio "Geny" Lopez, Jr., publisher of the *Manila Chronicle,* was arrested on November 27, 1982, along with Sergio Osmeña III, the son of Marcos' political rival. Although it was claimed they were part of a plot to assassinate Marcos they were never charged. With a promise that Geny would be released, the family signed over their Manila Electric Company in 1974 to interests controlled by the Marcos and Romualdez families. To make things appear legal the Lopez family received a $1,500 down-payment for $20 million worth of shares in the electric company. Despite this, Geny Lopez was never released, but he and Osmeña did manage to escape in October 1977.[7] Only after his escape and the threat of an international lawsuit were any further payments made for the "sale."

Alfredo "Bejo" Romualdez is another brother of Imelda. He controlled the gambling monopoly for the entire country. Before martial law, gambling was legal and flourished throughout the country. At the advent of martial law, Marcos ordered all casinos closed down. Shortly thereafter, however, gambling was soon made legal again, but only through Manila Bay Enterprises, owned by Bejo. He then proceeded to take over the Philippine Jai Alai and Amusement Corporation, owned by Enrique Razon and worth an estimated ₱400 million ($20 million) in annual revenues, without paying for it. Bejo's greed got worse. He then took over 60 percent of Razon's shipping company in 1978, also without paying. In 1981 he used the company as a front and borrowed $30 million. The loan, arranged through the Central Bank, was blatantly illegal in that it was supposedly for the purchase of equipment for a company project in Saudi Arabia although the company's contract specifically stated that only manpower needed to be provided. The money was reportedly funnelled back to Marcos.[8] Takeovers of a similar nature happened a number of times but on a smaller scale.

Alita, Imelda's sister, was involved in a hotel and shopping center. Eduardo, a cousin, was a former ambassador to the U.S.

and involved in the agri-business. He was also chairman of the Philippine Airlines after it was taken over.[9]

Philippine Airlines was owned by the Toda family. In 1976, Marcos received a bill for ₱17 million ($2.3 million), for planes chartered by himself and Imelda. Shortly thereafter, in October 1977, Benigno Toda, president and majority stockholder of the airline, was informed that the Government Service Insurance System (GSIS) would take control.[10]

Marcos didn't forget his friends in the military either. On October 28, 1972, he directed the Minister of Defense "to take over and control the assets of the corporations owned by Fernando Jacinto in the national interest." The 15 companies were involved in steel, publishing, broadcasting, insurance, mining, and chemicals. It seems a government investigation of these companies had turned up financial anomalies and the Development Bank of the Philippines foreclosed on the companies shortly afterward. However, no charges were ever filed. Instead they were taken over and run by a group of Army officers.[11]

Those seeking favors came and went. Some fell out of favor and others took their place. A few loyalists deserve special mention.

Antonio Floirendo is a shrewd businessman. He has sided with every government in power since the Garcia administration in the late 50's. He helped Marcos in the 1965 and 1969 presidential campaigns and was a loyal supporter. In the early 70's he was awarded the lease of some Davao Penal Colony land for his banana business, which allowed him to use very cheap prison labor on his plantations.[12] In 1976, Floirendo also served as the agent for SuCrest, one of three U.S. sugar refineries that contracted with the government — controlled Philippine Exchange Corporation for the country's sugar. He made more than a million dollars in brokers fees that year. Then, in 1977, he purchased the SuCrest refineries in New York, Boston, and Chicago for $11.8 million, and formed the Revere Sugar Corporation. Revere then took over SuCrest's contract to buy Philippine sugar. During the period 1978-1980, Revere paid $2.9 million in brokerage fees to a Hong Kong company called Thetaventures Limited. The company's listed agent was Vilma H. Bautista. Ms. Bautista worked for the Philippine Mission in New York and was also Imelda's personal secretary. Several very expensive New York properties turned up in her name in an investigation of Imelda's wealth.[13]

Marcos was clever enough not to have his name involved in any investments. Rolando Gapud took care of most of these details. He was the personal financial adviser to Marcos and his son, and treasurer of the Marcos Foundation, the very secret foundation housed in an eighteenth century Spanish villa next to Malacañang Palace that managed the Marcos wealth. His name seems to turn up everywhere there is an investigation of the Marcos wealth. Beginning around 1977 he incorporated more than a dozen companies which were the fronts used for Marcos' business and financial deals, including the Independent Realty Corporation, one of the biggest holding companies for Marcos' investments. He was the chairman of Security Bank & Trust Company in Manila and a member of the board of directors of the Redwood Bank in San Francisco, which was purchased in 1980 by Dewey Dee and two other prominent Filipino Chinese with close ties to Marcos. He served as an adviser to Floirendo when he purchased SuCrest in 1977.[14]

Jose Y. Campos is one of Marcos' closest friends. He is the baptismal godfather of Marcos' son. He owns United Drug Laboratories, a pharmaceuticals firm in Manila which had an exclusive contract to provide all medical supplies to the Ministry of Health.[15] He was also a large stockholder in Security Bank & Trust Company, where Gapud was chairman,[16] and has several real estate investments in the U.S., including a $9.18 million project in Seattle.[17] Beginning as far back as 1968 Campos set up scores of companies used as fronts for Marcos' business and financial dealings. Gapud was involved with many of these beginning in the late 70's.

Roman Cruz was the general manager of the Government Service Insurance System. It took over Philippine Airlines and he was made president. His father was the judge who convicted Marcos in the celebrated Nalundasan murder case.

Geronimo Velasco was Marcos' enery czar. He had worked for Harry Stonehill in the 60's before Stonehill was forced to

depart the Philippines. Marcos made him chairman of the
Philippine National Oil Company, the country's largest business
enterprise. It was set up by Marcos in 1973 during the oil crisis,
and imported more than 50 percent of the country's oil
requirements. It was exempt from public accountability. Later
government investigations would uncover a kickback scheme
involving hundreds of millions of pesos. A commission
of 5 to 8.5 percent was charged on every shipment of crude oil and
coal made by PNOC from 1974 until the revolution. Monthly
shipments of crude oil amounted to approximately ₱1.4 billion
per month. Coal shipments varied too much to make an estimate.
This so-called commission was never entered on the books of
PNOC and is unaccounted for.[18]

Marcos and Imelda bestowed special favors on these people.
Others deserve more attention because of their achievements,
dubious or otherwise.

CHAPTER TWENTY-ONE

The Capitalists

The names Cuenca, Disini, and Silverio are synonymous with the term "crony capitalism." They stand out because of the empires they built and the spectacular way each one failed. Between them the government loaned or guaranteed more than $1 billion and lost it all. They were the nouveau elite in Marcos' New Society. Herminio Disini was a public accountant married to Imelda's personal physician and cousin. Rodolfo Cuenca may have been a college dropout but his father was the Public Highways Commissioner, implying the best of connections in the most notorious of businesses. He was also a fundraiser for Marcos' presidential campaign in 1965. Ricardo Silverio's friendship with Marcos was rewarded with cheap, government-backed loans and high-level contacts with blue chip foreign firms. There was no doubt who their patron was. Marcos drove Disini's competitors out of business by decree; he rewarded Cuenca with government construction contracts; and he exempted Silverio from restrictions placed on all other automobile manufacturers.

Marcos could do all that but he couldn't run their businesses for them and he couldn't guarantee their success. Their greed and incompetence slowed their meteoric rise. Then another friend of Marcos, a Chinese Filipino, insured their failure by teaching them a lesson in finance they would never forget.

Until the early 70's about 70 percent of Central Bank loans to financial institutions went to private commercial and rural banks.

Then in the late 70's, as commercial credit grew faster, an increasing proportion of loans went to government financial institutions. This ultimately led to the concentration of loanable funds in the Philippine National Bank, the Development Bank of the Philippines, the Land Bank, and the Philippine Veterans Bank. In addition to the four government banks there were eight private commercial banks, called "political banks" because of their special relationship with the group in power, which enjoyed similar privileges. The total assets of the government and "political" banks made up 53 percent of the entire commercial banking system.[1] Companies owned by Marcos loyalists had access to credit from these institutions throughout this period.

Foreign borrowings in the 70's were facilitated by a highly liquid international capital market flooded with dollars from the Organization of Petroleum Exporting Companies (OPEC). So the government borrowed. They borrowed from every available source. In 1974 they borrowed $165 million from the World Bank. They had only borrowed an average of $30 million a year for the previous five years.[2] It is interesting to note that it was about this time that Imelda began to get more involved with the government, receiving several appointments and heading up large projects costing large amounts of the government's money. In 1976 the pattern of lending changed. The U.S. passed the Human Rights Amendment to the Foreign Assistance Act, which curtailed lending to countries engaged in human rights violations. As a result, bilateral aid to the Philippines dropped considerably and World Bank borrowings increased dramatically.[3] The borrowings got bigger every year. Foreign debt grew, from $2.6 billion in 1975 to $10.5 billion in 1980. Credit was readily available to the cronies.

By 1979 the worldwide economic recession reduced the demand for Philippine exports, and inflation in other countries increased the price of imports. The shrinking volume of petrodollars began to limit the availability of funds. Many foreign banks reached their country lending limit to the Philippines. By 1980 the country became the International Monetary Fund's most indebted Third World borrower, owing almost $1.6 billion.[4] As the foreign debt grew bigger, it became more and more difficult to obtain credit, and low revenues from exports and foreign investment made it difficult to meet its foreign obligations.

Herminio Disini was the most ambitious. His business ventures began in 1970 with the Philippine Tobacco Filters Corporation. It quickly captured more than 90 percent of the market for cigarette filters, mostly at the expense of Filtrona Philippines, another large tobacco filter company jointly owned by U.S. and British companies. Disini hired the son of the then director of the Specific Tax Division of the Bureau of Internal Revenue, which was responsible for the collection of cigarette and alcohol taxes, to sell his filters. Soon most cigarette makers switched their business to Disini, allegedly because of an implied threat of investigation by the BIR. Then, on July 21, 1975, Marcos signed Presidential Decree 750, which imposed a 100 percent duty on all imports of acetate tow, the raw material used to make cigarette filters. This applied to every cigarette filter company except Disini's. For his the tax was 10 percent. As a result Filtrona was driven out of business. The U.S. Embassy issued a formal complaint but to no avail.[5]

That was the start of the Herminio Disini group of companies called Herdis. His notoriety surfaced again in 1976. He was accused of being the key figure behind a stock market manipulation. In what was called the "Seafront Scandal," he paid ₱5 million ($675,000) for ₱70 million ($9.5 million) worth of authorized but unissued shares of an oil exploration company shortly before Marcos went on national television to publicly announce that oil had been found. The price fell 65 percent when some of these shares were dumped after the announcement in anticipation of a quick profit. Stockholders accused Disini of being too greedy and destroying the credibility of the stock market.[6]

Helped along by incentives, government loans, and loan guarantees of at least $163 million from the government banks, Disini had 33 companies with assets of $200 million by 1978. He was in everything, from charter airlines, oil exploration and petrochemical manufacturing to textiles, construction, and insurance. And once again he became the center of attention.

In February 1976, after almost two years of negotiations, a contract was signed, awarding the construction of a nuclear power plant in the Philippines to Westinghouse in the United States. This was somewhat of a surprise since the National Power Corporation had conducted feasibility studies on the project and was ready to sign a contract with General Electric's local representatives in June 1974. They had offered to construct two reactors for a cost of $700 million. However, at the last minute a decision was made to accept Westinghouse's offer instead, to construct one reactor for a cost of $1.1 billion. Just before this contract was awarded, it seems that Disini purchased Asia Industries, the Westinghouse representative in the Philippines. His commission from the contract was reported to be between $25 and $40 million.[7] Marcos is rumored to have received the majority of that.[8] By January 1981, Disini had a conglomerate of 70 companies with assets of $1.1 billion. He was at the pinnacle of his success, but he owed a lot of money, short-term, at high interest rates.[9]

Rodolfo Cuenca began the Construction and Development Corporation of the Philippines in 1966, merging 16 Filipino contractors to build a major expressway running north from Manila. Through government connections, the company secured every conceivable kind of contract: the North Luzon Expressway, the Manila South Expressway, the San Juanico Bridge, the Pantabangan Dam, and the Candaba Viaduct. It expanded and won contracts abroad in Jeddah, Dannon, Saudi Arabia, Kuala Lumpur and Kota Kinabalu in Malaysia, Jakarta in Indonesia, and Port Gentil and Libreville in Gabon. Then it diversified into other fields, including aviation, mining, agriculture, real estate, trucking, and shipping. In 1973 the company was awarded the Manila-Cavite Coastal Road and Reclamation Project, to reclaim 2,700 hectares (6,669 acres) along Manila Bay, at a cost of ₱8.7 billion ($116.1 million). The company would receive one-half of the land as repayment.[10]

At this point CDCP was one of the biggest builders in Asia and a diversified conglomerate of 17 corporations with assets of more than $600 million. It was also beginning to experience financial difficulties. The company was not being paid by the government for the contracts it was performing, and was balking at paying the extra charges due under escalation charges to cover inflation. Then there was a delay in the release of the land it was supposed to receive as payment for the reclamation project. All this, coupled with the underbidding to win the Middle East projects, had caused a serious cash shortage. The company then began borrowing short-term funds at high interest rates.[11]

Ricardo Silverio was a textile merchant until 1961 when, at the age of 31, he founded Delta Motors Corporation which became the sole assembler and distributor of Toyota cars. From this base he started his own conglomerate, expanding into ceramics, banking, air transport, logging, shipping, life insurance, construction equipment, gold mining, and the manufacture of television sets, refrigerators, and integrated circuits. By 1981 he had 32 companies with sales of $500 million.[12]

His special status became known to the automobile manufacturers in the early 70's. The government had lured Ford and General Motors to the Philippines by promising that if they manufactured components for export this would offset the local-content requirement for cars they assembled and sold in the country. After General Motors invested $17 million in a transmission plant, and Ford spent $36 million on a body stamping plant, the government changed the rules. Their exports could offset only 15 percent of local content. Toyota was exempted from this rule.[13]

With an advantage like that, Delta was the industry leader for most of the decade. Then it decided to expand into truck manufacturing. This required considerable investment for plant and equipment and by then credit was getting tight. So it borrowed short-term at high interest rates. Delta's short-term liabilities increased from ₱85 million in 1979 to ₱520 million in 1980. By 1981 its earnings were no longer able to service its debt.[14]

Silverio also owned Philippine Underwriter's Finance Corporation. It issued commercial paper collateralized by promissory notes from blue-chip corporations such as Caltex Philippines, Pilipinas Shell, Philippine Airlines, and Marcopper. Only in 1981, when the company couldn't meet its financial obligations, did investors find out about the massive fraud perpetrated by the company. The commercial paper was counterfeit.[15] At the time of its collapse it owed ₱600 million ($80 million) to its 700 creditors. A long, drawn-out and very slow investigation was begun but no one was ever brought to trial.[16]

Dewey Dee is a Chinese Filipino whose family was prominent in the Philippine business community. His Continental Manufacturing Corporation had once controlled about 80 percent of the acrylic yarn used in the export trade, and he was a banking entrepreneur with a reputation as a financial genius of-sorts. He was also a friend of Marcos. In 1980 the Security Bank and Trust Company in Manila was purchased by some investors which included Dee and two other Chinese Filipino friends of Marcos, Ramon Siy and Philip Ang. The chairman of the bank was Rolando Gapud. Another stockholder was Jose Y. Campos.[17] In March 1980 a company in the Virgin Islands, Empire Holdings, purchased the Redwood Bank in San Francisco for $15.3 million. Empire had three shareholders—Dee, Siy, and Ang. Gapud served on the board of directors of Redwood Bank.[18]

In January 1981 Dee disappeared. It seems that he had gotten into serious financial trouble by gambling. He gambled in Las Vegas and Macau. He gambled on the stock market and the commodities market in Hong Kong. The extent of his losses is not known, but when he departed the Philippines, he left behind debts estimated at ₱635 million ($84.7 million). Most of this money had been borrowed using nothing more than his name as collateral.[19] Before he left he did manage to sell his shares in Security Bank. He also signed over his shares in the Redwood Bank to Siy and Ang without any compensation.[20] The Chinese community was especially upset because Dee had brought shame to their race and to the Dee family name, but one scholar suggested that he had merely collected reparations for all the injustices visited upon the Chinese in the Philippines, which included an occasional slaughter.*

---

* In 1603, provoked by Spanish oppression, the Chinese rose up in protest in Manila. As a result almost the entire Chinese community of 20,000 was slaughtered. In 1639 it happened again, with another massacre of 24,000. In 1764, after Spain recovered Manila after two

Dee later surfaced in Canada in 1983 and applied for an immigrant visa. He then claimed that Marcos was a secret partner in both Security Bank and the Redwood Bank.[22]

This was the largest financial scandal in Philippine history, and it caused a severe crisis in the banking system. The banks panicked. Credit, already tight, was tightened even further. The automatic roll-over of loans was virtually stopped, and three of the biggest borrowers of short-term loans were caught in a credit crunch.

Just exactly how or when Disini got into trouble is not known. Herdis was a privately owned company and financial data was not publicly available. In 1981 Herdis' financial subsidiaries—Atrium, Apcor, Interbank, and First Summa—owed ₱1.3 billiion ($133 million) they couldn't repay, some of it at interest rates as high as 36 percent. Shortly thereafter Asia Industries folded with ₱400 million ($45 million) in debts. All were taken over by the Development Bank of the Philippines.[23]

Cuenca's problems were similar in that he had also borrowed hundreds of millions of pesos short-term at interest rates as high as 30 percent. After the Dee crisis the government injected ₱1 billion into the company to keep it afloat in exchange for 30 percent equity. In 1982 it contributed another ₱1.2 billion in exchange for 500 hectares of the reclamation project, and in 1983 the Central Bank loaned it ₱300 million, but it just wasn't enough. When CDCP folded in 1983, it had debts totalling $650 million.[24]

Delta Motors lost ₱21 million ($2.3 million) in 1980 and ₱78 million ($8.5 million) in 1981.[25] Silverio admitted having $100 million in short-term debt in 1981 he couldn't repay.[26] In 1982 Delta defaulted on at least ₱200 million ($24.4 million) in matured loans to the Philippine National Bank.[27] When the bank finally took over the company, it was owed ₱700 million ($63 million).[28]

It is interesting to note that the government poured more

___

years of occupation by the English, the authorities accused the Chinese of collaboration, and another massacre ensued, but on a smaller scale.[21]

than a billion dollars into the companies of Disini, Cuenca, and Silverio, yet they were never asked to publicly account for the loss of so much money despite the fact that these were public funds. In the case of CDCP, the biggest failure, the bailout was done without consultation with the government institutions involved and without notifying or seeking approval of the shareholders. There were other anomalies. Marcos ordered the return of all collateral to the principal shareholders. They were not required to make good on any personal guarantees or to surrender any personal assets they had put up as collateral. The Philippine National Bank had also violated a Central Bank regulation by investing 70 percent of its net worth in one company — CDCP. The maximum allowed was 15 percent.[29]

The Dee scandal should not have come as a surprise. The Philippine banking system was an accident waiting to happen. In 1973 Presidential Decree 117 was signed to encourage bank mergers and consolidations with foreign banks because it was claimed that local banks lacked professionalism in their management. The decree also required the local banks to increase their capitalization to a minimum of P100 million ($14.8 million). Most banks could not afford to do this without a foreign partner. Of the ten overseas banks that were attracted to this scheme, six were gone by 1979. The reason most given for the breakup in the partnerships was the "difference in management style and motivation." In reality the main reason was the practice of local banks of lending to their own directors, officers, relatives, and shareholders without collateral or even a credit investigation.[30]

Rational economic planning was abandoned because of the government's support of the business interests of Marcos' friends. The over-rapid expansion of these crony conglomerates was founded on easy access to funds from the government and so-called political banks, and resulted in the loss of more than a billion dollars that could have been used to prime a very sick economy. This loss plus the Dee scandal placed a severe strain on the country's financial system. A lot of companies were in trouble, especially those run by the cronies of Marcos. There were more failures and more bail-outs by the government. The total government expense in bail-out funds, as of 1983, would amount to ₱30 billion ($3 billion). All this gradually destroyed the confidence of international bankers and ultimately brought the country to the brink of bankruptcy.[31]

CHAPTER TWENTY-TWO

A Controlled Economy

A major concern of the private sector in the Philippines during this period was the overregulation of business. Despite Marcos' assurances that he supported free enterprise, there was too much evidence to the contrary. The issuance of exclusive rights to import, export, or exploit certain areas, or the preferential treatment of certain firms in an industry were commonplace. Also the government owned or controlled numerous enterprises which were normally the baliwick of the private business sector and better left to free market forces.

The Ranis Report* was prepared by a group of international and local specialists in economic problems with permission of the Philippine government. Headed by Yale's Professor Gustav Ranis, it came out in 1974 with a series of recommendations aimed towards creating more employment opportunities in the country and distributing the fruits of growth more equitably. Among other things, it recommended the reform of interest rates, liberalization of import restrictions, tariff reforms, reduction of fiscal incentives, and a wages policy. Bernie Villegas described the reaction to the report: "Many of the recommendations of this report were rejected as irrelevant to the Philippines. It was claimed that the Ranis mission used a free market economy as a

---

* *Sharing In Development*. Report of an inter-agency team financed by the United Nations Development Program, (Manila: National Economic and Development Authority, 1974).

framework for policy-making. Ironically, the businessmen were espousing a managed economy."[1]

The petroleum industry was nationalized under the control of Geronimo Velasco; the logging and wood-processing industries under Marcos and Romualdez relatives; the shipping and construction industries under Cuenca; and the airline industry under Romualdez. Agricultural monopolies were created, including sugar under Roberto Benedicto and coconut under Eduardo Cojuangco. The Philippine Cement Corporation regulated that industry; the National Food Authority regulated trade in rice, corn, wheat, and other cereals; the Fertilizer and Pesticide Authority regulated those trades; and the National Coal Authority did likewise. With rare exception mismanagement, inefficiency, and corruption were typical in anything owned or controlled by the government.

Jess Estanislao, head of the Center for Research and Communication, had tried to point out the inefficiency of such companies. He noted that the slow unbusinesslike grind of regulatory agencies usually resulted in decision delays and unnecessary paperwork, especially in export-related industries. It was also pointed out that such agencies could not have the full understanding of individual company, or even industry-wide, peculiarities. The cement industry was a good example. Government agencies set the selling price and all exports were controlled by the Philippine Cement Corporation. The selling price hardly ever reflected the current rise in production costs until a year later—if ever. As a result, producers would sometimes be forced to sell at a price that didn't cover their cost of production. Hence there was no incentive to produce. To the contrary, it was incentive not to produce, and production would fall. This had happened many times in industries in which the government had intervened. Intervention in agriculture to control prices for consumers or to nationalize the processing and marketing of food and commercial crops had constantly had a detrimental effect on producers.[2]

In addition to intervening wherever it wanted, the government offered protection to crony companies through legislation. Large segments of the manufacturing sector were protected through import restrictions, the imposition of tariffs, and indirect taxation. The government refused to prod manufacturers out of their protected-home-market mentality. The main purpose of this overprotection, of course, was to favor the cronies engaged in manufacturing, but it offered no incentive to compete internationally. The results were predictable — inefficient industries producing inferior and shoddy products at high prices. Economist Richard Hooley of the University of Pittsburgh, in a study on the productivity of the manufacturing sector in the Philippines from 1956 to 1980, concluded that government intervention had resulted in higher prices and restricted output, slower growth of employment and real wage rates, and failure to expand market opportunities.[3]

In 1973 there were five public utility corporations, seven financial institutions, and 39 other corporations, self-governing boards, commissions and agencies in the public sector (defined here to cover national and local government and public corporations). By 1982 there were more than 100, and by 1984 there were approximately 260 government owned or controlled corporations, of which 45 were listed in the top 1,000 corporations in the Philippines according to the *Business Day* publication in Manila. These companies were engaged in agriculture, mining, manufacturing, construction, utilities, transportation, communications, banking, and services. They accounted for 20 percent of the gross revenues of the top 1,000 but their aggregate net income was minus ₱16 million.[4] Philippine Airlines had managed to lose ₱3.52 billion ($276 million) during the four year-period 1980 thru 1983.[5] In stark contrast 54 multinational corporations that accounted for 18 percent of the gross revenue of the top 1,000 earned more than ₱1 billion in net income,[6] and they did this despite the government's somewhat ambivalent attitude toward foreign investment.

The Philippines had always officially welcomed foreign investment but very little was ever done to provide a conducive atmosphere. Most foreign companies setting up in the Philippines were forced to accept Filipino partners, with the most attractive partnerships going to members of the Grand Coalition. In addition, the efficiency of its bureaucratic process was underwhelming.

Mountains of paperwork and redundant administrative requirements boggled the mind. Red tape and bribes were the
rule and not the exception. All that was combined with an
infrastructure that featured unreliable and costly communications, prolonged power interruptions, high energy costs, transport
problems, and bad roads. An enormous amount of time, money,
and effort was lost just contending with bureaucratic and
infrastructure problems.

In 1978 American and European investors had complained
about the government "changing the rules of the game,"
particularly with regard to legislation about the patent laws,
which was prominent at the time, as well as increased taxes and
restricting local borrowings. Then Minister of Industry and Board
of Investment chairman Vicente T. Paterno replied, "In the
Philippines foreign investments are considered as supplementary
tools for development. Change is necessary according to the
conditions and needs of the national economy, and foreign
investment is only one among many considerations in running a
developing country."[7] He had made it quite obvious that foreign
investment was not a major consideration at the time. In fact, it
appeared that the government considered foreign borrowings
much more important than foreign investment.

In December 1978, Michael Armacost, then American
Ambassador to the Philippines, commented that the Philippines
should rely more on foreign investment than on foreign loans to
boost the economy. Singapore, Hong Kong, and Taiwan
aggressively seek foreign equity investment, and they have
experienced the most rapid growth, while the communist
countries, which are least open to foreign investment, are the least
prosperous, he had said. The Philippines, on the other hand,
relied on foreign investment for only two percent of its net
financial inflows and 98 percent upon borrowings, and had thus
achieved the lowest growth rate in the Association of Southeast
Asian Nations (composed of Singapore, Thailand, Indonesia,
Malaysia, the Philippines, and, as of 1983, Brunei), Armacost
noted. Despite such eminent advice the government continued to
borrow, and continued not only to neglect but to criticize foreign
investment.[8]

In 1979 the Technology Resource Center, a government agency, submitted a 300-page manuscript to the American Chamber of Commerce in Manila. Entitled "Multinational Corporations in the Philippines," it requested the Chamber to read it and give their comments, which would be published with the book. There were nine chapters with each chapter written by a different author. Each author had taken one aspect of foreign investment and multinational corporations, such as technology transfer, capital movements, labor and restrictive business practices, and had proceeded to depict the multinational corporations as completely negative contributors to the economy. The Chamber provided its own commentary, which disproved with facts the manuscript's dramatic presentation. Subsequently the book was never published. However, there was no doubt that the Technology Resource Center had made every effort to criticize and belittle the multinational corporations in the Philippines. At the same time there was a smear campaign going on in the local pro-government newspapers. The multinational corporations received constant negative exposure in the media during this period. Another book was published about the same time by the University of the Philippines Law Center. Entitled *Philippine Perspectives on Multinational Corporations*, the book was more factual than the other, but still provided a very pessimistic view of the role of the multinational corporations in the Philippines.

In 1980 the attitude toward the foreign investor improved somewhat. The difficulty in borrowing dollars was forcing it to reconsider foreign investment but it wasn't desperate yet. The Ministry of Trade invited the four international business groups in the Philippines—the European Chamber of Commerce, Japanese Chamber of Commerce and Industry, American Chamber of Commerce, and the Australian Business Group—to air their views on improving the system of regulations and administration of incentives regarding investments and exports. In their letter, dated August 11, 1980, they mentioned several problems: overlapping requirements and responsibilities, constant revision of rules, and serious infrastructure problems involving electricity brownouts, inadequate telecommunications, and transport problems. According to Bernie Villegas, "The proposal zeroed in on the obstacles to the rapid expansion of exports and investments during the seventies. The majority of complaints hammered on the incredible red tape that potential exporters and investors had to wade through." Unfortunately, conditions changed very little and the letter elicited no action. Despite numerous dialogues with the government, there was little improvement in the bureaucracy or the infrastructure.[9]

About the same time Richard Robinson, former head of the International Division, Chamber of Commerce of the United States, published his study on investment programs in the Third World. It noted that the Philippines only extended a selective welcome to foreign investors. The plethora of laws regulating foreign investment was described as "One of the world's most complex set of rules and regulations regarding foreign invest-ment...The very complexity of the system invites criticism. Indeed, members of the [Board of Investment] staff admitted that they themselves did not have a full understanding of all laws, regulations and procedures. One suspects that, given this complexity, almost any project (assuming that foreign ownership be held within the appropriate limits) could be justified on some basis."[10] Commented one U.S. official: "It [the Board of Investments] was good at creating red tape and then helping companies cut through the mess it created for something in return."[11]

Inadequate infrastructure and a complex bureaucracy were big problems in the Philippines but the "something-in-return" was probably the biggest of all. Corruption was a way of life. It permeated every level of government and was written about openly in the pro-government newspapers. A foreigner doing business in the Philippines found it impossible to avoid. Bribes had to be paid to expedite matters ranging from the processing of papers to the shipment of goods. A 1982 study estimated that more than a billion dollars a year was lost to corruption, with half of that spent to expedite paperwork and half lost due to malversation and mishandling of government funds.[12]

The government did very little to encourage foreign invest-ment. In fact, it seemed to discourage it. Not until it began to experience difficulty in borrowing and encountered the financial crisis of 1981 did it seem to realize its predicament. Crony capitalism resulted in lost bailout funds totalling more than $3 billion, and state capitalism resulted in a controlled economy characterized by mismanagement, inefficiency, slow growth, impeded expansion, and restricted output. In addition, the country's agricultural exports, particularly its major dollar earners, coconut and sugar, were singled out for special attention by the government. It is estimated that during the period they were under government control, approximately $2.1 billion was lost.

CHAPTER TWENTY-THREE

The Coconut Monopoly

In 1973 there was a commodities boom in the Philippines. Export earnings hit $1.87 billion, double the level of 1969. One of the country's major exports is coconut oil and the demand for it that year caused a domestic crisis. The price of cooking oil was driven up and out of reach of the housewife. Marcos decreed that local manufacturers be subsidized in order to offer the oil at an affordable price locally. A levy of ₱15 ($2.05) per 100 kilograms of copra was charged to exporters. The crisis dissipated but the levy remained. The government, through the Philippine Coconut Producers Federation (Cocofed), realized it could raise large sums of money via the levy. Cocofed was organized in 1947 as the semi-official coconut farmers' organization but only gained recognition as their spokesman in 1971. It was never a grass-roots organization, being dominated by large landowners.[1]

The largest dollar earner for the country in 1973 was coconuts, at $370 million. It edged logs that year, which earned $303 million. This must have attracted the attention of the number one logging and timber industry entrepreneur, Juan Ponce Enrile. He had helped Marcos in his 1965 presidential campaign. As a result he was appointed Commissioner of Customs and later Secretary of Justice. He had run for the Senate in 1971 but lost in a close race. Marcos then appointed him Minister of National Defense. He was one of the prime architects of martial law. When it was declared, he was placed on the board of directors of the Philippine National Oil Company. He would receive many such appointments, attesting to his closeness to Marcos. Another of his responsibilities was cracking down on illegal loggers. While doing this he acquired at least seven lumber or wood-based companies.[2]

In 1974 Marcos decided that those huge dollar earnings in the coconut industry required government administration. He created the Philippine Coconut Authority and made it the government body with decision-making powers in the industry. Cocofed was given three seats on the PCA board. Its first chairman was Enrile. The PCA was made responsible for the levy, which was then raised to ₱100 ($13.70) per 100 kilograms. Before the levy had only been used for subsidizing the consumer. Now part of the levy would go toward the government's "vertical integration" program. Two projects were envisioned. First, according to the government, Philippine bargaining power in world markets would be strengthened by unifying the trading and milling of coconut. Secondly, a replanting scheme would replace old coconut trees with a new high-yielding variety. It was an ambitious project.[3]

The replanting scheme was absolutely essential. Most of the coconut trees in southern Luzon were 50 years old or older and nearing the "menopause" state. The trees in Mindanao were younger but were of the same variety, with a lower yield per tree and a shorter productivity period than the proposed new variety. The government awarded the contract to supply the seedlings to Eduardo Cojuangco, Jr. He was also made a director of PCA.

"Danding" Cojuangco is from Tarlac. Twenty years before he had been defeated in a congressional election by his first cousin, Jose Cojuangco. Although he had been backed by then Senator Marcos, who was campaigning for president, Jose was backed by the political machine of Tarlac Governor Benigno "Ninoy" Aquino, Jr. Jose won. His sister, Corazon, married Ninoy. Thus a family feud began out of political differences in a province known more for its Death March than for its politics. But things would change and the whole world would find out soon enough who Ninoy and Cory were.

Cojuangco's wealth stemmed from family interests in banking and sugar. Another source of wealth was the ties he had cultivated with Marcos while serving as a representative in

Congress. (He was finally elected in 1969.) He became the baptismal godfather, along with Jose Campos, of Marcos' son. The friendship grew as did Cojuangco's power and prestige.

In 1976 the replanting program was started with ₱1.15 billion (about $153 million) from the Coconut Industry Development Fund, and 133 pilot seednut farms were set up. In 1980 the actual program was started. The seedlings were distributed free to the farmers by the Philippine Coconut Authority. However, PCA had to purchase them from Cojuangco at ₱7 (about 97 U.S. cents) per plant from the levy funds. His annual profit was estimated at ₱40 million ($5.5 million).[4]

The levy generated a substantial amount of funds, so it was decided that a bank should be purchased for the farmers. The Cojuangco family held controlling interest in the First United Bank. The family offered to sell its equity to Eduardo, who offered it to Enrile. On June 30, 1975, the First United Bank became the United Coconut Bank. (It later changed its name to United Coconut Planters Bank.)[5] The bank purchase was paid for out of levy funds. PCA bought 72.2 percent on behalf of the farmers. Of this Cojuangco inexplicably received 10 percent, or 7.2 percent of the total shares, free of charge, making him the largest individual shareholder. The remaining 27.8 percent represented outstanding shares of the bank. Levy funds were also used to increase the bank's capitalization to ₱140 million ($19.3 million), and a management contract was concluded between the bank and Cojuangco, making him its president. Cojuangco thus became a shareholder and profit-sharing president of the bank, which received all replanting funds and levy funds as interest-free deposits, part of which was lent back to the farmer, but with interest. The chairman of the board was Enrile.[6]

Others present at the meeting on June 30, 1975, were eight of the senior partners of Angara, Concepcion, Cruz, Regala and Abello—the ACCRA law firm. It had been founded by Enrile and Edgardo Angara, who had been fraternity brothers at the University of the Philippines Law School. However, Enrile was no longer formally conncected with ACCRA at the time of the meeting. The eight partners were stockholders of record of the First United Bank, and retained 1.9 percent of the new bank through a company called ACCRA Investments.[7] Two years later, in April 1977, five partners of the ACCRA law firm incorporated the United Coconut Mills (Unicom). It remained virtually dormant until 1979. At that time Marcos, in a presidential letter of instruction dated September 3, 1979, declared a "national policy of oil mill rationalization," and directed United Coconut Planters Bank to invest in a private corporation, on behalf of the farmers, for the "buying, milling, and marketing of copra and its by-products."[8] The next day the bank bought into Unicom. Cojuangco was made its president.[9]

Critics, led by Assemblyman Emmanuel Pelaez of the KBL party from northern Mindanao, claimed that, through a series of manipulations by the five original stockholders of Unicom, their ₱5 million ($676,000) investment grew by ₱95 million ($12.8 million) to ₱100 million during its two years of dormancy, and the bank's ₱495 million ($67 million) investment on September 4, 1979, had shrunk by ₱95 million, to ₱400 million ($54.2 million) in just a matter of weeks. The farmers had effectively lost almost $13 million through corporate sleight-of-hand.[10] Pelaez was not your average run-of-the-mill assemblyman. He had more than thirty years in politics. Beginning in 1949, he was elected as a congressman; then as a senator; then as vice-president from 1961 to 1965; then another term as congressman in 1967; and another term as senator until martial law was declared. Pelaez was a man to be reckoned with, and he was speaking out against a powerful group. He was rewarded for his efforts on the evening of July 21, 1982, when his car was run off the road and riddled with gunfire. Though seriously wounded he survived, but his driver was killed. The criticism stopped.[11]

Unicom then proceeded to buy more than two dozen oil mills throughout the Philippines, and took over the operations of three coconut oil trading firms in the U.S.[12] It would eventually control more than 85 percent of coconut milling capacity[13] and 93 percent of all oil exports.[14]

Another subsidiary, United Coconut Chemicals, Inc. (Unichem), was incorporated in 1980 and a $100 million cocochemical complex was built. Since 70 percent of coconut exports are from oil, the industry decided to diversify its end products. Marcos then decreed that the import of chemical derivatives used in soap and detergent manufacturing be banned. However, if Unichem could not supply enough of these raw materials to other manufacturers then petrochemicals could be imported but only through Unichem. There were complaints. Each manufacturer of soap would have to spend millions of dollars in new equipment in order to implement the new process, thus entailing added costs to consumers. As usual the complaints fell on deaf ears.[15]

At that time the Philippines provided 85 percent of the world's coconut oil, so a plan was devised. The three U.S. based trading firms began buying up all the coconut oil from Unicom and hoarding it in warehouses in the U.S. until the price rose. The scheme backfired however. What no one apparently took into consideration was that there were plenty of oil substitutes. Coconut oil comprises only eight percent of the world's vegetable oil market. Consumers merely switched to other oils. As a result more than 43,000 tons stockpiled were sold at a loss of over $10 million.[16] In February 1981 the U.S. Justice Department sued the U.S. based Philippine trading companies for alledgedly conspiring to create a shortage of coconut oil to maintain its price. It was called the "Cocopec Scandal."[17]

Shortly after this incident Cojuangco was made an ambassador. He was due to make a trip to Cancun, Mexico, in October 1981 with Marcos. The entourage would land in the United States on the way. There was a warrant of arrest for Cojuangco because of the Cocopec scandal, but of course an ambassador with diplomatic immunity could not be arrested. Ambassador Cojuangco made the trip without incident.

The complaints about nationalizing the industry were legion: The Cocopec scandal which cost the farmers $10 million; the $12.8 million anomaly when the bank shares were recapitalized; and the $5.5 million in annual profits from the replanting scheme which should have gone to the farmers but didn't. (It would later turn out that the particular hybrid Cojuangco had chosen was not suitable for some parts of the country, resulting in tremendous unnecessary cost which could have been prevented if other varieties had been tested at the same time. In any event the whole operation was suspended indefinitely in early 1983 without explanation although new plants are desperately needed.)

The levy was the biggest source of complaints. Officially the levy was to be paid by the exporter, but these government owned and controlled companies illegally passed this cost back to the farmer. These collections totalled almost a billion dollars during the ten years it was implemented. (It was finally scrapped in August 1982.) There was never any public accountability of the funds and how they were disbursed. The United Coconut Planters Bank never distributed all the shares due to the farmers, claiming that there was a problem in determining an equitable distribution.[18]

The levy collection was a serious burden to the coconut farmer. More than a third of the country's population derives some income from coconuts and their by-products. In 1982 there were 500,000 coconut farms of which 75 percent were parcels of less than 10 acres each. Poor subsistence farmers comprised 72 percent of the industry.[19]

A study by the Institute of Labor and Manpower Studies in Manila concluded: "Coconut farmers were minimal benefactors of the United Coconut Planters Bank, which had garnered unprecedented government incentives in the name of the coconut farmers...welfare benefits from the levy such as scholarships and insurance represented but a trickle of the whole package of benefits."[20] Another study by the Philippine Institute for Development Studies noted that the great majority of contributors to the fund could not meet the criteria in order even to qualify for those benefits.[21]

Even the size of the subsidy was in question. Critics once estimated that, at a world price of 25 U.S. cents per pound, and a levy of of ₱50 ($6.67) per 100 kilograms, Unicom should have paid the farmers ₱196 ($26.13) per 100 kilograms. But Unicom claimed it could only pay ₱157 ($20.93), which was its break-even point. The difference led to questions involving the accounts of Unicom and the United Coconut Planters Bank. It was then announced that a caucus of the KBL would be held to air all the facts about the levy accounts. However, it was not to be. Marcos stepped in, announced there would be no caucus, and ordered those concerned to stop arguing. As a result the matter was hushed up, and all mention of the subject vanished from the press.[22]

None of this seemed to affect the coconut king himself. Cojuangco continued to expand his business interests which everyone suspected were also the business interests of Marcos. One of his nicknames was "Pacman," earned for his penchant for gobbling up companies. In 1983 he purchased 16 radio stations becoming one of the largest radio networks throughout the country. In addition to his prominent role in the coconut industry, he was chairman and chief executive officer of San Miguel Corporation, the nation's largest brewery and Coca Cola distributor. He also owned controlling interest in the company that bottled Pepsi Cola. Coke and Pepsi were the top two soft drinks in the country. In his trademark cowboy boots, polo shirt, and sport coat, he could usually be seen dashing around Manila in his gold Mercedes or his helicopter; or, if it was an out of town sortie, he would hop aboard his private Falcon jet. He also had political clout, being chairman of Marcos' KBL party. He was even considered as a possible vice-presidential candidate for Marcos.[23] Although private armies were supposed to be outlawed since the beginning of martial law, he had his own private army of several thousand trained by Israelis brought into the country as "agricultural experts."[24]

The secrecy surrounding the accountability of the monies collected by the levy, the reluctance of the United Coconut Planters Bank and Unicom to submit any report to the farmers, and allegations of price manipulation, greed, and corruption all led to justifiable criticism of a monopoly that benefitted only those in power who showed nothing but disdain for the source of their greed — the coconut farmer.

CHAPTER TWENTY-FOUR

The Sugar Monopoly

Much of the modernization of the Philippines took place around the sugar export industry beginning in the latter part of the nineteenth century when sugar became big business. Deep-water ports and harbor facilities were developed, railroads built, and telegraph lines extended. The country had virtually free access to U.S. markets up until the Laurel-Langley Act expired in 1972. This made the exporters wealthy. In turn, the sugar bloc, which includes the owners of the sugar centrals and the planters, became one of the most powerful groups in Philippine society.[1]

After the coconut industry was nationalized, the government turned its attention to the sugar industry with its enormous dollar-earning capacity. Beginning in 1974 all sugar trading was handled by a government body called the Philippine Exchange Corporation (Philex), which was a subsidiary of the Philippine National Bank. The chairman of the bank at that time was Juan Ponce Enrile.

From the start there were complaints against Philex. One complaint was that it held on to the sugar stocks, hoping the price would go up. This was confirmed in a study by the Philippine Institute of Development Studies, which concluded that the sugar stocks of Philex were largest when the world price was the highest while its sales were largest when the world price was the lowest.[2] Another complaint was that the fixed price paid to the farmer did not increase even when the world market price increased. Philex argued that it had to make a profit on export sales in order to be able to subsidize local consumers. The criticism continued. Marcos finally directed Philex to stop profiting from its exports and to increase the price paid to the sugar producers.[3] The farmers were appeased but only for awhile. What they didn't know was that Marcos had other plans for the industry.

In mid-1977 he abolished Philex and announced the establishment of the new Philippine Sugar Commission (Philsucom). Roberto Benedicto was appointed commissioner. Philsucom took over the operations of Philex. It also absorbed the Sugar Quota Administration and the Philippine Sugar Institute, as well as taking over the price-fixing function of the Price Stabilization Council. It also had the power to take over any mill or refinery that failed to meet its financial and other contractual obligations or was deemed to be operating inefficiently.[4]

Philsucom obviously had much broader powers than Philex. It also stopped reporting of any kind, so there was no way to tell whether it profited from operations or not. Philsucom would be funded by the producers themselves. The marketing arm would be the National Sugar Trading Corporation (Nasutra). Its first act was to assume an outstanding loan of ₱1.887 billion ($251.6 million) from Philex, which had reported that amount in operational losses when it was abolished.[5]

At the time of his appointment Roberto Benedicto was ambassador to Japan. He had been Marcos' classmate at U.P. High School and University of the Philippines Law School as well as a fraternity brother. Like Cojuangco he would rise in wealth and prestige as Marcos rose in power. A former president of the Philippine National Bank, his corporate empire extended from the Philippines to the United States and beyond. His offshore holding company in the Netherlands Antilles, Bequel Corporation, acted as the front in several of his bigger purchases. His conglomerate of approximately 50 corporations were engaged in banking, finance, insurance, hotels, the media, transportation, agriculture, food processing, real estate, mining, and sugar milling and trading. They included two banks, Traders Royal Bank in Manila and Overseas Bank of California in Los Angeles; a Holiday Inn hotel in Manila; the *Daily Express* newspaper in Manila; and 12 companies engaged in shipping and transport, including Northern Shipping Lines.[6] He owned seven sugar mills and four companies engaged in sugar and molasses trading, which should have been a conflict of interest, but Marcos didn't seem to mind.[7] Nor did he seem to mind when Benedicto's Kanlaon Broadcasting System took over 13 provincial radio stations, bringing his total network to 36 stations, and five provincial television stations owned by the family of former vice-president Lopez in 1973.[8] He also owns the controlling interest in three sugar trading firms in New York — the Czarnikow-Rionda Company, Ragos Trading Company, and the Philippine Sugar Trading Corporation.[9]

Most of his enterprises profited from an infusion of cheap credit from the government banks and from government connections. In 1977 he was allowed to import television sets duty free, supposedly for distribution by several government ministries to be used in rural areas for dissemination of government news. However, they immediately began showing up in stores in Metro Manila. Only after the local manufacturers complained for several years about unfair competition, did Marcos finally relent and stop this practice.[10]

Nasutra controlled both the domestic trading and the export of sugar. During martial law the average dollar earnings was $420 million. However, starting in the year the industry was national-ized, its earnings gradually shrank, from a high of $727 million in 1974 to a low of $197 million in 1978. Although part of the decline was due to a drop in world prices there was also a drop in production. Philex' policies had caused serious dissension among the farmers and Nasutra only compounded these problems. When it took over in 1977, the price the farmers were paid for their crops was below the cost of production. The farmers' constant appeals for a better pricing policy fell on deaf ears. They then began to cut back on their sugar crop and substituted other crops. After Nasutra took over, there were four consecutive years of a decline in production. From 2.34 million tons in 1977, it declined three to 400,000 tons a year. These declines were especially felt in 1980 when the price of sugar doubled on the export market. Earnings jumped to $624 million but they could have been much bigger.[11]

There were slight increases in production in 1981, 1982, and 1983, but dollar earnings dropped because of a slump in world prices. In 1983 they had to buy sugar on the world market in order to honor their export commitments.[12] In 1984, 287,000 tons had to be imported because of a domestic shortage. This was done at a time when Nasutra could not even pay the farmers for their harvest, citing a lack of funds as the reason.[13] It had already fallen behind in payments, owing an estimated ₱500 million ($27.78 million) to the very people it relied on for production.[14]

From the start of nationalization there was a constant litany of appeals to the government to restore sugar trading to the private sector. The Philippine Chamber of Commerce joined with the Philippine Chamber of Industries [the two have since been combined] and the Federation of Filipino-Chinese Chambers of Commerce in protesting the low price paid by Philex to the farmers.[15] Later various groups in the business sector, including the prestigious Philippine Business Conference, appealed to the government to abolish Nasutra and encourage free trade. However, the appeals were ignored. The sugar monopoly remained.[16]

The complaints against Nasutra were numerous and varied. The domestic distribution system was often criticized. Only sugar quota holders of Philsucom could trade in the domestic market, and almost all the quota holders were non-sugar producers. In fact, most of the quota holders were engaged not in sugar trading but in quota trading.[17] This system resulted in a very inefficient method of distribution and made billions of pesos for the "paper traders" which should have gone to the farmers. Even industrial users were not allowed to buy their sugar needs directly from private refiners. Even though the farmers had the capability to package sugar in household quantities, they were not allowed because they were not accredited sugar traders. So it was packed, and later repacked, and went through a trader to a wholesaler before reaching the retailer. This resulted in waste through spillage and waste through additional charges by middlemen. There were constant complaints about the blatant inefficiencies, but the distribution system remained.

The complaints that the price was not enough to cover the

cost of production have been noted. When the farmers asked Nasutra to account for the price they received, there was no response. However, in 1980 Nasutra finally began giving export rebates on profits it made on exports after deducting its handling charges.[18] Although the export profits should have all been paid to the farmers, they actually only received 50 percent. The other half, according to Nasutra, went toward the repayment of loans. In another disagreement Nasutra claimed that, for crop year 1980-81, 50 percent of sugar exports had been contracted at a fixed price of 22 U.S. cents per pound and the remaining 50 percent of exports had been sold on the open market at 28 U.S. cents. The National Association of Sugar Producers charged that this was not correct. Only 40 percent was sold at 22 U.S. cents per pound and the remaining 60 percent at 28 U.S. cents. The 10 percent difference amounted to a $15 million discrepancy.[19] Nasutra issued a denial but no monthly data on volume and value of exports were ever provided. The books remained closed to the farmers and no inspection was allowed.[20]

Such an accounting system, or lack thereof, invited criticism. The Center for Research and Communication conducted a study based on data from the government's National Census and Statistics Office. According to their statistics the export volume from January to August 1980 was 1,171,450 metric tons, and the export value was $377.15 million; but Nasutra claimed it only exported 795,692 metric tons for a value of $300.57 million. There was a discrepancy of $76.58 million.[21]

Another complaint stemmed from the cost of trading. In February 1981 the sugar farmers were informed by Nasutra that they owed ₱2.78 billion ($370.6 million). The farmers were aware of the ₱1.887 billion ($251.6 million) which they had been forced to assume from Philex in 1977, and which they resented, but now there were also accrued "trading costs" which seemed unduly high. For crop years 1979 and 1980 Nasutra charged 2 U.S. cents per pound, and 3 U.S. cents per pound for each succeeding crop year. This represented an effective 8 to 17 percent of the average selling price and 11 to 21 percent of the average purchase price from the farmers. The industry average had been about 8 percent before the monopoly.[22] This brought severe criticism but the trading costs remained.

It would be several years before detailed studies on the sugar industry could prove that Nasutra and Philsucom systematically cheated the sugar producers of billions of pesos over the years by imposing their power through price control, excessive trading charges, sugar imports, and the dumping of smuggled imported sugar into local outlets, forcing prices to very low levels and compelling producers to agree to the restoration of Nasutra's control over local sugar trading. The studies would also reveal that so-called paper traders had been allowed to make billions of pesos in profits simply because of their influence with the government.[23] It was estimated that farmers lost between ₱11.6 and ₱14.4 billion (about $1.1 billion) because of the monopoly.[24]

During this period most of the farmers were forced into a hand-to-mouth existence. Despite the obvious abject poverty facing them, the government did little to help. That is when the church stepped in. To the majority of Filipinos the church represented the last bastion of hope. It did what it could but the gulf between the wealthy landowners and the poor farmers became ever wider. When the church cried "oppression," the government, instead of trying to help, countered with its own charges of "subversion."

Soon all this would not matter. By the time the greed of Marcos, Imelda, and the Grand Coalition had effectively bankrupted the country, and Marcos realized the only major source of dollars left was foreign investment, it would be too late. As the economy worsened events were shaping up in the Philippines that would once and for all prove that Marcos' claims of a free market, a free press, and a free country espousing democratic principles were nothing but lies.

CHAPTER TWENTY-FIVE

The State Visit

Washington supported Marcos throughout his reign. Even when he declared martial law, the U.S. government continued its support but let it be known that dictatorships were frowned upon. In the mid-70's Marcos didn't care what the U.S. thought was best for his country. He was on a roll then, everybody kowtowing and wanting to lend money. He and his Grand Coalition pillaged the country to their heart's content. The conspicuous consumption of the new rich became an embarassment as the number of poor increased dramatically. Now the economy began to falter and the country was slowly going bankrupt as he became more and more desperate. Now he really needed U.S. dollars and U.S. support, and he desperately needed a visit to Washington to plead his case. He was invited to an economic summit to be held in Cancun, Mexico, in October 1981. There he would meet with President Reagan. He had already ended martial law and the Pope had visited the Philippines. In addition, presidential elections were scheduled for June. It was hoped that, with all this show of democracy, he might receive an invitation to visit the U.S. But that is all it was — show. Marcos was very careful about making certain that nothing really changed.

As soon as martial law ended, he announced that a new constitution, supposedly based on the French model, would better serve the people. Another plebiscite was held that April before the June presidential election, and the new constitution ratified. Several new provisions were included. One granted Marcos and all government officials lifetime immunity from any legal action.[1] Another set the minimum age to run for office at 50. This effectively excluded Ninoy Aquino, who would be 49 that year, from entering the presidential election.[2]

The election in June could only be described as farcical. After Marcos announced he was a candidate for president, nobody wanted to run against him as it was apparent the whole thing was a sham. The coffee shops of Manila were rife with rumors that Marcos would pay handsomely for somebody to run against him. Finally an ally of Marcos, Alejo Santos, 69, from the Nacionalista Party, which generally supported the Marcos regime, agreed to run. To insure a big turnout Marcos decreed that failure to vote was a crime punishable by six months' imprisonment. Even so, many refused to vote. Of those, some were jailed and some were shot.

Marcos was elected to a new six-year term. The U.S. wasted no time in showing its support. Former Secretary of State Alexander Haig, in Manila for an ASEAN conference the day after the election told him: "You are going to find America with you, not in a dominating way, not in a pedantic way, but in a true partnership of equality and friendship."[3] Vice-President George Bush flew to Manila in July for Marcos' inauguration and toasted him: "We love your adherence to democratic processes."[4] Practically the whole democratic world blanched. The day after Bush's remark the editorial page of almost every major newspaper in the U.S. asked, "How could you do that?" There was no official comment but the answer was obvious: the bases.

In a paper on U.S.-Philippine relations, Larry Niksch of the U.S. Congressional Research Service, Library of Congress, reported that "[during this time] the primary goal of the administration was to solidify the good relationship with the Marcos government as a prelude to the upcoming base negotiations...Human rights issues and other internal problems in the Philippines seldom if ever occupied the Assistant Secretary of State for East Asia or the Secretary of State...The bases' domination of U.S. policy increasingly overshadowed consideration of the Philippine internal situation."[5]

Marcos' human rights record apparently wasn't a concern for the U.S. There was no doubt about the oppression. The State Department and Amnesty International had the proof, but Marcos continued to receive not only support but praise. This so-called "Quiet Diplomacy" stance harkened back to Roosevelt's simple philosophy in a simpler time: "He may be an SOB, but he's our SOB." Such a posture would have tragic results but for then the game plan was simple. The bases came first.

Strategically, since Cam Ranh Bay fell to the North Vietnamese, Subic Naval Base and Clark Air Base are the two most essential overseas U.S. bases in the world. They are the only U.S. bases from the Aleutians to the Indian Ocean, and sit astride the vital sea and air lanes of the western Pacific and the gateway to the Indian Ocean. They were built before World War II and retained after Philippine independence in 1946. They grew in importance as world tensions increased. Subic is a major refitting and supply depot for the U.S. Navy and Clark Field can respond to any crisis in the western Pacific, Indian Ocean, or Persian Gulf. In 1979 Washington had signed an agreement to give the Philippines $500 million compensation over a five-year period in return for the use of the bases. The treaty didn't expire until 1991, but it was due for review in 1984.

After the election Marcos continued to run the country as before — as a dictator — and continued to receive open support of his oppressive regime from the U.S. He went to Cancun in October 1981 and received his invitation for a state visit to Washington.

Before the state visit several U.S. senators had criticized U.S. support for Marcos' oppressive regime, including Edward Kennedy, who had told President Reagan: "The security of the United States does not require our support for the repression of the Filipino people...There is convincing evidence, confirmed by the Department of State, that the government of President Marcos...has engaged in persistent persecution of the press, labor, church, students, and business leaders."[6] Kennedy's words fell on deaf ears. Quiet Diplomacy remained.

In July 1982 a confidential World Bank report was leaked to the world press. It stated that the country had reached its effective upper limits on foreign borrowings. It also complained that too much was being spent on inefficient government corporations (over ₽18 billion [$2.1 billion] had been spent on 33 government banks and corporations the past two years) and that an intolerable balance-of-payments problem could occur if the government didn't spend more equitably and efficiently.[7]

Marcos must have realized that the excesses of his regime had gone too far. Foreign investment had begun to decline for the first time. It was decided that, after the state visit, he and his ministers would go to New York and once again convince the captains of U.S. finance and industry that the Philippines was an ideal place for investment.

Now the trip took on new importance. It is estimated that somewhere between $5 and $20 million was spent in preparations for the trip for such things as picnics, luncheons, dinners, festivities, receptions, entertainment, seminars, public relations, government publications, advance teams, and security personnel.[8] It is interesting to note that the government publications all trumpeted the praises of Marcos the war hero. In addition, several Philippine government officials wined and dined officers from the U.S. Army Department of Military History. The reason for the attention was that Marcos still wanted a U.S. Congressional Medal of Honor. These overtures were ignored.

Imelda's brother, Kokoy, was appointed Ambassador to the United States and three more diplomats with ambassadorial rank were sent to Washington for four months to assist in preparing for the visit. In July Imelda flew in to make sure all arrangements were being handled properly, and paid courtesy calls on Vice President Bush and CIA Director William Casey. The Philippine Embassy began publishing an English language newspaper, *The Monitor*, and distributed it free to the one-million Filipino-Americans living in the United States. Manila's leading corporations and advertising agencies dispatched their top public relations executives to Washington to help with the "image problem." (How do you present a dictator in a good light?) Philippine consulates all over the U.S. staged celebrations, flying in Filipino movie stars, starlets, and entertainers. It was an elaborate and costly attempt to buy a good media image.

In Manila, Marcos made a few special plans of his own before the trip. In August he ordered the arrest of three labor leaders and scores of "anti-government agitators" because they had threatened to strike. Strikes had been illegal during martial law. Although they had now been legalized, all organized labor was still considered by the government to be leftist or communist. In a news conference Marcos claimed there was evidence of a "communist plot to carry out strikes, bombings, assassinations, and the armed overthrow of the government." His "preemptive action," he claimed, had thwarted the plot.[9]

At the same time he created a force of 1,000 "secret marshalls" empowered to kill suspected common criminals. When 47 suspects were killed and only six captured in two weeks, he had to restrict their powers.[10] The crackdown, said a Marcos aide, "served as a reminder to everyone concerned of who is in charge, whether he [Marcos] is in the country or abroad."[11]

Before he departed he drew up a succession plan that bore the markings of a dynasty. At his prodding the National Assembly approved a law clarifying the constitutional provisions for a 15-member Executive Committee to succeed him in the event of his death or disability. He appointed Imelda as a member, which meant she would obviously dominate and, perhaps, even emerge as president if anything happened to Marcos.[12]

For the trip to Washington, Marcos and Imelda's entourage numbered about 700. It included more than 100 journalists, all pro-Marcos, of course; about the same number of security men; three personal physicians; their daughters' hairdresser; personal friends; several leading businessmen and industrialists; and numerous government officials. One magazine commented: "The official delegation included virtually the entire Philippine government."[13] When the circus of 700 descended on the nation's capitol, the extravagance shocked even the jaded Washington press corps.

On September 16, 1982, Marcos arrived in Washington on his second state visit. The first had been 16 years before, during the administration of Lyndon Johnson. Now, five U.S. presidents later, Marcos was still in power. As he stood by Ronald Reagan in front of the Washington Monument, the President of the United States assured him of his warm friendship.

The herald trumpeters along the steps announced the arrival of Marcos and Imelda as they pulled up to the White House in a black limousine. Reagan used all the pomp and ceremony the Presidency could muster. Marcos was delighted, especially at the praises and the phrases heaped upon him: Liberty...Democracy...Justice...Equality.[14] He replied, "At the risk of our fortunes, our lives, but most important of all, our honor, [we] will stand for the ideals of democracy that is our legacy from the United States of America."[15] It was a bit effusive even by Washington standards.

The welcoming ceremony was seen live on Philippine television via satellite and must have rankled more than a few members of the opposition and church. At the risk of *their* lives, they had provided evidence to an Amnesty International team of investigators that revealed conditions in their country far different from the democracy Reagan and Marcos were describing. The results were released in a report just before the state visit and detailed the brutalities of the Marcos regime. It included every manner of human rights abuses imaginable—torture, disappearances, and summary executions, all carried out with tacit government approval.[16] In addition, there was a $30 million lawsuit filed in Seattle in which Marcos and Imelda were charged. Two young union leaders, anti-Marcos activists, had been gunned down by killers allegedly acting on the orders of Marcos' agents, to halt their efforts in establishing ties with opposition trade union movements in the Philipines.[17]

Reagan, Marcos, and their advisers met for almost an hour. Significantly the human rights question was never brought up even though Amnesty International had just released its lastest report on the Philippines. The modernization of the armed forces was discussed and the U.S. agreed to play a key role. Thus in less than an hour Marcos was assured there would be no interference in matters regarding human rights and that his military forces would become stronger. Those were ominous signs of what was to come.[18]

That evening about 149 guests were entertained at the White

House. They dined by candlelight in the Rose Garden under the stars. One newspaper described the scene as "being somewhere between a Christmas image and a South Seas fantasy."[19] Across the street more than a hundred demonstrators protested the visit, but the large numbers promised by the protestors did not materialize. Only about a dozen had been at the Washington Monument when Marcos arrived, and only about 75 had attended the protest rally at Lafayette Park that afternoon.[20]

The next day Marcos met with members of the House Foreign Affairs and Senate Foreign Relations Committees. When asked about the recently released Amnesty International report, which documented hundreds of human rights abuses, Marcos criticized Amnesty International, the recognized pre-eminent authority on human rights, as not being an accurate judge. "There has been no violation," he proclaimed.[21] One can only wonder at how he could make such a brazen, and obviously incorrect, remark to such an august audience. The answer is that he had a lot of practice. In the first place, very few abuses were ever reported by the media in the Philippines; and if they were, very little detail was given; but if it ever got to the point where Marcos had to publicly answer a charge, it would go away and cease to exist as soon as he denied it. It may be difficult to believe that one person's affirmation could carry with it such absolute finality, but Marcos had that kind of power in the Philippines. Such denials in the United States, however, did nothing to enhance his credibility.

Marcos had hoped to discuss the extradition treaty that had been negotiated but not ratified.[22] In 1973 he had decided that an extradition treaty with the U.S. was needed. Extradition is the formal surrender of a person by a state to another state for trial and punishment. Salonga, in his monograph on the subject,* noted that before martial law the Philippines had neither sought nor considered such a treaty, but suddenly in 1973 it was extremely important. However, the U.S. government informed Marcos that, because of martial law, perhaps it wasn't the time to

---

* "The Extradition Treaty Between the Philippines and United States: Facts and Implications," Philippine Occasional Studies Paper No. 5, Philippine Studies Program, (Honolulu: University of Hawaii, Center for Asia and Pacific Studies), August 1982.

negotiate such matters. Thus when martial law was ended and
Marcos was reelected in June, negotiations were resumed in
September, and the treaty was finalized and approved by
President Reagan within a month. Almost immediately the treaty
drew widespread criticism. It was fairly obvious that Marcos
wanted the treaty to enable him to eliminate his opposition now
living in the U.S. There was already considerable sentiment
against it because of his human rights record, and his performance before the two committees only reinforced that sentiment.
He was advised that it was not a good time to discuss the matter.
Congress refused to ratify the treaty.

In other discussions with government officials it was agreed
that the talks regarding the future of the bases would start the
following April, eight months early. This pleased Marcos, who
wanted to raise the rent as soon as possible. He had previously on
occasion threatened to throw out the bases but this was more
bravado on his part than anything else. Subic's 1982 local
expenditures ran to $96.9 million and Clark's $100 million, a
boost to any economy. This didn't count the $500 million in rents.
(The talks would be concluded in May 1983. The rents were raised
to $900 million over a five-year period beginning October 1,
1984.)[23]

One of the goals of the state visit was to improve Marcos'
poor image in the U.S. Along with the elaborate public relations
campaign, journalists had received books and a sheaf of press
releases praising Marcos, the soldier and statesman. There were
also regular embassy luncheons for the media. Marcos met with
the editorial boards of the *Washington Post* and the *New York
Times*, appeared on the "Meet the Press" television program, and
spoke at the National Press Club. The results were not what his
campaigners had envisioned.[24]

The Amnesty International report was brought up again. At
a news conference, reporters, a more brash bunch than the
congressmen and senators, asked him to answer the charges in the
report about the disappearances, torture, and executions. He once
again denied the charges. He was obviously unaccustomed to such
treatment by the media, who would not accept his contant litany
of denial. He finally acknowledged that "there probably were some

human rights violations but these cases were investigated immediately and the guilty punished."[25] Outside, across the street, Ninoy Aquino was leading the demonstrators in protest. The absurdity of Marcos' comment would only be fully realized years later when, after the brutal murder of Aquino at Manila International Airport, all those indicted for the killing would be absolved of complicity in a trial stage-managed by Marcos.

Back home Cardinal Sin scoffed at Marcos' remarks. In a speech he stated: "I should not believe what I see with my own eyes because the truth is very different from what I see or feel or hear...I should not believe there is malnutrition in the Philippines even if, in the centers run by the Archdiocese of Manila, children are daily snatched from the jaws of death because of starvation...I should not believe that there are political detainees held for months and years without charges even if the families of these detainees regularly come to me for help...I should not believe that there are military abuses even if the victims themselves—or the widows of the victims—related to me what they saw with their own eyes."[26]

In Manila the *Bulletin Today* newspaper praised Marcos for handling himself so well in front of his critics. It reported that his decision to face the media critics head on "using wit and forthrightness (sic) [had] changed the hostility in American media attitude to the Philippine situation."[27] *We Forum* saw it a little differently: "To think the Americans really believed him is to insult their intelligence as a people."[28] (They would pay dearly for such remarks a few months later.) The *New York Times* did not agree with the *Bulletin*'s assessment either: "Mr. Marcos' main service to democracy has been to demonstrate how much of it his countrymen have lost."[29]

The visit was judged a success by the newspapers in Manila. Marcos and his Cabinet and, of course, Imelda, were all praised. As usual *We Forum* saw things from a more realistic perspective. It spoke of human rights, and noted that in view of "Reagan's failure to bring this matter to the attention of Mr. Marcos...expect, therefore, a harsher repression of human rights and curtailment of civil liberties of Filipino citizens."[30] And, as usual, they were right.

CHAPTER TWENTY-SIX

Blitzkrieg

After the state visit was officially over the entourage departed for New York. They checked into the Waldorf Astoria, occupying 100 rooms. Marcos took the Presidential Suite and Imelda the Royal Suite. She arrived with more than 300 suitcases. Bellboys there welcomed her with enthusiasm, knowing well her propensity toward $100 tips and the standing order that her suite be kept full of fresh flowers. The cost to her government for this caprice was $1,000 a day.[1]

Marcos took his government officials with him to New York. They included Prime Minister and concurrent Minister of Finance Cesar E. Virata, Foreign Affairs Minister Carlos P. Romulo, Minister of Trade and Industry Roberto Ongpin, Minister of Defense Juan Ponce Enrile, Minster of Agriculture Arturo Tanco, Jr., Minister of Energy Geronimo Velasco, Minister of Tourism Jose Aspiras, and Solicitor General Estelito Mendoza. Their mission was to bolster the image of the Philippines as a great place for investment. This would not be easy.

The country had a huge foreign debt and, with the release of the World Bank report, parallels were being drawn between them and the recent economic debacle in Mexico. In addition, international businessmen had worried publicly about the political stability of the country, and foreign investment had declined at a time when it was most needed. At the Cancun economic summit in Mexico the previous October, eight of the world's richest nations and fourteen less developed countries had met to

discuss the economic plight of the Third World. Reagan told
those gathered that the era of massive American handouts was
finished.[2] Marcos knew that if no more aid were forthcoming, and
if they couldn't borrow anymore, then foreign investment had
suddenly become very important.

Thus he had come to New York to assuage all doubts about
the stability of his economy and his government. First there was a
dinner for 1,400 at the Waldorf Astoria. The guests, who paid
$125 each, represented the cream of American industry and
finance. After dining on filet mignon and California Gamay wine,
they listened to Marcos assure them that "Whether I am president
or not, the rules will not be substantially changed. No private
investment is going to be confiscated, and nor will we stop the
remittances of profits or payments or the amortization of
indebtedness."[3] Later there was a dialogue among members of the
Cabinet, led by Minister Virata, and 60 businessmen. Virata
assured them: "The Philippines is very reliable in terms of both
political and labor stability."[4] He advised them of the numerous
incentives available and assured them of the country's ability to
service its debts, saying "We have not defaulted on our loan
repayments...the borrowing situation must be in accordance with
our capacity to borrow."[5]

The businessmen could not help but be impressed by Marcos'
zeal in the combative defense of his regime; and Virata and the
Cabinet spoke with equal conviction about the soundness of their
economy. However, these performances were remarkable for two
reasons. One, it was almost a total about-face from the way the
foreign investor had been treated by the Philippines in the 70's;
and, secondly, almost everything that was said in New York was
not true. The claims and promises given to these astute
businessmen were lies and Marcos knew it.

As the economy worsened, the official explanation was that
it was all due to external factors. Everything was blamed on the
world economic recession. Undoubtedly it did slow the growth
rate. After the boom year of 1973 the economy slowed to an
average growth rate of about 6.5 percent a year for the rest of the
70's. As already noted the reduced demand for exports coupled

with inflation and an increase in the price of imports, including oil, did hurt the economy.

However, there was another side to this proverbial coin. The government had, in fact, discouraged exports through restrictive and complicated policies, and local industry was more protected than in any country in Asia except Indonesia, thereby restricting imports. This protectionism was designed for only one purpose—to enrich Marcos and his cronies. The government borrowed itself into a gigantic debt trap and inhibited its ability to repay by limiting its ability to earn dollars.

In addition to the warning in the World Bank report about the country's reaching its effective outer limit on foreign borrowing, there was also its pattern of spending. During the period 1970-1983, most of the monies spent on government capital expenditures were wasted. Capital outlays for infrastructure projects, such as roads, bridges, schools, and irrigation, totalled ₱48.259 billion (about $6.27 billion); corporate equity investments, which included contributions to the Central Bank, the Philippine National Bank, the Development Bank of the Philippines, the Land Bank, and the National Development Corporation, totalled ₱47.248 billion ($5.96 billion); construction by ministries other than the Ministry of Public Highways and the Ministry of Public Works and Transportation Commission totalled ₱18.974 billion (about $2.39 billion). The second item, corporate equity contributions, went mostly toward the takeover or extension of new loans to distressed companies of Marcos' cronies. Most of the last item comprised Imelda's pet construction projects. With few exceptions these outlays had little social or economic justification and, as usual, there was no public accountability for their cost, leading to allegations that the book value (original cost) of each project far exeeded the actual value. Such overpricing was common in any Philippine government project, made necessary by the kickbacks expected in order to win the bids for such projects.[6]

Overpricing was also a frequent occurrence with just about any item imported into the Philippines. Whether it was weapons, oil, machinery, or consumer goods, it was common practice for the local buyer, be he government, military, or private importer, to request the foreign seller to overprice the item(s) and demand a kickback. This overpriced amount would then be deposited in an account abroad. This was typically referred to as "dollar salting." Another common practice was for the importer to underdeclare, or even reclassify by prior arrangement, the value of the imported goods in order to reduce or remove entirely the import taxes.

Jaime Ongpin, prominent Filipino industrialist, noted that there was a "deep-seated propensity on the part of too many Filipinos for instant gratification," in explaining that much of the "equipment and construction costs for some textile mills, sugar mills, copper mines, etc. were overpriced to enable the project promoters to get most of their money back even before the projects started operating, or in some cases, even when the projects never operated at all."[7]

Then there was the government's propensity for "making adjustments" when it was to its advantage. In May 1982, it was announced that the format for reporting the country's external debt was to be changed. Revolving credits, which were mostly short-term borrowings, would be excluded. Under the old format the outstanding debt was $16 billion; under the new it was $11.5 billion. They had lowered the country's outstanding debt by $4.5 billion by a change of definition.[8] When foreign creditors complained, Finance Minister Virata defended the change, stating, "There is a feeling that the revolving credits inflate our debt figures too much."[9] This comment would prove to be somewhat of an understatement.

In 1982 the Central Bank definition of the debt-service ratio was changed to keep within the 20 percent lending limit. In 1970 it had voluntarily set a debt-service ratio of 20 percent on the amount it could borrow from abroad. Annual foreign borrowings could not exceed 20 percent of the average annual export earnings over the past three years. This was later changed to 20 percent of the previous year's earnings. In 1982, the definition changed again. Short-term loans were excluded (thus decreasing the numerator), and foreign borrowings were added to export earnings (increasing the denominator). Effectively this could allow them to borrow short term loans ad infinitem without disturbing the ratio. It also made their capacity to repay their loans dependent on their ability to borrow, and not vice-versa, as is normally the case.[10]

It was an Alice-in-Wonderland strategy. To quote Humpty Dumpty telling Alice scornfully, "When I use a word it means just what I choose it to mean — neither more nor less." The routine obfuscation of government data continued. In October 1982, it was announced that the base year for determining the Consumer Price Index had been changed to 1978. Before, the base year had been 1972. In addition, the composite of the market basket that comprised the index was reduced from 644 to 393 items, with many of the items now under price control. Thus, the Consumer Price Index for mid-1982 was 28 centavos under the old method, and 59 centavos under the new. They had raised the purchasing power of the peso by a change in the base year.[11]

After "lowering" the external debt and "raising" the purchasing power with strokes of the pen, and changing the definition of its debt-service ratio so that it could borrow short-term ad infinitem, the stage was set. As the foreign debt grew bigger it became more and more difficult to obtain credit. In early 1982 the government, unbeknown to its foreign lenders, began to resort to overnight borrowing to cover some of its external payment shortfalls. As the country's credit rating dropped, interest rates rose and maturities grew shorter. Then the government began to sell its international reserves. This continuous drain on the reserves, along with low revenues from exports and investments, started them on a downward spiral. They kept borrowing...at shorter terms...at higher interest rates.

At the same time the government decided to "dress up" the accounts again in order to look good for its creditors. It falsified the international reserves accounts in order to be able to borrow more. They had started doing it in 1981. Such fabrication over a three-year period, until they got caught, could not have occurred without approval at the highest levels of government.

This was not the first time Marcos had tinkered with the international reserves. He increased them in 1977 by changing the definition. Originally it was "All gold, foreign exchange assets of the Central Bank, and net foreign exchange holdings of the commercial banks."[12] Expressed in dollars, by that definition the international reserves could cover about two months' import requirements. As a rule of thumb, international creditors would like to see enough international reserves to cover three or four months of import requirements. So, on January 1, 1977, the net foreign exchange holdings of the commercial banks, which had become quite a large negative figure, were excluded from the definition. In addition, the Central Bank's own borrowings would no longer be excluded from its foreign exchange assets. Thus, with the stroke of a pen, the value of the international reserves almost doubled, from $844.7 million to $1.525 billion, which was about 4.7 months of import requirements.[13]

Because of such financial sleight-of-hand the Central Bank's relationship with its commercial lenders was less than smooth. Also, the supposedly close relationship it had with the World Bank and the International Monetary Fund was a myth. So was the way each commitment of funds was presented in the Philippine newspapers as an endorsement of the government. In fact, the World Bank had reported, in 1977, that it regarded 30 percent of all projects to which it had provided assistance as "problem projects." By 1979 that figure had grown to 63 percent, substantially above the figure for the whole East Asia and Pacific region.[14]

In financial circles there was serious doubt cast on the ability of the Monetary Board, the highest monetary policy-making body in the Philippines, to function as the institution accountable to international authorities for the country's fiscal responsibilities. There was strong evidence that the board, like almost everything else, was being controlled from Malacañang Palace. For example, in January 1981, when the Dewey Dee scandal had the banking system in chaos, a ₱5 billion ($630 million) fund established by the World Bank and government to boost industrial investment was diverted to a "rescue-of-troubled-companies" fund. The ceiling for the rescue financing of the crony companies was set at $193 million. Access to the fund was premised on the selloff of subsidiaries not related to their basic business. However, in defiance of World Bank guidelines, the Philippine authorities allowed the $193 million to balloon to almost $400 million. This provoked the IMF to veto the government's request for standby credit in 1982.[15]

It was after the Dee scandal and the financial crisis that the government started playing its deadly games — falsifying data and changing definitions. The World Bank and the IMF had to have known what was happening, but perhaps protocol prevented them from being overly critical except in extreme cases such as the incident in early 1982. The government's claim of a 4.9 percent increase in Gross National Product for 1981 was disputed by the IMF. According to their figure, the growth rate was zero. Virata complained vigorously. A diplomatic compromise set the figure at 2.5.[16]

About the same time as the growth rate dispute, Virata announced a freeze on government spending in order to keep the government deficit at ₱10.5 billion. It had ballooned from ₱1.1 billion ($114 million) in 1980, to ₱12.1 billion ($1.36 billion) in 1981. The IMF had doubted the projections on the freeze, and, true to form, the government deficit for 1982 amounted to ₱14 billion ($1.6 billion). They were 40 percent off target.[17] The balance of payments projection was off even more. The initial estimate was $600 million. The final official figure was $1.6 billion.[18]

When Marcos came to New York, he already knew he was in trouble. That is why almost his entire Cabinet was with him, and they had their instructions. Promise anything but attract the investors. And hurry. They were running out of dollars; they were running out of lenders; and they were running out of time. That Kokoy Romualdez, Philippine Ambassador to the U.S., was put in charge of the campaign to promote U.S. investment in the Philippines was a sort of confirmation that they really were desperate. All of a sudden they were ready and willing to solve any problem for the foreign investor. Committees were formed. The promotion was headlined in the papers. It was impressive. But it was too late. An infrastructure that had been neglected for more than 20 years could not be refurbished overnight. Too many roads had to be repaired; too many phones fixed; too many brownouts alleviated. Also, two generations of bureaucrats, skilled only in the art of red tape and how to complicate a transaction in order to be paid to uncomplicate and expedite it, could not be taught efficiency overnight. The campaign fizzled. It was now 1983 and Marcos had some big financial problems.

In February the government again requested standby credit worth $336 million from the IMF. The request was approved after they agreed to certain terms. In the middle of 1983, a mid-term review was held to determine if they were performing in accordance with those terms, which was to keep the balance of payments deficit below $600 million and the budget deficit within 2 percent of the gross national product. They had projected a deficit of $560 million. They were found in violation, and the drawdowns were stopped after disbursing $125 million of the standby credit. The deficit would hit $2.5 billion by the end of the year. For some reason the government could not or would not adhere to the policies they agreed to. After so many incidents it can be safely concluded that the government would agree to anything to get their hands on the dollars and worry about compliance with the conditions later if at all.[19]

At first it was camouflage. Then gradually the obfuscation of data became routine. Finally there was outright falsification of figures. This was done because the government wanted its lenders to believe that the Philippines was in good shape economically in order to be able to continue borrowing. In keeping with their "management by illusion" concept, looking good became more important than being good. And, for some reason, the country valued its ability to borrow more than its ability to produce. The explanation for such an irrational policy would only become obvious during the investigation of the hidden wealth of Marcos and his Grand Coalition.

So Marcos' political appointees sat in Washington in their Western coats and ties, speaking English without an accent, and negotiating for dollar loans in the language of international high finance. Then they went home, put on their barongs, and dispensed this money in accordance with their own customs, which probably predate most banking and commercial concepts.

Afterwards, it was the responsibility of their monetary authorities, also appointed, to insure that it all looked proper in the eyes of the World Bank, the International Monetary Fund, and other commercial lending institutions. That was the way the government worked.

It has already been pointed out that superstition played a prominent role in the palace. Lucky numbers were a part of this. Imelda chose to testify before the Agrava Commission on July 2, her birthday, always a lucky day. Marcos also had his lucky number. The tags of all the palace automobiles sported "777" tags. At least one of his companies was named the 777 Corporation. Also, if there was an auspicious occasion, the date of the event would be considered of special importance. At least three events in Marcos' life would occur on the 21st day of the month. Two have already been mentioned — August 21, 1971 and September 21, 1972. The third date is August 21, 1983.

EPILOGUE
Assassination

CHAPTER TWENTY-SEVEN

Martyrdom

In 1896, Jose Rizal was a young man of 35. He was brilliant: medical doctor, skilled linguist, classical scholar, novelist, and essayist. He was a man of peace who espoused evolution, not revolution. And he was about to pay the ultimate price for his beliefs. The Spanish colonialists had just tried and convicted him of insurrection, and he was to die by firing squad. On the eve of his execution he was moved to the prison chapel to spend his last hours saying goodbye to his family and friends, and to make peace with himself and his God. There was no sign of fear or anguish of that coming December dawn. Instead the man that would become the Philippines' national hero calmly composed a beautiful 14-stanza poem at his Last Farewell.*

My dreams, when life first opened to me,
My dreams, when the hopes of youth beat high,
Were to see thy lov'd face, O gem of the Orient sea,
From gloom and grief, from care and sorrow free;
No blush on thy brow, no tear in thine eye...

My Fatherland ador'd that sadness to my sorrow lends,
Beloved Filipinos, hear now my last goodbye!
I give thee all; parents and kindred and friends;
For I go where no slave before the oppressor bends,
Where faith can never kill, and God reigns e'er on high!

* The poem was unnamed. Later the Rizalists titled it "Ultimo Adios" (The Last Farewell). English Translation by Charles E. Derbyshire.

Eighty-seven years after Rizal was martyred, another Filipino, full of trepidation, decided to stand up for what he believed in and to do what he thought was right. Very few people ever get the chance to test the courage of their convictions and even fewer, when given the chance, rise to the occasion. Ninoy Aquino always seemed to be testing his. He became a war correspondent in Korea at the age of 17. In 1954, at age 22, he negotiated the surrender of Luis M. Taruc, the rebel commander of the Huks, for President Magsaysay. That same year the lady he had been courting for several years finally accepted his proposal of marriage. He and Corazon Cojuangco were married in Our Lady of Sorrows Church in Manila on October 11, 1954. They moved back to Tarlac, the home province of both families, and began to raise a family. Aquino became interested in politics. In succession he quickly became: the youngest elected mayor, of Concepcion, Tarlac, at 22; the youngest elected vice governor (Tarlac province) at 27; and the youngest governor (Tarlac province) in 1961 at age 29. During this period he served as an executive assistant to three presidents: Magsaysay (1953-1957); Garcia (1957-1961); and Macapagal (1961-1965). In 1967 he became the youngest elected senator. In his maiden privelege speech in the Senate, he denounced Marcos' "gradual and steady development of a 'Garrison State.' " He was the shining star in the Liberal Party, which was Marcos' political rival. That, in essense, was his crime. That, and uttering such communistic slogans as "Without criticism no government can survive, and without dissent, no government can effectively govern."[1]

He was arrested on September 23, 1972, and taken to Fort Bonifacio. There he languished for 11 months without being charged. Finally, in August 1973, he was charged with murder, subversion, and illegal possession of firearms. The trial was long and tedious. He refused to participate and to defend himself because he found it "not only anomalous, immoral, unjust, and unjustified — but an unconscionable mockery of justice, an obscene farce!"[2] On November 25, 1977, he was sentenced to death. The reaction worldwide was immediate. People everywhere expressed outrage at the sentence. Marcos backed off while Aquino appealed his conviction to the Supreme Court. In 1980, he suffered a heart attack and an examination revealed he was in urgent need of a delicate triple by-pass heart operation. He refused to allow the military doctors to perform the surgery. Marcos was in a quandary. If he forced the operation on Aquino and he died, the consequences could be drastic. The only other choice was made and on May 8, 1980, in what the newspapers called a "humanitarian" gesture, he allowed Aquino to depart for the United States for the operation. He had been in solitary confinement seven years and seven months when he left.

He survived the surgery and was safely ensconced in the United States, where he could speak out against the Marcos regime without fear of reprisal, but he felt he was needed at home. Home, where he had spent almost eight years in solitary confinement and might have to do so again if he returned. Home, where those in power had pointedly warned him that he wasn't welcome and might be killed. Home, where he was still under a sentence of death. Yet he came.

Marcos was a very sick man in 1983. It is rumored that he has systemic discoid lupous, a debilitating disease that affects the body's internal organs, usually the kidneys. Marcos' kidneys were failing. Dialysis machines were installed in the palace and in his mobile medical unit to cleanse his blood of impurities, a function his kidneys could no longer perform. On August 7, he underwent a kidney transplant at the National Kidney Foundation in Manila. The doctor was flown in from Georgetown University Medical Center.[3]

Marcos had enough problems on his hands at that time. Events were getting out of control. The economy was in shambles; he was running out of cash to feed the countless projects which were the bread and butter of the Grand Coalition; the business-men and academics were becoming more vocal despite intimida-tion; the non-government press was exhibiting more independence in publicizing these problems; and he was a very sick man. Another problem wasn't needed right then. Aquino wasn't wanted, and he was advised of this in the strongest possible terms. The reaction to the announcement that he was returning can only be surmised. Marcos was never weaker and more vulnerable. He was very aware that if anyone had the ability to organize the opposition into an effective force, which would cause even more problems and possibly even expose him, it was Aquino. It was in this atmosphere of paranoia that an order was given for the assassination. It may never be known who gave the order, but it was a way to regain control, serve as a warning, and perhaps discourage others who were less resolute.

By now everyone has heard about what happened on that fateful Sunday, August 21, 1983. The China Airlines flight from Taipei arrives in Manila in the early afternoon and docks at Gate Number 8. A military escort party boards the plane and picks up Aquino. All others on board, including the reporters and friends who had accompanied him from Taipei, are prevented from leaving the plane. The escort party rushes Aquino out the door, into the tube, and down the stairs. Then the gunshots. First one. Then an interval of about three seconds. Then a second and third shot, and another one-second interval. Then a fourth shot, and a two-second interval. Then a fifth. Then screaming and shouting, panic and pandemonium for about 17 seconds. Then a last fusillade of about 23 shots.

In 1899, the Americans took their turn at colonizing the Filipino. During what the U.S. called the "Philippine Insurrection," American General Arthur MacArthur (father of General Douglas MacArthur) was bivouacked with his 4,800-man division in the town of San Fernando, Pampanga, on June 15, 1899. Don Emilio Aguinaldo, the charismatic young leader of the revolutionaries, had surrounded the town with his entire force of 7,000 men, and was determined to inflict a mortal blow on his American enemy. Aguinaldo's forces were divided into small groups spread apart at such distances that they wouldn't be discovered by the "yanqui" patrols. The plan was for each to rush the enemy outposts at exactly 3:00 A.M., enter the town from all directions, and capture the Americans. The plan was brilliant. But it didn't work. Not a single rebel unit reached its place at the appointed time. As soon as one outpost was hit, all the others were warned and were able to prepare for the surprise attack. Some rebel units didn't arrive until the fighting was over. Their individual commanders simply failed to realize the necessity of launching a simultaneous attack at the prescribed hour. Aguinaldo was not that surprised. It had happened before. This was not the first time, nor would it be the last, that "Filipino Time" had reared its ugly head.

Anyone who has ever lived or worked in the Philippines has experienced "Filipino Time." A Filipino agrees to a two o'clock appointment. He shows up at four with no excuse and no apology. Why should there be? Whether the occasion is business or social makes no difference. He has done nothing wrong. There is no insult intended. That's just the way it is. Not all Filipinos practice this but enough do to consider it a Filipino trait.

They might have gotten away with it. Wait until his feet touch the tarmac. Then shoot him. Have Captain Valerio's men storm out of the Aviation Security Command (Avsecom) van as soon as the first shot is fired. Have Captain Kavinta's team take out Galman at the same time. Good plan. But it didn't work that way. "Filipino Time" destroyed it and helped expose a conspiracy. It would be a year before a method was derived from all the madness that day. Audio recordings ultimately refuted the claim that "a lone communist gunman" by the name of Rolando Galman ran up and shot him from the rear. Sequenced photographs, along with the audio recordings, proved that Aquino was shot as he descended the stairs and that Galman was shot a few seconds later. All that happened during the first five shots. The other 23 shots were meaningless except to make more obvious the attempt at a coverup. Both Aquino and Galman had been laying on the tarmac, already shot, for 17 seconds, which is an eternity in a firefight, before the men in the Avsecom van decided to open the rear door and jump out. That 17 seconds was enough time for the photographers to overcome their panic and react to the situation. Most tape recorders were already running. They recorded those men coming out of the van, seeing Galman and Aquino lying there motionless, and pumping over 20 bullets into Galman. It was almost funny. Almost. These men were murderers.

The assassination touched off more massive demonstrations and once again the people asked Marcos to resign. There had been opposition before but nothing like this. Hundreds of thousands took to the streets, shouting and protesting. Taxi drivers in tee-shirts and businessmen in barongs marched side-by-side in the largest anti-Marcos rallies ever staged in his 19-year reign. During the rioting Marcos ordered two battalions to Manila. Soldiers patrolled the streets and citizens were frisked. Military checkpoints were set up and bars and restaurants were raided. Imelda announced a plan to arm 70,000 city workers with riot batons to control crowds and gather "community intelligence." Prosecutors were instructed to accuse youths seized in street demonstrations of "sedition" and "inciting to rebellion," charges that could carry the death penalty.[4] When 500 foreign and Filipino business leaders, attending a Chamber of Commerce conference in Manila, publicly criticized Marcos' record on human rights and his economic performance, he retaliated by ordering that 33 of the industrialists be charged with economic sabotage.[5] The situation was tense.

The State Department called the slaying a "cowardly and despicable act which the United States condemns in the strongest possible terms."[6] The Reagan administration also issued a statement, saying that it expected Marcos to bring to justice all those found to be involved, "no matter who they may be."[7] Reagan, observing the assassination aftermath, knew a potential powderkeg when he saw one. Scheduled to visit the Philippines in November, he decided to cancel his trip, citing "unexpected changes in the domestic legislative agenda" in Washington.[8] This infuriated Marcos who had almost worn out the film footage of his state visit showing Reagan praising him to the heavens and, thereby, endorsing his rule. Marcos, in a veiled threat, hinted that if the United States didn't support him in his hour of need then perhaps the Russians might—rather strange talk for a sworn anti-communist. The U.S. politely ignored that remark, having heard it before from Marcos, but it found it could no longer adhere to its Quiet Diplomacy stance after the worldwide publicity that brought even greater attention to the military and their suspected involvement. The U.S. Congress voted to cut military aid to the Philippines. Marcos' reaction to this was, by now, typical. There was no sign of retribution. Instead there was another threat to get rid of the bases and a renewed attack on "subversive elements," which primarily meant the church.

The assassination was on page one of every newspaper in the world. Every newspaper, that is, except the government owned or controlled newspapers in the Philippines. It would be the lead story on every television and radio news program in the world, except in the Philippines. Marcos could not have done the Filipino people and the world a bigger favor. The lack of a story was greater news than the story itself. It also proved what every Filipino was afraid to admit—that acts in the defiance of tyranny were no longer part of his psyche.

Steinberg had written about Marcos in 1982, "Sacrifice has been mocked. The consistency of General Artemio Ricarte, who refused to surrender at the turn of the century, and the martyrdom of Chief Justice Jose Abad Santos by the Japanese have been cheapened by the apparently successful, pragmatic triumphs of other leaders."[9]

Ninoy Aquino returned because he wanted to help his country, and he was murdered. Why couldn't Marcos at least have recognized this as an ultimate act of patriotism by a fellow countryman? Why couldn't he dignify what happened with the respect due to a Filipino slain in the service of his country? Apparently there was only room for one hero in the Philippines. Marcos had worked long and hard to develop his hero-saviour image, and anyone that disputed it was in a lot of trouble. Aquino's death was treated the way most events were that might tarnish this image. The whole affair was ordered to be treated as a non-event.

That was a mistake, a fatal chink in the Marcos armor. A man had just been martyred—given his life in the service of this country—and it was on page 14. The insult raged inside the Filipino like the fires of Prometheus and became the catalyst for the first outright active rebellion of Marcos' rule.

CHAPTER TWENTY-EIGHT

The Non-Event

The assassination of Ninoy Aquino once again focused world attention on the Philippines. Hundreds of journalists and radio and television reporters converged from all over the world to cover his funeral. An estimated two million people lined the streets to pay their last respects. As the foreign media observed the event, they had to have recalled Marcos' remarks the previous September in Washington when he expounded on the freedom of his local press. The local radio and television stations, as well as the pro-government newspapers, had apparently been ordered to down-play the funeral. Only the brave little small-circulation anti-government newspapers gave the event full coverage. Jose Burgos and his *Malaya*, which took the place of the *We Forum* when the government closed it down, was still around; *Veritas* was backed by the Catholic Church and a few enlightened businessmen; and *Mr. & Ms.* magazine still risked repression by publishing the truth.

Ninez Cacho-Olivarez risked her job and possibly more when she wrote in her column: "Was there fair play when a crony newspaper chose to give more prominence to a tree that was felled by lightning instead of focusing on the phenomenal and massive people turnout during a funeral — the likes of which Filipinos have never experienced in their history?"[1]

She was responding to Marcos' attack on the foreign media and his claims that they didn't play fair. He had said that "they have been trying for the past dozen years to destabilize me and the government that I head, and have failed. This has angered and frustrated them to the point where they can no longer write and report about the Philippines with integrity and impartiality." He had asked them to stop serving as "the tools and lackeys of the Communists and the opposition in this country, and to start going back to the basic principles of honorable journalism—honesty, fair play, and objectivity."[2] After the assassination he displayed his own sense of honesty, fair play, and objectivity by closing another newspaper, the *Philippine Times*, on September 19, and jailing its editor, Rommell Corro, for suggesting that the military might be involved in the assassination.[3]

The reporting, or rather the lack of reporting, on the assassination resulted in a boycott of the three major pro-government dailies—the *Daily Express*, the *Bulletin Today*, and the *Times Journal*. Newspaper bonfires were held in universities and colleges all over Metro Manila as a protest against media repression. Circulation was down considerably.

Another example of what Marcos called media "objectivity" was demonstrated right after the assassination. Within days all television stations began showing a film of the government's version of the assassination. Interspliced with real film footage of Aquino's arrival at the airport was another film, complete with suspenseful music, showing an actor portraying Aquino as he descends the steps and makes his way onto the tarmac. Another actor, portraying Galman, suddenly runs up and shoots him from the rear and is gunned down himself. This film received more air time than Aquino's funeral.

Phil Bronstein, of the *San Francisco Examiner*, was sent to Manila to cover the assassination aftermath. It was his first trip to the Philippines. He provided some fresh observations about the local television: "There are always half-hour TV documentaries extolling President Ferdinand Marcos' programs. Television news is unabashedly pro-government. Charges by Marcos and government officials are given wide play, but anti-government speeches and demonstrations get little notice. Appearances by the president and his wife are often covered live, as is his birthday celebration and a pro-Marcos rally in his home area of Ilocos, while major events like the funeral of slain opposition leader Benigno Aquino are sandwiched between dozens of other short reports."[4]

Imelda was just as effusive as Marcos in her attacks on the foreign media. In a press conference held at the Manila Hotel in September following the assassination, she had called the foreign press "racist and sexist," and said "We have lost our credibility because of the media."[5] The Philippine delegation attending the Asian Inter-Parliamentary Organization in Singapore, followed up the attack in early October. "Oppressed and biased reports" and "gloomy forecasts about the future heavily contributed to the rash of violent demonstrations that threaten to wreck the Philippine economy and credibility of the government," they charged.[6] Their timing couldn't have been more perfect. The following weekend the Philippine government sent out telexes to all its foreign creditors requesting a moratorium on its principal payments. They had defaulted and the ensuing investigation would prove they had been lying to their creditors for quite a long time. They had also lost their credibility.

On October 25, the U.S. House of Representatives passed a resolution that called for full freedom of the press in Manila.[7] It isn't known whether the resolution was intended as a direct answer to the Philippine delegation in Singapore, but it was an acknowledgment that the world disagreed with them about the non-event, and that a lack of press freedom still existed.

The church viewed the assassination in a different light. Cardinal Sin said it created a miracle and that he had witnessed "The incredible transformation of a people from a nation of sheep to a nation of militants, keenly aware of their rights, clamoring insistently and vigorously for a return to democracy."[8] He met with Marcos after the assassination and proposed as "the last alternative to a bloody revolution," free elections, a free press, an independent judiciary, and a national council of government, church, opposition, and private leaders to guide the government.[9]

This wasn't the first time Sin had pushed his "national council" idea. In early 1983, Marcos, repeating a proposal he made back in 1965 at the beginning of his presidency, suggested that "all sectors in our society, especially those belonging to our various religious groups—Muslim, Catholic, Protestant, Iglesia ni Kristo, the Philippine Independent Church and other religious sects—should actually participate in the implementation of the government's socio-economic reforms." Sin responded by suggesting a ten-member Council of Reconciliation that would include three government members, three from the Catholic Church, two from the opposition political parties, and two from the private sector. Such a council, he explained, would help to solve what he saw as a "growing mutual distrust between government and the private sector." Sin's proposal was turned down. In reality, all Marcos had wanted was for the churches to endorse Imelda's KKK and thought this was a clever way to propose it.[10]

The new proposal for a national council was greeted by Marcos with about the same enthusiasm. Obviously the meeting didn't go well. Afterwards Sin, apparently piqued, commented that Marcos "is a man who believes he is the only intelligent human being in the world."[11] Shortly afterward Marcos appeared on television and warned the priests, nuns, and teachers to quit preaching what he called "hatred against Marcos" in Roman Catholic schools.[12] Such a statement from a man who had gone so far to control children's minds as to rewrite textbooks to include propaganda messages about the "Hero from the North," and who had formed a junior Kalibapi in the guise of a children's organization, the Kabataang Barangay, with one of his daughters as national chairman, reflects not a small amount of paranoia. Sin issued a denial. Church schools, he said, taught social science classes to inform young people about contemporary events so they could learn to think and cope for themselves. It was unfortunate, he said, that such events put Marcos in a bad light.[13] The church-state rift continued. Marcos was now under extreme pressure and a lot of it was due to what he thought were unwarranted attacks by the church.

CHAPTER TWENTY-NINE

Aftermath

Marcos had wanted everyone to believe that the crisis in the Philippines was the result of a series of unfortunate events, related mostly to economics, over which he and his government had no control, and which were exacerbated by the assassination. He was half right. The assassination did exacerbate the crisis, but there had been a very serious financial problem all along. Short-term credits had already begun drying up, with many international creditors asking for full payment instead of allowing a roll-over. Reserves were depleted at an alarming rate. The default would have occurred anyway.

This sent shock waves through the halls of international finance. During its investigation the International Monetary Fund found that the Central Bank had exaggerated its reserves figures by $264 million in 1981, $823 million in 1982, and $1.2 billion in 1983. It was also discovered that short-term debt had gone from $4.5 billion in May 1982 to almost $10 billion in 1983, which was 40 percent of its total debt. As a rule of thumb, the World Bank and the IMF expected short-term debt not to exceed 20 percent of overall debt.[1] Virata had been correct. The revolving credits did inflate the foreign debt figures, and for good reason.

Virata announced that foreign debt was $24.6 billion as of October 17, 1983.[2] This was quite a revelation considering the fact that early in September that figure was quoted at $18.1 billion. Two weeks later he announced it had risen to $19.1 billion.[3] And a few weeks later, it was announced to be $24.6 billion, a $6.5

billion increase in five weeks. It is ironic that, earlier in the year, the Central Bank stated in a published report that the Philippines was the only country in the world that compiled and published accurate information about its foreign debt.[4]

The moratorium requested by the government was granted, and the Bank Advisory Committee (composed of the 12 largest banks, which represented the 483 commercial banks that lend to the Philippines) decided to investigate. An economic subcommittee was sent in. That is when the fabricated international reserves was discovered.[5]

What the people suspected all along was now confirmed—the government had been lying to them. There was a renewed public outcry for Marcos' resignation. Marcos refused, claiming he had been given a mandate by the people. What the people didn't know, could not have known, at the time was that during this period, while the country was reeling from the double shock of an assassination and an economic crisis, Marcos moved to consolidate his own private wealth. He instructed Rolando Gapud to organize things and began negotiations on the purchase of hundreds of millions of dollars worth of New York real estate.

In the meantime, in order to placate the people somewhat, a commission, headed by Chief Justice Fernando, was appointed to investigate the assassination. This was expected. Marcos knew what he was doing—conduct an investigation and raise the communist spectre once again, as it was done on so many previous occasions where force and violence seemed to be out of proportion to the problem at hand. The strategy was based on at least two Filipino traits which politicians had always worked to their advantage: Filipinos have a short memory for unpleasantness, and they are forgiving by nature. The announced "investigation" was based on this short memory. The front page of local newspapers had announced numerous investigations of dastardly deeds over the past decades. And then no more was ever mentioned or reported. The Plaza Miranda bombing was a classic example. Aquino's murder was supposed to fit into this mold, and over a period of time all would be forgiven and forgotten.

Cardinal Sin was asked to serve on the Fernando commission, but he refused and publicly expressed strong doubts about the military's version of the killings. The commission had to be dissolved after a few weeks because of the public clamor that it was packed with Marcos puppets. A new commission was appointed later, headed by retired appellate court judge Corazon J. Agrava.

In October 1983 the peso was devalued by 21 percent, from ₱11 to $1 to ₱14. Business leaders and the church alike, already reeling from the assassination and the new Central Bank scandal, were now openly critical of the country's economic performance. The coconut and sugar farmers hoped that the higher peso value of their crops would generate some windfall profits to combat the current rampant inflation. It was not to be. Instead the government charged additional export taxes which took most of the windfall.[6]

After the assassination, as the public demonstrations continued, the attacks on the church were stepped up. Marcos seemed to become more and more paranoid, and blamed the church for all his problems. Now it was knock-down, drag-out and no-holds-barred. All the stops were pulled out as Marcos became determined to triumph over his nemesis.

One week before Christmas 1983, Marcos went public with captured communist documents which, according to him, pointed to the existence of a "clergy-bourgeois clique" bent on toppling the administration. This "unholy alliance" between the church and big business was made public just a few days after Sin, in his strongest attack ever on Marcos, had publicly accused him of "wanton extravagance...spending precious and borrowed dollars in an orgy of waste and ostentation here and abroad."[7] The "clique" was denied by both sides. Cardinal Sin admitted that some church and business leaders had teamed up to work together to seek national reconciliation and political reform. Marcos viewed this as some sinister plot.[8]

As the economy worsened, businessman-banker Ramon del Rosario exemplified the frustrations of the Filipino trying to deal with the harsh realities of an economic crisis, while, at the same time, reading in the pro-government newspapers that nothing was wrong. In a speech before the Philippine Economic Society in January 1984, he lashed out at government efforts to "bombard the public with optimistic pronouncements" which were in "utter disregard of realities. Some may call it 'politics of optimism;' others with rare candor, 'management by illusion;' I call it deceit," he had said.[9]

In February Imelda kicked off another of her projects to help the poor with all the fanfare of a major political rally. This one was "a program of national productivity and economic libera- tion," and called Sariling Sikap (Self Reliance). By now her neatly catchworded mammoth projects designed to eliminate all suffer- ing were considered a joke. A recent study had shown that more than 70 percent of all Filipinos still lived in poverty and could not even afford the barest of necessities, such as food, clothing, shelter, and medical care.[10]

While Marcos was in power, the population increased by 12 million, from 38 million in 1965 to about 50 million in 1983. During the same period the number of Filipinos living below the poverty line increased by 17 million, from 18 million in 1965 (48 percent of the population) to 35 million in 1983 (70 percent of the population).[11]

Income inequality worsened also. In 1980 the top 12.9 percent of the population received 22.1 percent of total income; the bottom 11 percent received 16.6 percent. The gap widened in 1981. The same top 12.9 percent now received 36.3 percent of total income, while the bottom 11 percent received only 11.4 percent.[12] By 1983 the gap was even wider. The top 12.9 percent of the population now received 45.5 percent of total income, while the bottom 11 percent received only 6.4 percent.[13]

Another cause of poverty was related to the development strategy of the country. The World Bank had commented on the fact that most developing countries have a concept of progress, which has been conditioned by their colonial past. They pattern their economy after a model of a highly industrialized society and talk about "catching up." Marcos' plans in the late 70's to set up 11 major industrial projects costing about $4 billion was a classic example of this. The benefits of such projects would have been concentrated on modern sectors of the economy, which further increased income inequality. Also, by now the Marcos pattern of investment was obvious. These projects would have been placed in the hands of cronies and mismanaged and pillaged until they were bankrupt, leaving the government with another huge debt. Luckily, most of the projects were never implemented.

Another serious flaw in Imelda's social programs was the lack of an adequate land reform program. In 1972, at the start of martial law, Marcos decreed all tenants to be owners of the rice and corn lands they worked, provided the area of that land was within carefully prescribed limits. However, that was the scope of the program—rice and corn lands—which occupied about 55 to 60 percent of total farm area but only included about 14 percent of the arable land.[14] Marcos exempted the sugar and coconut lands owned by his cronies. The large hacienda crops were excluded from the program, and the overall holding of wealth in the agricultural sector was not dramatically affected. This doomed the program from the start.[15] In addition, there was gross negligence in administering to the tenants who were recipients of the program. The government did not arrange for any credit facilities for the tenants which the landlord had previously supplied. Nor was there a marketing system to replace the previous system of the landlord. Failure to do these things guaranteed the failure of the program.[16]

Mahar Mangahas, of the Development Academy of the Philippines and former full professor at the University of the Philippines, School of Economics, was the foremost Philippine expert on social indicators. He conducted extensive research on the poor. In one of his studies he noted that the Philippine government "does not recognize any official level [of poverty] and does not use the [poverty line] concept in its development planning—either in the 1978-1982 Plan, where it was stated that the 'conquest of mass poverty becomes the immediate, fundamental goal of Philippine development (page 3),' or in the draft 1983-1987 Plan, which is rhetorically more subdued."[17] In other words, the conquest of poverty was no longer part of their development plan. Probably no one envisioned that it would get so bad since the "trickle-down" effect had worked for so long. The rich were becoming richer but they provided less and less for the poor, and the poverty got worse and worse.

In early 1984 Marcos, under increasing pressure from the World Bank and the IMF, announced that the government monopoly on sugar would be dismantled. A decree was signed which freed domestic trading from Nasutra's jurisdiction but retained export trading under it indefinitely. However, Nasutra, in a catch-22 situation, refused to purchase sugar from a farmer unless he also agreed to sell his sugar allocated for the domestic market.[18] Once again there were protests, and once again Marcos did nothing.

In March 1984, Imelda announced she would not run for reelection in the National Assembly in May. The public clamor had already forced her to resign from the Executive Committee, which had been abolished right after she resigned, leading to the suspicion that it was created as a vehicle for her to perpetuate the dynasty should anything have happened to Marcos. The irony is that all this was caused by the assassination. Ninoy Aquino, in death, had become her nemesis larger than he ever had in life.

The elections proved to be hopeful. Although there was the usual fraud, violence, and ballot-box stuffing, an independent group called NAMFREL (the National Movement for Free Elections), headed by Jose Concepcion, sent volunteers, composed mostly of priests and nuns, to observe the voting. This, plus the fact that there were more than 300 foreign media who seemed to be everywhere also observing, tended to hamper the cheating somewhat. As a result, the opposition was able to win more than a third of the 187 elected seats. (There were actually 200 seats but Marcos' constitution allowed him to appoint 13.) Although Imelda had bowed out of the race, she campaigned vigorously on behalf of the KBL ruling party, and predicted a clean sweep of all the races. When the opposition candidates won in 16 of the 21 contested seats in Metro Manila, she was reported "dumbfounded" and took to her bed.[19]

In a related development, Mahar Mangahas had conducted another survey right before the elections. The results showed the public's dislike of certain government programs which they perceived as ineffective in promoting general economic welfare. Imelda's programs were at the top of the list. Mangahas suddenly left the DAP in July. No reason was given for his departure.[20]

During this period General Ver and the others suspected of being involved in the conspiracy to assassinate Aquino were giving testimony to the Agrava Commission. They were anything but repentant and consistently perjured themselves with impunity. As if to underscore the previous findings of Amnesty International, initially no witnesses wanted to testify about the shooting, fearing reprisals or being killed when taken into custody. There were more than 100 arriving passengers on the China Airlines flight that arrived with Aquino. On board and on the ground was the China Airlines crew. There were 1,200 security and military personnel at the airport, including at least 70 in the immediate area and 20,000 more people in the terminal and beyond. Yet, for more than six months, only the military would admit to seeing anyone shoot Aquino. They all insisted it was Galman, and at least four persons who could give evidence about Galman disappeared during the investigation—his common-law wife, his girlfriend, his girlfriend's sister, and a friend of the sister.[21] The only witness who claimed to have witnessed the shooting, and said it was the military, was Kiyoshi Wakamiya, a free-lance Japanese photographer who was on the plane with Aquino. However, he was deported as an undesirable alien and was unavailable for testimony. There were other, more subtle, forms of intimidation. Eduardo Cojuangco and General Ver filed a ₱220 million ($12.2 million) suit against *Panorama* magazine for printing an interview with Lupino Lazaro, the lawyer of Galman. In the interview, Lazaro intimated that both may have been involved in the assassination.

Virata, when asked in June 1984 how long did he think the crisis would last, replied, "Well, I do not know what they mean by crisis...They [the people] never had it so good."[22] Such absurd pronouncements, even from the Prime Minister, were now commonplace, and only added fuel to a very volatile situation. The church kept up its assault on the Marcos regime.

Cardinal Sin, in the United States about this time to receive an honorary degree from Brandeis University, warned, "Our vigilance is all the more necessary since those who will design economic policies devoid of social justice and go about militarizing government machineries behind the facade of law and order, are individuals whose outward demeanor and motives are just as rational and neighborly as the dutiful Mr. Eichmann."[23] (Eichmann was one of Hitler's more famous subalterns who was tried and executed for killing Jews.)

Marcos reciprocated. On July 19, 1984, a military court charged Father Jose Dizon, a Roman Catholic priest, and five others with subversion. They had been arrested on June 28 when his house in Metro Manila was raided. The military alleged that it was a "distribution center for subversive publications." Dizon's house was the headquarters of the National Alliance for Justice, Freedom and Democracy, whose chairman was the former Senator Lorenzo Tañada, 86, the "Grand Old Man of Philippine Opposition." Thus Dizon and the five began the same ordeal that Brian Gore and his colleagues had undergone.[24]

The church countered. In a pastoral letter read in masses all over the country on July 15, Cardinal Sin urged the abolition of "all authoritarian decrees and powers," amnesty for political prisoners, and an end to the feared summary killings of suspected criminals. This last reference was in reaction to a rash of killings of suspected holdup men and other criminals by a special police force known as the "secret marshals," which Marcos had used once before in 1982 and had reinstated.[25]

Marcos, in a speech to the Philippine Association of Judges in August, told them to work hard for an "independent, vibrant, strong, and dynamic judiciary," as the failure of the judiciary would mean failure of the entire concept of democratic government.[26] The year before, he had implemented the Judiciary Reorganization Act. Under it, all existing courts, except the Supreme Court, were abolished and their judges ceased holding office. They were replaced by new courts with different names but substantially the same duties. All the new judges were Marcos appointees.[27]

The attack continued. In August more "captured communist documents" were disclosed, citing numerous allegations of infiltration by the communists of religious-based institutions, and reported instances of priests and nuns joining the Communist Party of the Philippines and the New People's Army "...confirm-

ing the extensive efforts of the CPP to infiltrate the religious
sector." It noted that "some churches and parishes," particularly
those in the country side, have become "subservient to communist
activities." The documents named the AMRSP, Task Force
Detainees, the National Secretariat for Social Action, Christians
for National Liberation, and the Katipunan ng Kristohanang
Katlinagban (the church's Basic Christian Communities). There
had been a marked increase in human rights abuses, including
murder and torture, with the finger pointed mainly at the
military. Needless to say, all these groups had been actively
critical of the government in these areas.[28]

On August 17, the Supreme Court denied the petition of
Renato Cañete. Cañete, a 19-year-old farmhand, had been
arrested on April 3, 1982, and a Presidential Commitment Order
was issued April 21, 18 days later, against him for subversion,
illegal possession of firearms, and illegal possession of subversive
documents. The first two charges were dropped. On February 25,
1983, the trial court dismissed the case for insufficient evidence on
the final charge and ordered Cañete's release. The military refused
to honor the order. The reason given was that only the president
could order his release since he was detained by a PCO. A petition
for writ of habeas corpus was filed. The military, through the
Solicitor General, gave the same reason. The Supreme Court then
dismissed the petition for being "moot and academic" since he had
already been released by then. Justice Teehankee dissented. He
noted that, under a PCO, "A person can still be detained
indefinitely without judicial recourse, contrary to the basic
precepts of human rights and freedom." He urged that the court
rule squarely that a PCO cannot prevail against a judicial order of
acquittal. The court would not. Marcos' absolute powers were still
alive and well two years after the reported demise of martial law
and two months after so-called democratic elections.[29]

A year after the assassination, on August 21, a crowd
estimated at 500,000 gathered at Luneta Grandstand and Rizal
Park in Manila to celebrate the first anniversary of Aquino's
death. Most wore yellow tee-shirts, scarves, or dresses, which had
been the unofficial color of the Aquino supporters since the
assassination. The demonstrations were orderly and peaceful in

response to Cardinal Sin's plea for a non-violent demonstration. This demonstration, more than any since Aquino's death, demonstrated how deep-rooted was the faith of the Filipino and how persuasive the influence of faith can be in maintaining the sobriety of the people in such difficult times. This demonstration would reap huge rewards, and another miracle, in due time.

Sometime in November 1984, Marcos had to undergo another kidney transplant because he had rejected the first one implanted in August 1983. Another American doctor was flown in to perform the surgery. Rumors were passed around once again about his failing health and, once again, the palace vehemently denied them. In December a photograph of Marcos was released which showed him holding his shirt up to dispel the rumors. This proved nothing, of course, since the scarring could have been below the belt line. However, the palace continued to brand as "preposterous" all rumors of his health and his operations. It was apparent that Marcos did not like such talk.[30]

Government corruption appeared to increase in 1985. A World Bank Report, released in September 1984, was made public. It stated that $3.1 billion of an unspecified amount of foreign loans contracted from 1978-1982 failed to reach its supposed beneficiaries.[31] Also, a preliminary congressional report found that more than $100 million in American military assistance to the Philippines had been wastefully spent and that the United States was limited in tracing the funds or influencing how they were used.[32] In addition, USAID officials also reported that Philippine officials took an $18 million U.S. grant earmarked for building typhoon-resistant schools and invested it in a money market instead.[33] It had already stopped giving financial assistance to the National Electrical Administration after an audit discovered that the NEA padded a $1.45 million disaster relief fund for the rehabilitation of typhoon-wrecked electric power lines. They had submitted false vouchers and other documents amounting to $108,441.[34] Finally, the IMF delayed payment on the third installment of its loan, totalling $113 million scheduled for September 1985, because Marcos had not fulfilled his agreement to institute substantial reforms, particularly in tax collection procedures, budget, and agriculture.[35]

It appeared that, as the economic crisis worsened, more dollars were being misappropriated or disappearing at an alarming rate. Later, it would be discovered that during his last 90 days in office, Marcos transferred $100 million from the government to private Swiss bank accounts.

In October the Agrava Commission released two final reports of its assassination investigation. Both rejected the claim of Marcos and the military that Ninoy was killed by a lone gunman and alleged communist, Rolando Galman, who was also gunned down shortly after Ninoy was shot. Both reports stated that he was shot by one of his military escorts as he descended the stairs, but did not state which one. The reason for two reports was that Corazon Agrava, the head of the five-man investigation panel, disagreed with the other four members on several points. Since there could be no reconciliation, two reports were rendered—hers and the report of the other four. Judge Agrava and Marcos had been classmates at the University of the Philippines Law School. She had graduated in 1938; he in 1939.

Judge Agrava's report specifically stated that General Ver was not implicated in the assassination, and named only seven persons, which included the chief of the Aviation Security Command, who was in charge of airport security, the five-man escort party, and one eye-witness.

The majority report found 26 suspects to be "indictable for the premeditated killing of former Senator Aquino and Rolando Galman."[36] Their report named the following: General Fabian Ver; Major General Prospero Olivas, Chief of Staff of the PC Metropolitan Police Command (Metrocom); Brigadier General Luther Custodio, chief of the Aviation Security Command (Avsecom), who was in charge of security at the airport when Aquino arrived; Colonel Arturo Custodio, who picked up Galman at his house on August 17, six days before the assassination; Colonel Vicente Tigas, PC Press Relations Officer, who was in charge of the 14 journalists who were invited to the airport to cover Aquino's arrival, but prevented them from observing the shooting; Captain Felipe Valerio, who was in charge of the four SWAT teams deployed around the airplane, was also leader of the Alpha SWAT team, and was sitting in the front seat of the Avsecom van that was parked at the foot of the stairs when the assassination occurred; Captain Llewelyn Kavinta, leader of the Delta SWAT team, who was supposed to secure the area in front of the plane; Captain Romeo Bautista, who was in charge of security at the airbridge and tunnel which led from the plane to the airline terminal; Second Lieutenant Jesus Castro, aide-de-camp to General Custodio, and in charge of the escort party which boarded the plane and arrested Aquino; the escort party, which included Tech Sergeant Claro Lat (who was on Aquino's right going down the stairs), Sergeant Arnulfa de Mesa (who was to the immediate left rear of Aquino going down the stairs), Constabularyman First Class Regelio Moreno (who was behind Aquino going down the stairs), Tech Sergeant Filomeno Miranda (who was behind Moreno going down the stairs); Sergeant Armando dela Cruz, who was positioned at the top of the stairs, and was filmed looking down the stairs as the five shots were fired, but denied seeing anything (he was the eye-witness indicted by Judge Agrava); Staff Sergeant Pedrito Torio, who was on the tarmac but claimed he only fired a warning shot; Sergeant Prospero Bona and Airman First Class Aniceto Acupidio, who were with the security detail at the airbridge (the airbridge extended from the tunnel to the aircraft); Sergeants Pablo Martinez, Tomaz Fernandez, and Leonardo Mojica, who were on the tarmac in the area of the shooting; civilian Hermilio Gosuico, who was with Colonel Custodio when Galman was picked up; and the soldiers of Alpha SWAT team who alighted from the Avsecom van, allegedly to shoot Galman after he supposedly shot Aquino (they fired the second volley of 23 shots, mostly at Galman), who included Staff Sergeant Ernesto Mateo, Sergeant Rolando de Guzman, Airman First Class Cordova Estelo, and Tech Sergeant Rodolfo Desolong. Audio and video recordings proved that they did not alight and begin firing until 17 seconds after everything was over and Galman was already lying on the tarmac. As soon as the report was submitted, General Ver took a leave of absence.

Based on the findings of the commission, Criminal Case Nos. 10010 and 10011 were filed on January 23, 1985. There was a trial, or rather a semblance of one, that began on February 22.

Rulings by the three-man panel of judges seemed to reinforce that view. The judges considered the Agrava Commission's photo-chronology findings as "ballyhooed;" and new evidence regarding the statements of several U.S. Air Force personnel, on duty that Sunday at two jointly-manned air force installations, that two Philippine Air Force jets were scrambled to find Aquino's plane, was ruled inadmissible. The whole affair appeared to be stage-managed and everyone knew who the director was. There were more demonstrations and more demands for Marcos' resignation. Once again he refused, claiming he had been given a mandate by the people. President Reagan was concerned enough about the unrest to send Senator Paul Laxalt to Manila in October. The pro-Marcos newspapers seemed to reflect the building tension between Marcos and the U.S. "Good Riddance," stated one of the headlines when Laxalt departed.[37]

On November 1, 1985, the body of Doctor Potenciano Baccay was found with 19 stab wounds. Five men had broken into his house around ten o'clock the previous evening, and waited two hours for him to come home. They then took a microwave oven, a Betamax video recorder, some rubber shoes, and cash, and left with Baccay in his van. The van was found sixteen hours later with Baccay inside, along with the items that were stolen.

Baccay had been a personal physician of Marcos and vice-president of the Kidney Foundation of the Philippines. Before he died, it was learned, Baccay had revealed to journalists of the *Pittsburgh Press* in the U.S. that Marcos had had kidney transplants in August 1983 and November 1984. The Manila police caught the alleged killers a short time later and claimed it was a simple matter of robbery and killing. The palace once again vehemently denied there was a connection to the killing and Marcos' health.[38]

On November 3, Marcos, being interviewed live on U.S. television, announced that there would be a snap presidential election. His term didn't expire until 1987, but he was prepared to have an early election to settle what he called the "silly claim" that his government was inept. He first announced it would be held on January 17, but later changed it to February 7.[39] Perhaps it was just that a wizened old politico like Marcos probably felt that some gesture might be in order, something to placate the people until things cooled down; or perhaps the announcement was designed to take the sting out of the next announcement. On December 2, all those on trial for the murder of Aquino were found not guilty and Ver was immediately reinstated. There were howls of protest and more demonstrations.

On December 3, Corazon Aquino, Ninoy's widow, announced her candidacy for president in the upcoming election. Marcos probably could not have been happier. He had watched as the various opposition candidates jockeyed for position. They were a sad lot—disorganized, unfinanced, and demoralized—and now they had chosen a woman to run against him. Marcos pulled out all the stops.' He knew how to "run" an election—whom to bribe, whom to promise, whom to threaten.

He was totally confident and more than a little arrogant. Despite Namfrel, the foreign media, and hundreds of official foreign observers, Marcos proceeded with his plan. Over the next two-months he pumped about ₱10 billion ($500 million) into his campaign, most of it going to pay off the voters. Most of this money was newly printed by the Central Bank. In addition, many of the notes bore the same serial number. This wasn't a new trick. He had used it in every election and, in fact, he had bankrupted the economy once before using the same tactic.

In the 1969 presidential election Marcos spent more than ₱1 billion ($250 million) on his campaign. The overspending brought about a severe liquidity crisis, which was overcome by borrowing abroad, short-term, at high interest rates. The interest commitments increased. The loans reached maturity. Foreign exchange resources were scarce. Repayment schedules became difficult. Then the Central Bank couldn't meet its foreign exchange requirements for its capital goods importations. Finally the government had no other recourse. It had to negotiate for the roll-over of its maturing obligations and seek stabilization loans. Thus, in 1970, the IMF agreed to extend $27.5 million in credit, subject to the condition that it allow the peso to float free. It was devalued on February 21, 1970. So Marcos had bankrupted his country once before, but this time the amount—$500 million—was unprecedented. So was the fraud and violence.[40]

The elections were held on February 7. On Saturday night, February 15, the National Assembly finished its official tally and announced Marcos the winner. While this was going on, the foreign media were reporting to the world of the incredible fraud being perpetrated on the Filipino people. Apparently they got the message. Only the Soviet Union sent Marcos a message of congratulations. Defying Marcos' claim and proclaiming herself the people's choice, Cory announced that a "People's Victory" rally would be held the next day, on February 16.

Field Marshall Douglas MacArthur (that was his rank as head of the Philippine armed forces) used to pace the balcony of his palatial residence on the top floor of the old Manila Hotel at sunset in 1941 while looking out on beautiful Manila Bay with Corregidor in the distance. The same view today is still just as breathtaking. A slight turn to the left reveals the old Army-Navy Club still there just as busy as it was in pre-war days, and the old Governor General's residence, now the American Embassy, can be seen just beyond the club. Directly below is the Luneta Grandstand with Rizal Park across the street to the left where Jose Rizal fell before a firing squad on December 30, 1896. The Luneta and Rizal Park were full on August 21, 1984, when the people came to pay their respects to another fallen hero. There had been a massive outpouring, all peaceful, of love and support for Ninoy Aquino and what he stood for. Now, on a Sunday afternoon, February 16, 1986, there was another gathering. Only this time the crowd was bigger. A vast sea of yellow overflowed the Luneta and Rizal Park, and extended past the Army-Navy Club and beyond the American Embassy. Cory, flanked by members of the church, delivered her message: The elections were over and the people had chosen her, not Marcos. Now it was up to the people to see that justice prevailed. Marcos must step down. No one who was there will ever forget the people's response. A crowd, estimated at between 500,000 and 1 million began shouting CORY! CORY! CORY! The pro-government newspapers down-played it the next day as usual. Marcos matter of factly stated that there was always a lot of people in the park on Sunday out for a stroll.

The following week several measures were implemented to

demonstrate to Marcos the people weren't conceding defeat. There was a boycott of all the crony-owned banks and all the crony-owned media; the delayed payment of water and electric bills was urged; and, certainly the most painful of all measures to prove their mettle, all Filipinos were urged to boycott all products of San Miguel Corporation, the maker of San Miguel beer. In addition, a nightly noise barrage reminiscent of Aquino's LABAN chant on election eve of 1978, and a national work stoppage on February 26, was called for.

President Reagan's trouble-shooting envoy, Philip Habib, arrived on February 17 to try and defuse a tense situation made worse by Reagan's comments after the election that there had been cheating on both sides. He met with Cory and her vice-president, Salvadore Laurel, and asked if they would consider working with Marcos if he agreed to make reforms and step down after a fixed period of time. Cory flatly rejected the idea. Habib also met with Marcos that day. Marcos presented proof of voter fraud and violence by the opposition. Apparently the proof wasn't convincing enough. On February 19, the U.S. Senate passed a resolution condemning the election. The lines were drawn. On one side was a dictator known for his ruthlessness; on the other, a housewife known only for her God-fearing iron-willed spirit.

At first Marcos offered a few conciliatory gestures but they were all flatly rejected. By then everybody knew how credible such gestures were. Then he threatened force. That didn't work either. The boycotts and other measures were beginning to take their toll. A state of anarchy was fast approaching. A bloody revolution loomed as a very real possibility. Habib continued to meet with both sides but to no avail. He had breakfast with Enrile on Saturday morning, February 22, before he departed. At that time, according to Habib, "We were not surprised but did not know exactly what would happen that day."[41]

CHAPTER THIRTY

Contrition

The military establishment during martial law seemed to represent the forces of evil, a huge black monolith reaping misery, violence, and death. "The military" was responsible for the human rights abuses. "The military" shot Aquino. That was their image and they had to live with it. Or did they?

There were some young military officers who were very aware of the lack of professionalism in the armed forces and scorned what General Ver, their Chief of Staff, stood for. They knew that the integrity of the whole military establishment had been brought into question because of the acts of a few unprincipled elements; that the oppressive and criminal acts of a few soldiers had brought discredit to the entire corp of the professional soldier; that they bore the brunt of the derision caused by a few; and that their patriotism and loyalty to their flag and country meant nothing anymore.

They knew about the graft and corruption and that Ver was behind most of it. In addition, Ver had allowed all officers who were Marcos loyalists to remain on active duty and the armed forces became top-heavy with aging colonels and generals long due for retirement. The military had, over the years, become nothing more than a huge warlord army headed by Marcos and Ver. That was the situation. Any soldier who didn't like the way things were could jeopardize not only his career but his life as well by complaining. Despite the threatening circumstances dissension in the ranks continued to grow. The young officers began to talk among themselves of how it should be, how it could be, how it must be. The reform movement was born.

The first signs of dissatisfaction emerged on February 17, 1985, at a Philippine Military Academy homecoming when some of the alumni issued a manifesto critical of the military establishment and corruption in the ranks. On March 15, eighty officers issued a statement calling for higher standards, better training, and loyalty not to one man but the Constitution.[1] On March 21 at PMA graduation rites, 300 alumni hoisted a banner that proclaimed "Unity Through Reforms," and sported "We Belong" tee-shirts.[2] For the first time the names of the leaders became known: Lietenant Colonel Gregorio Honasan and Vic Batac, Navy Captain Rex Robles, Colonels Eugene Ocampo, Hector Tarrazona, and Red Kapunan, and Captain Felix Turingan.[3] Others would become known later: Lieutenant Colonel Babao Flores, Major Napoleon de los Santos, Captain Alejandrino, and First Lieutenants Tadeo, Abello and Catapang.[4] By February 7 they had grown to about 1,200 and had picked up some unlikely support along the way.[5]

Marcos was well aware of the reform movement. It had come under increasing scrutiny by Ver's intelligence organizations. On election day Captain Robles, one of Enrile's assistants, was called in for questioning and informed that he and all of the reformists would be arrested if they didn't cease their troublemaking.[6] However, unbeknownst to them, secret plans were already being drawn up for their arrest.[7] As conditions worsened over the next two weeks while Cory implemented her boycott and other measures, Marcos plotted his own counter-measures. Orders were drawn up. Beginning Saturday, February 22, Cory, her advisers, members of the reform movement, church leaders (including Cardinal Sin), civic leaders, and opposition leaders were to be arrested. The final total came to over 10,000. Ver also ordered some soldiers to prepare the barren Islas de Caballos (Island of Horses) near Corregidor, the site of Fort Hughes during World War II, as the place of detention.[8] In addition, he planned to close down all opposition newspapers the following Monday, including the *Daily Inquirer, Malaya, We Forum, Veritas, Mr. & Ms., New Manila Times, Business Day* and *Free Press.*[9] Afterwards, Marcos thought, a peaceful inauguration could be held.

Enrile had known for quite some time that his political star was in eclipse. Ver had gradually usurped his powers, Imelda had begun to give him the cold-shoulder treatment, and Marcos had isolated him from any important military function. As if to be certain he got the message, Marcos publicly announced in his speech on August 8, 1983, at the PC (Philippine Constabulary) Day celebration at Camp Crame that the Minister of Defense was no longer in the chain of command of the Armed Forces of the Phillippines. General Ver, as Chief of Staff, was now at the head of that chain and reported directly to the Commander-in-Chief.[10] When Ninoy was assassinated the following August 21, Enrile was never accused or implicated because everyone knew he no longer had any power. He had tried to resign afterward but Marcos wouldn't accept, preferring to keep him in limbo. He knew he was no longer trusted and that Ver was having him watched. As the election neared, several events transpired that foretold his imminent departure from the inner circle. Marcos called him to the palace and warned him that the NPA were out to assassinate him. Then in February a meeting of the top military brass was held at the palace. Enrile had not been invited.[11] It was one more sign of his fall from grace. After the elections all cabinet members tendered their resignations as a formality so that Marcos could start with a fresh mandate. It was obvious that Enrile's would be accepted, if he survived that long. Despite all this, he appeared to remain loyal and delivered his province's tainted and stuffed ballot boxes to Marcos. Appearances can be deceiving, however.

Enrile had taken up the cause of the reformists and supported them all along. Most were members of his staff. Honasan, the leader, was his intelligence chief. In April 1985, he and General Ramos persuaded Marcos to meet with them to air their grievances. Marcos listened but nothing productive came out of the meeting. That was unfortunate. The reformists then approached Enrile and suggested a coup. It only took him a week to decide. From then on the recruiting and planning was in earnest. The date was set for Christmas or New Years Day. Then in November Marcos announced the snap elections so the coup was put on hold. Marcos was declared the winner on Saturday,

February 15, and the people reacted. The following Friday,
February 21, at midnight the plotters met at Enrile's house. It was
decided that the time had come. The go signal was given. At 2:00
o'clock early Sunday morning the Palace would be assaulted and
Marcos and Imelda either killed or captured. Enrile would then go
on the air and declare himself head of the new government, called
the "National Reconciliation Council." The implementation included three battalions of rebels, participation by the air force,
navy, and marines, and involved blowing up the building in which
Ver slept. It was a good plan, but like a chain that is only as strong
as its weakest link, it had a fatal flaw. His name was Major Edgardo Doromal. He had been approached to join the coup. He was in
charge of perimeter security at the Palace so his participation was
critical. At first he refused; then he agreed. Then, in January, the
pressure apparently became too much. He broke down and exposed the coup. Ver asked him to become a double agent. The planning continued but now Ver and Marcos were kept appraised, and
drew up their own plans.

After the midnight meeting on Friday, a pre-dawn recon-
naissance revealed that another battalion of marines had been
added to the Palace gates. Malacañang had been turned into a
fortress. At two o-clock that same morning, 15 security guards
were arrested at Fort Bonifacio.[12] It was obvious that something
was awry. The coup had somehow been compromised. Frantic
messages were sent out to stop the Sunday attack.

Later that morning, after breakfasting with Habib, Enrile
was in the Atrium coffee shop in Makati when Roberto Ongpin,
Marcos' trade and industry minister, called and asked why some
of his security personnel had been arrested. Enrile called his
ministry to find out what was going on, and went home for lunch.
While there, he was contacted by Honasan and informed of
events. The coup was off. Now it became a matter of survival.
Enrile knew that it was only a matter of time before he and the
reform movement leaders were arrested. He made his decision in-
stantly. He then called General Ramos and asked him to join
them. Ramos did not hesitate either, answering "I am with you all
the way." The word was passed and those who could made their
way to the Defense Ministry at Camp Aguinaldo on E. Delos

Santos Avenue. At seven that evening they called in the press and within minutes the world knew that Enrile and Ramos and a small band of troops had revolted.[13] No mention was made of a coup. A Death Watch was begun, for it was a foregone conclusion that the gesture was futile with little hope of success. Even Enrile spoke of it as his "act of contrition," a final gesture of goodness. The last rites were given to this motley band. They made peace with their God. Now they were ready to settle with Marcos.

In military parlance the pucker factor was '10.' There were about 200 defenders in the camp when Enrile arrived. This would grow to a little under 400 during the night and Camp Crame, directly across the street, was also occupied. Marcos and Ver had not planned for this contingency but they obviously had the upper hand, and about 260,000 troops. The press were bandying about words like "futility" and "stupidity." "Bravery" wasn't mentioned much. Still they continued to work their field radios into the night, calling on commanders to support their cause. The pace was frantic. No one wanted to even think about how much time they had left.

One of the books Enrile had brought with him to the siege was Sun Tzu's *The Art of War*. Written 2,500 years ago, his strategic concepts still apply today. Enrile had very little going for him and may have recalled some of those lessons.

> The art of war is of vital importance to the State. It is a matter of life and death, a road to either safety or to ruin.

> If you know your enemy and you know yourself, your victory will not stand in doubt; if you know Heaven and Earth, you may make your victory complete.

> Soldiers, when in desperate straits lose the sense of fear. If there is no place of refuge, they will stand firm. If they are in the heart of a hostile country they will show a stubborn front. If there is no help for it they will fight hard.

At least one of those concepts was in his favor. As one of the architects of martial law and a close confidant for more than a decade, he knew his enemy. He knew how cunning and clever Marcos could be, and he knew one thing for certain. Marcos was utterly ruthless and could not be trusted. Any agreement with him was out of the question. The die was cast. It was him or Marcos.

Cory was in Cebu in the southern Philippines, attending a workshop on planned civil disobedience on Friday night, February 21. The next day she received word of Enrile's defection. Her aides advised her to go into hiding as a precaution. She chose the Carmelite Convent. There she could seek spiritual guidance while awaiting the outcome of this strange new twist in their struggle. Was her husband's jailer really turning against Marcos? She telephoned him that night. Yes, it was all true. What could she do? "Just pray for us," Enrile replied.

Marcos held a press conference later that evening. In an attempt to regain the initiative, he accused Ramos and Enrile of treason and of attempting to assassinate him and his wife, Imelda, as part of a coup d'état. He warned Enrile and Ramos, "You are vulnerable to artillery and tank attacks," but added, "I would rather talk about it than shoot each other."[14] Enrile and Ramos quickly made it quite clear that there was no assassination attempt and no planned attack on the palace. Most importantly, they emphasized that their revolt was not a military coup d'état. They recognized Cory as the duly elected President of the Philippines and demanded the resignation of Marcos.

In those first moments of revolt there was a lot of jostling for position, each adversary feeling the other out. Marcos sent Colonel Rolando Abadilla to the camp to ask Enrile to call him. He refused. "It's too late," he replied. Abadilla delivered the message and came back again. Marcos still wanted Enrile to call him. He again refused but agreed to talk to Ver. Their telephone conversation was testy. Enrile accused him of planning to arrest himself and the members of the reform movement. Ver vehemently denied it. Finally Ver agreed that he wouldn't attack Camp Aguinaldo in exchange for a promise that Malacañang would not be attacked. They agreed to talk again after daybreak Sunday.[15]

About the same time Ver was giving his solemn word not to attack, General Fidel Singson, Ver's chief of military intelligence, was already on the way to Camp Aguinaldo with 60 marines. He had orders to blow up Enrile's helicopter which might be used for escape, and then proceed to Radio Veritas and destroy its transmitters. He arrived at Aguinaldo and worked his men to within 200 yards of the objective, but he couldn't help but observe all those people arriving at the gate. He and his officers were uneasy and perplexed. These people were not their enemy. He called for more men as a delaying tactic.[16]

Marcos controlled the airways almost totally during the election. As a result, it was difficult to obtain accurate information about the returns. The only reliable radio station was Radio Veritas, owned and operated by the church. It was considered a minor bother by Marcos and was generally left alone. Agapito "Butz" Aquino, brother of Ninoy, was at a party when he heard of the revolt over this station. He excused himself and left for Camp Aguinaldo. There he found Enrile and asked what he could do. "Tell the people to come and support us," Enrile replied. Butz went on the air at Radio Veritas at eleven o'clock that evening and asked for the people's support. In particular, he asked members of his political action groups— ATOM (August Twenty-One Movement) and BANDILA (an acronym meaning flag in Tagalog)—to assemble immediately. At midnight, he led 10,000 people down E. de los Santos Avenue chanting "CORY! CORY! CORY!" They were the first. Later on that night Cardinal Sin came on the radio. "Our two good friends have shown their idealism. I would be very happy if you could support them now," he appealed. And they responded. They came to the camp—and stayed—and their ranks grew—to fifty thousand, then a hundred thousand, and then a million.

Marcos held another televised press conference early Sunday morning. This one was vintage Marcos—perfectly stage-managed. With all his loyalist generals seated behind him, he presented "proof" of the assassination and coup attempt. Several army officers were brought out and their confessions read describing the planned attack on Malacañang. Four aides of Enrile, all members of the reform movement. were named as the leaders. Marcos now took a different tack. Stating that the revolt led by Enrile and Ramos was not part of the coup attempt, he implied that the blame would be placed on the young officers if Enrile and Ramos surrendered.[17] No one surrendered.

Brigadier General Artemio Tadiar was the commanding general of Marcos' marines. On Sunday morning his tanks came rumbling down the wide boulevard. They came closer and closer and then had to stop. They would have to kill a lot of people—innocent men, women and children—to get to the camps. The people rushed to meet them with flowers and food and rosaries. There seemed to be priests and nuns everywhere. The marines, dressed in full combat gear, ordered them out of the way. The people stood their ground. Their prayers grew louder. What manner of warfare was this? There were threats, then pleading, but no one gave way. The marines finally boarded their tanks, turned back, and drove away. The people had won their first victory.[18]

Sunday evening the State Department cabled Ambassador Stephen Bosworth at the U.S. Embassy in Manila with a message for Marcos, which was passed on immediately. It was an appeal not to use force to remain in power.[19] At the same time Bosworth alerted Brigadier General Teddy Allen, of the Joint U.S. Military Assistance Group (JUSMAG), Philippines, to begin preparations for a possible evacuation of Marcos and his family.

Marcos called Enrile the same evening, and Enrile finally agreed to speak to him. Marcos implored, "We'd better settle this problem. Tell your boys I have no intention of punishing them. We'll go through a pro forma investigation and trial and if they're convicted I'll pardon them." Enrile replied that he would talk to his men and get back to him. He knew Marcos too well, knew his cunning and treacherous ways better than anyone. He didn't call him back but did send a message through intermediaries—the troops had refused and they wanted Marcos to step down.[20]

Radio Veritas continued to broadcast news of the revolt all day Sunday. About six o'clock that evening it was attacked and the transmitter blown up. The people no longer had their vital communications link. Father James Reuter, head of Radio Veritas, immediately went into action. He needed another radio station and ultimately settled on DZRJ in Sta. Mesa, not far from Malacañang Palace. He then called a friend who had helped broadcast the results on Radio Veritas during the election to see if she could help out again.

June Keithley had been an amateur actress and appeared on various radio and television programs before she got her big break as a hostess on a televised children's show. Now she was thrust into the role of her life that would earn her a presidential Legion of Honor. She had spent the previous night and day at the barricades. So, with little sleep and plenty of apprehension, she began broadcasting on "Radio Bandido" at 11:45 that evening, playing an old record, "Mambo Magsaysay," which had been a theme song for another president in another era and was now identified with Radio Veritas, hoping that the people would recognize it and tune in to the new station. She was well aware of the reprisals if the station were located as it was the only communications link with the opposition. Her only security was the nuns who sat on the stairs and refused to let anyone pass that they didn't recognize. She would continue to broadcast for the next 11 hours — "the longest night" of her life, she would later exclaim.[21]

Marcos came back on television just after midnight Sunday. He had apparently received Enrile's message. He was furious, pounding the table and blaming Enrile for trying to grab power for himself. "They say that [I should step down] one more time and I'll send the tanks and artillery on them," he warned, and swore he would never resign or leave the country.[22]

General Singson's reinforcements had arrived during the night on Saturday but he still delayed his attack. All day Sunday and into the night they watched and waited. The crowd outside the camp continued to grow. Finally he called a pre-dawn meeting on Monday and gave his officers three minutes to "search their own consciences," but refused to express his own view. A vote was called. It was almost unanimous. They sent word into Camp Crame that they were coming in, and 160 men climbed over the walls and defected.[23]

Enrile and Ramos had evacuated Camp Aguinaldo on Sunday in preparation for General Tadiar's attack that had fizzled. Now they were all concentrated in Camp Crame and preparing for another attack which Radio Veritas had reported was coming. Before dawn the 3rd and 5th Marine Battalions and the 4th Marine Provisional Brigade occupied Aguinaldo by coming in the back door via the Logistics Command compound. They set up their mortars and recoilless rifles, and trained them on Camp Crame. Despite several orders to fire their commander, Colonel Braulio Balbas, delayed at first and then refused outright.

Around 6:00 A.M. the defenders at Camp Crame cocked their ears. A far-off sound was heard that gradually grew louder, and it wasn't the lumbering noise of tanks. It was the distinct thump that helicopters make as their rotors slice the air. Then they saw them, in formation—three, four, five Sikorsky gun-ships— circling overhead.   The silence on the ground was deafening. Dry mouths hung open and clammy hands gripped weapons as the choppers peeled off and came in low over the trees...and landed. Colonel Antonio Sotelo, commanding officer, Tactical Operations Group, 15th Strike Wing, had defected along with his men. There was pandemonium as soldiers laughed and cried and hugged each other. In addition to the five gunships, two rescue choppers and one utility chopper defected.[24]

Then another shock came. Around 7:00 A.M. Radio Veritas broadcast that Marcos had left Malacañang and was on his way out of the country. The crowd went wild, screaming, hollering, and honking horns. Some observers claim they saw Enrile with his head bowed and tears streaming down his cheeks. It was only the second time anyone had ever seen him cry in public. The first time was when he had seen Ninoy Aquino's body in the morgue after the assassination. Things had changed somewhat since then. Now here he was prepared to die for the lady who had refused to allow him to attend Aquino's funeral. At least he had tried. Nobody else in Marcos' Cabinet had.

The celebration was short-lived when it was discovered to be a hoax. Marcos came on television at nine-thirty that morning with his family to prove he was still there in the palace. He announced that he was still taking his oath the next day as planned, and that the policy of "maximum tolerance" was over. No one who viewed this scene will ever forget Ver, in full combat gear, pleading with Marcos to let him use his artillery and air power to attack Camp Crame. When Marcos ordered him to use only small arms fire, he was visibly upset. There had always been whispered rumors of Ver being a killer, but no one expected to witness such a spectacle on nation-wide television. A few minutes before ten o'clock the television screen went blank. An hour later a chopper flew over the palace, fired off six rockets, and departed. They exploded in Imelda's room, the palace garden, and the parking lot. Six people suffered minor injuries. If they had not thought about it before, those inside probably finally realized that an attack on the palace was a very real possibility. One can only wonder what that small act of defiance did to anyone inside the palace with a fertile imagination.[25]

After the Radio Veritas transmitter was blown up it was decided that two could play that game. On Monday morning at 9:00 A.M. the government's Maharlika Broadcasting System complex in Quezon City, which housed a television station, three radio stations, and the government's news agency, was attacked by the rebels. That is why the television screen had gone blank. The complex was secured by 11:30 A.M., and Radio Veritas was on the air fifteen minutes later using the MBS radio facilities. Channel 4 television was back on the air at 1:30 P.M., this time as the rebel station.[26]

Enrile and Ramos' appeals were finally beginning to pay off. Ver ordered Brigadier General Angel Mapua, commanding officer of the 5th Fighter Wing at Basa Air Base next to Clark Air Base, to bomb Camp Crame. He refused, and defected.[27] Ver had lost his jet fighters. Units were calling into Camp Crame from all over the Philippines announcing their support. The Philippine Navy Base at Cavite defected and was ready with several warships at the mouth of the Pasig River to bombard the palace if the order was given.[28] Tanks could be heard rumbling around the vicinity of Camp Crame but rebel intelligence reported no imminent attacks. They did report, however, that some of the marines were withdrawing from Camp Aguinaldo. The only troops Ver deployed were around the remaining television stations and around the palace.[29]

That evening at 6:00 P.M., Marcos was interviewed on Channel 9 television. Only the panel interviewing Marcos could be seen because they were in the studio and Marcos was in the palace. His television hookup was out. He was upset about the rocket attack on the palace and complained, "My family is cowering in terror."

The bad news just kept coming for Marcos. Habib had returned to Washington and a meeting had been held on Sunday morning at the home of Secretary of State George Shultz. In attendance were Secretary of Defense Caspar Weinberger; Admiral William Crowe, Jr., Chairman of the Joint Chiefs of Staff; Robert Gates, Central Intelligence Agency Deputy Director for Intelligence; John Poindexter, National Security Adviser; Michael Armacost, Under-Secretary of State for Political Affairs (and former Ambassador to the Philippines); Paul Wolfowitz, Assistant Secretary of State for East Asian and Pacific Affairs; and Richard Armitage, Assistant Secretary of Defense for International Security Policy. Sometime during this meeting, although the precise time wasn't recorded, Quiet Diplomacy was pronounced dead.

Blas Ople and Kokoy Romualdez, the Philippine Ambassador to the U.S., had left for the U.S. on February 20 to seek support for Marcos. On Sunday evening, February 23 (Washington time), they met with Secretary of State George Shultz and Under-Secretary Michael Armacost at the State Department. The message was blunt. Marcos had lost control of his army; troops still loyal to Ver were ineffectual; and if Marcos didn't step down, the Philippines could be headed for civil war. The same message was conveyed to Marcos by Bosworth on Monday. About the same time Marcos received a personal message from President Reagan: he, as well as his family and close associates, was welcome to live in the United States. The National Security Council also sent Ver a message advising him that it would not be in his best interest to make a military move. In other words, if he expected to be included in any rescue operation, there should not be any bloodshed.[30]

Tuesday morning at 3:00 A.M. (Manila time) Marcos called Senator Paul Laxalt in Washington. Laxalt had visited Manila in October as President Reagan's special envoy. Was it true what Ambassador Bosworth had said? Laxalt replied that it was. Marcos asked if he could stay on until 1987, when his term would end, or whether some sort of power-sharing arrangement could be worked out with Cory. According to Laxalt, Marcos was "...hanging on, looking for a life preserver. He was a desperate man

clutching at straws." Laxault agreed to talk to Reagan and Schultz
and call him back. At 5:15 A.M. (Manila time) Laxalt called back.
What should he do, Marcos asked. Laxalt replied: "Mr. President,
I'm not bound by diplomatic restraint. I'm talking only for myself.
I think you should cut and cut cleanly. The time has come." There
was a pause which lasted so long that Laxalt asked, "Mr. President, are you still there?" "Yes, I'm still here," came the voice on
the other end. "I am so very, very disappointed."[31]

While Marcos was expressing his disappointment to Laxalt,
Ramos continued to receive more phone calls from units
previously loyal to Marcos. By now over 90 percent of the military
had defected. The 1st Scout Ranger Battalion in Manila and the
Philippine Military Academy in Baguio announced their support.
The Scout Rangers immediately took over the job of taking out
the remaining television stations loyal to Marcos.

A hotline between the State Department in Washington and
the U.S. Embassy in Manila had kept everyone appraised of
developments during the revolt. It isn't known how quickly such
information was relayed to Camp Crame, but a fair assumption is
that urgency was the order of the day. In any event the decision
was made to hold the swearing-in ceremonies of President Cory
Aquino and Vice-President Salvadore Laurel that morning at
ten-thirty at Club Filipino in the Metro Manila suburb of Green
Hills. Just before Enrile left for the ceremonies, he received a call
from Marcos. Marcos just wanted a graceful exit out of the crisis,
he said. "He suggested he would cancel the last election, set up a
provisional government, and serve as honorary president until
1987. He told me, 'You run the government the way you want.' "
Marcos was still grasping at straws. Enrile left him grasping. "I
told him Mrs. Aquino was about to take her oath. He said, 'Ask
her if she can postpone that so we can discuss these problems.' I
told him I'd try." He never got around to speaking to Cory.
Associate Justice Teehankee swore her in. Wearing a simple
yellow dress, she proclaimed herself the rightful new President of
the Philippines. The ceremony was televised on Channel 4.
Viewers got an added bonus that day. They were witness to an
image they had never seen before in the newspapers or on
television. It was General Ramos. He was smiling. The soldier

had restored his honor.[32]

Marcos, belligerent to the end, announced his own inauguration would proceed as planned at 12:30 P.M. Channels 2,9, and
13 were set to telecast the event. As he was about to raise his right,
hand the screen went blank. The last pockets of resistance around
the television stations were being mopped up.[33] The ceremony
proceeded anyway, but afterwards Marcos called Enrile and
asked him to stop firing on the palace. Enrile said he had no
troops there. Marcos then asked him to contact Ambassador
Bosworth to find out if the U.S. could provide security in flying
out of Malacañang. Enrile promised he would take care of it.[34]

It isn't hard to imagine the scene in the palace during that
afternoon as everyone rushed around in a state of panic trying to
gather whatever possessions they thought important and preparing for an evacuation no one could have planned for.

The crowds outside began to swell in size and temperament.
The people could feel something was going on. Their numbers
grew as the evening wore on. On the front line, as always,
were the omnipresent priests and nuns. It was a beautiful
evening, cool and a bit windy with a full moon overhead. The
crowd was well disciplined at first. Then they heard choppers and
became more anxious, the atmosphere more charged. By eleven
o'clock their numbers were estimated at more than a million.
Then they began to move forward, slowly, hesitant at first. Then,
not meeting any resistance, they surged forward, scaled the fences
and stormed the palace, screaming and shouting. There was
pandemonium.

One-hundred-twenty people were evacuated from the palace
that night. Fifty-two, including Marcos and Imelda, were taken
across the Pasig River in boats and then picked up by four
helicopters and flown to Clark Air Base. The remaining 70
crossed the river and then travelled overland to the air base. Some
of those were guards who later decided not to remain with
Marcos. The final number of evacuees was 89, and included
Marcos, Imelda, the three Marcos children and their families,
General Fabian Ver, his three sons and their families, the
Cojuangco family, security guards, household staff, and two
medical doctors.[35]

The original plan was to evacuate the group back to Clark Air Base and then fly them to Laoag, Marcos' stronghold in Ilocos Norte, the next morning. However, events would dictate otherwise. At Clark the word quickly spread and crowds began to gather outside the gates. To further complicate matters, the Philippine Air Force had defected to the Aquino government and some of their personnel were staying in billets next to the Marcos party. The safety of Marcos' party was in question. In the meantime President Aquino had informed Bosworth that Marcos had to leave the Philippines. Thus the decision was made. The group was awakened before dawn, and they departed soon afterward for Guam and then to Hawaii.

Marcos had no say-so in this decision. He obviously didn't want to leave the country. His baggage will attest to that. Later on customs agents would impound more than 300 crates the exiles took with them to Hawaii, including 22 crates containing an estimated $1.2 million in pesos. An inventory later made public would yield a vast treasure trove of valuables, including gold, diamonds and other jewelries and stock certificates. But the most important discovery was more than 2,000 pages of documents which were made available to the Philippine government. The documents detailed the incredible wealth Marcos and Imelda had salted away over the years, including Swiss bank accounts and real estate all over the world. In retrospect, Marcos wasn't grasping at straws. He was trying to hold onto a treasure that may rival that of any king or potentate, past or present.

Cardinal Sin was at his residence at Villa San Miguel when he heard the news. "We must pray for Marcos," he said of the man who would have imprisoned him on a barren island if he had won. In defending the role the church had played in the revolution, Sin stated emphatically that the church never meddled in politics. "The issue was moral. It was a fight between the forces of good and evil."[36]

Sin had once used an allegory in expressing Marcos' situation. He said that Marcos was riding on a tiger and he couldn't get off. If he did the tiger would eat him. If there had been no noise that night at the palace, no screaming people and no noisy choppers, perhaps the people might have heard the victorious primeval scream of a jungle beast as he relished his prey. It would have been a fitting end for a ruthless dictator.

It was all over 77 hours after it had begun. The people were dancing in the streets and shouting, "Happy New Year!" The day after Marcos left, Noel Soriano, who had served on the steering committee throughout Cory's run for the presidency, was asked if he had ever truly believed that he could win. "That isn't the point," he replied, "I had to try, for my children."

It's your move, kids.

*

Notes

Part I

Chapter 1

1. Hartzell Spence, *Marcos of the Philippines,* (Copyright 1979, Ferdinand E. Marcos), p. 39.
2. *Ibid.,* p. 37.
3. Patricia R. Mamot, *People Power,* (Quezon City: New Day Publishers, 1986) p. 109.
4. William Manchester, *American Caesar,* (New York: Dell Publishing Company, 1985), p. 436.
5. Teodoro A. Agoncillo, *The Burden of Proof,* (Metro Manila: University of the Philippines Press, 1984), p. 166.
6. *Ibid.,* p. 165.
7. *Ibid.,* p. 187.

Chapter 2

1. Louis B. Morton, *The Fall of the Philippines,* Department of the Army, Washington, D.C., 1953, p. 245.
2. Report of Major General George M. Parker, Formerly Commanding, The South Luzon Force and the II Philippine Corps, from 8 December 1941 to 9 April 1942, (Washington, D.C.: National Archives, R.G. 407, File 98-USFI—0.3), p. 30.
3. Colonel Uldarico Baclagon, *Filipino Heroes of World War II,* (Makati, Metro Manila: Agro Printing & Publishing House, 1980), p. 39.
4. Morton, *op. cit.,* pp. 272-3.
5. *Ibid.,* p. 275.

Chapter 3

1. Uldarico S. Baclagon & Jose M. Crisol, *Valor,* (Metro Manila: Development Academy of the Philippines, 1983), p. 16.
2. Gregorio S. Cendeña, *Documents on the Marcos War Medals,* (Office of Media Affairs, Republic of the Philippines, 1983), p. 43.
3. Brigadier General Mateo Capinpin, History of the 21st Division (PA), untitled, (Philadelphia: Carlyle Barracks, U.S. Army Military History Institute), p. 35.
4. Morton, *op. cit.,* p. 277.
5. *Ibid.,* p. 591.
6. Colonel Ray M. O'Day, History of the 21st Division (PA), untitled, (Philadelphia: Carlyle Barracks, U.S. Army Military History Institute).
7. Baclagon, op. cit., p. 47.
8. Cendeña, *op cit.,* pp. 43-46.
9. *Ibid.,* p. 45.
10. Letter from Lt. Colonel Harrison Lobdell III, Department of the Army, dated 12 December 1985.
11. *Washington Post,* Outlook Magazine, "The Marcos Mystery: Did the Philippine Leader Really Win U.S. Medals for Valor?", by John Sharkey, Sunday, December 18, 1983.
12. Capinpin, *op. cit.,* p. 33.

Chapter 4

1. Cendeña, *op cit.,* p. 15.
2. *Ibid.,* p. 23.
3. Telephone interview with Colonel John R. Vance, 29 November 1985.
4. Morton, *op. cit.,* p. 289.
5. *Ibid,* pp. 287-288.
6. Parker, *op. cit.,* p. 35.
7. Morton, *op. cit.,* p. 291.
8. *Ibid,* pp. 291 & 293.
9. John M. Toland, *But Not In Shame: The Six Months After Pearl Harbor,* (New York: Doubleday, 1970), p. 169.
10. Morton, *op. cit.,* pp. 293-294.
11. Toland, *op. cit.,* p. 169.
12. Morton, *op. cit.,* pp. 293-294.
13. U.S. Army, Allied Translator and Interpreter Section, Southwest Pacific Area, Enemy Publication No. 151, (Washington, D.C.: National Archives, R.G. 407, File 98-GHQI-ATIS), p. 31.
14. O'Day, *op. cit.,* p. 30.
15. Toland, *op. cit.,* p. 169.
16. *Ibid.,* p. 174.
17. *Ibid.,* p. 175.
18. Baclagon, *op. cit.,* p. 104.
19. *Marcos of the Philippines,* (Manila: Raya Books, 1978), p. 50.
20. Toland, *op. cit.,* p. 187.

Chapter 5

1. Morton, *op. cit.*, pp. 427-429.
2. General Jonathan M. Wainwright, Report of Operations of USAFFE and USFIP, 8 December 1941 — 9 April 1942, (Washington, D.C.: National Archives, R.G. 407, File 98-USFI-0.3), p. 59.
3. Baclagon, *op. cit.*, pp. 120 & 122.
4. O'Day, *op. cit.*, p. 43.
5. Baclagon & Crisol, op. cit., p. 49.
6. Bonifacio Gillego, "Marcos By 'Affidavit,' " unpublished article, 4 July 1984, p. 6.
7. Morton, *op. cit.*, p. 435.
8. *Ibid*, p. 442.

Chapter 6

1. Toland, *op. cit.*, pp. 310-329.
2. Narciso Manzano, unpublished memoirs, Chapter VII, pp. 4 & 12.
3. Baclagon, *op. cit.*, pp. 233-235.
4. *Ibid.*, pp. 167-168.
5. Major General Charles A. Willoughby, U.S. Army (ret.), *The Guerrilla Resistance Movement in the Philippines*, (New York: Vantage Press, 1972.), pp. 450-451.
6. Letter from Ferdinand Marcos to Commanding General, PHILRYCOM, dated 2 December 1947, (Washington, D.C.: National Archives, R.G. 407, File 60, Box 298)..
7. Manzano, *op. cit.*, Chapter VI, p. 13.
8. *Ibid.*, Chapter VIII, pp. 2-3.
9. Willoughby, *op. cit.*, p. 48.

Chapter 7

1. Letter from John Sharkey, dated 7 February 1986.
2. Willoughby, *op. cit.*, p. 463.
3. *Ibid.*, p. 257.
4. *Ibid*, p. 201.
5. Letter from Ferdinand E. Marcos to Commanding General, PHILRYCOM, dated 2 December 1947, *op. cit.*
6. Willoughby, *op. cit.*, p. 172.
7. *Ibid.*
8. Whitney Papers, SWPA Message Traffic, 29 August 1943, Fertig to McArthur, NR 245. (Norfolk, Virginia: MacArthur Memorial Archives).
9. *Ibid.*, 6 September 1943, MacArthur to Fertig.
10. *Ibid.*, 11 September 1943, Fertig to MacArthur, NR 268.
11. Willoughby, *op. cit.*, p. 540.
12. Gerald S. Snyder, *They Never Surrendered*, (Quezon City: Vera Reyes, Inc., 1982), p. 207.
13. Whitney Papers, *op. cit.*, 17 November 1943, Andrews to MacArthur, NR 195.

14. *Ibid.*
15. *Ibid.,* 16 December 1943, Fertig to MacArthur, NR 486.
16. *Ibid.,* 16 December 1943, Fertig to MacArthur, NR 483.
17. *Ibid.,* 20 December 1943, Fertig to MacArthur, NR 510.
18. Maharlika History, (Washington, D.C.: National Archives, R.G. 407, File 60, Box 298).
19. Check Sheet of Captain E.R. Curtis, dated 25 July 1947, (Washington, D.C.: National Archives, R.G. 407, File 60, Box 298).
20. Whitney Papers, *op. cit.,* 22 April 1943, Fertig to MacArthur, NR 82.
21. *Ibid.,* 16 February 1944, Fertig to MacArthur, NR 705.
22. Toland, *op. cit.,* p. 158.
23. Cesar P. Pobre, The Resistance Movement in Northern Luzon (1942-1945), master's thesis, University of the Philippines, Graduate School of Arts and Sciences, March 1962, p. 65.
24. *Ibid.,* p. 68.
25. *Ibid.,* p. 55.
26. *Ibid.,* p. 59.
27. *Ibid.,* p. 61.
28. *Ibid.,* p. 62.
29. *Ibid.,* p. 32.
30. *Ibid.,* p. 68.
31. Toland, *op. cit.,* p. 363.
32. Russell W. Volckmann, *We Remained: Three Years Behind Enemy Lines,* (New York: W.W. Norton & Co., 1954), p. 83.
33. Pobre, *op. cit.,* pp. 72-73.
34. *Ibid.,* pp. 43-44.
35. *Ibid.,* p. 45.
36. Willoughby, *op. cit.,* p. 481.
37. Pobre, *op. cit.,* pp. 50-51.
38. *Ibid.,* p. 51.
39. Willoughby, *op. cit.,* pp. 481-482.
40. Pobre, *op. cit.,* p. 54.
41. Willoughby, *op. cit.,* p. 482.
42. *Ibid.*
43. Volckmann, *op. cit.,* pp. 138-139.
44. Telephone interview with Vincente Rivera, 22 November 1985 and 9 January 1986.
45. Willoughby, *op. cit.,* p. 483.
46. Volckmann, *op. cit.,* p. 82.
47. Pobre, *op. cit.,* p. 76.
48. *Ibid.,* p. 81.
49. *Ibid.,* p. 82.
50. Willoughby, *op. cit.,* p. 482.
51. *Ibid.*
52. Volckmann, *op. cit.,* p. 40.
53. *Ibid.,* p. 119.
54. Pobre, *op. cit.,* p. 89.
55. Volckmann, *op. cit.,* p. 154.

56. Ernesto R. Rodriguez, Jr., *The Bad Guerrillas of Northern Luzon*, (Quezon City: J. Burgos Media Services, 1982) pp. 35-59.
57. Volckmann, *op. cit.*, p. 180.

Chapter 8

1. Pobre, *op. cit.*, p. 120.
2. Letter from Teodoro A. Agoncillo to Bonifacio Gillego dated 19 November 1982..
3. Telephone Interview with Romulo Manriquez, 21 November 1985 and 9 January 1986.
4. Willoughby, *op. cit.*, p. 488.
5. *Ibid.*, p. 102.
6. *Ibid.*, pp. 389-398.
7. Letter from R.W. Volckmann to C.G. SWPA, dated 20 November 1944, (Washington, D.C.: National Archives, R.G. 407, File 60, Box 298).
8. Check Sheet, from G-3 Operations, General Headquarters, SWPA, dated 2 December 1944, (Washington, D.C.: National Archives, R.G. 407, File 60, Box 298)..
9. Willoughby, *op. cit.*, p. 45.
10. *Ibid*, pp. 187-188.
11. *Ibid.*, p. 189.
12. Spence, *op. cit.*, p. 176.
13. *Ibid.*, p. 181.
14. Maharlika History, *op. cit.*
15. Report of Lt. Pete C. Breaz, dated 4 August 1947, (Washington, D.C.: National Archives, R.G. 407, File 60, Box 298).
16. Willoughby, *op. cit.*, p. 209.
17. *Ibid.*, p. 450.
18. *Ibid.*, pp. 457-458.
19. *Ibid.*, p. 450.
20. *Ibid.*, p. 428.
21. Report of Captain Elbert R. Curtis, dated 25 July 1947, (Washington, D.C.: National Archives, R.G. 407, File 60, Box 298).
22. Report of Lt. William D. McMillan, undated, (Washington, D.C.: National Archives, R.G. 407, File 60, Box 298).
23. Maharlika History, *op. cit.*
24. *Washington Post*, "New Doubts on Marcos' War Role," by John Sharkey, 24 January 1986.
25. Whitney Papers, *op. cit.*, 19 August 1944, Anderson to MacArthur, NR 64.
26. Spence, *op. cit.*, p. 171.
27. Affidavit of Ferdinand E. Marcos, dated 15 February 1945, (Washington, D.C.: National Archives, R.G. 407, File 60, Box 298).
28. Maharlika History, *op. cit.*
29. Letter From Ferdinand E. Marcos to Commanding General, PHILRYCOM, dated 2 December 1947, *op. cit.*

30. Letter from William Saunders to Commanding Officer, Luzon, dated 26 July 1944, (Norfolk, Virginia: MacArthur Memorial Archives).
31. Spence, *op. cit.,* p. 183.
32. Willoughby, *op. cit.,* pp. 457-458.
33. Volckmann, *op. cit.,* p. 131.
34. Willoughby, *op. cit.,* p. 353.
35. *Ibid.,* p. 457.

Chapter 9

1. Willoughby, *op. cit.,* p. 110.
2. Affidavit for Philippine Army Personnel, signed by Ferdinand E. Marcos, dated 6 February 1946, (St. Louis, Missouri: U.S. Army Records Center).
3. Manchester, *op. cit.,* p. 489.
4. Spence, *op. cit.,* p. 187.
5. *Ibid.,* p. 184.
6. *Ibid.,* p. 187.
7. Report of Lt. Pete C. Breaze, *op. cit.*
8. *Washington Post, op. cit.*
9. Letter from Vincente Rivera to Bonifacio Gillego, dated 5 July 1982.
10. Spence, *op. cit.,* p. 187.
11. *Ibid.,* p. 191.
12. *Ibid.,* p. 190.
13. *Ibid.,* p. 192.
14. Baclagon, *op. cit.,* pp. 181-182.
15. Letter from Vincente Rivera to Bonifacio Gillego, *op. cit.*
16. Baclagon, *op. cit.,* p. 185.
17. Spence, *op. cit.,* p. 194.
18. *Ibid.,* p. 185.
19. Spence, *op. cit.,* p. 194.
20. Baclagon, *op. cit.,* pp. 182-183.
21. Letter from Vincente Rivera to Bonifacio Gillego, *op. cit..*
22. Spence, *op. cit.,* pp. 194-195.
23. *Ibid.,* p. 195.
24. Vincente Rivera, History of the 14th Infantry Regiment, USAFIP NL, unpublished.
25. Telephone inverviews with Romulo Manriquez and Vincente Rivera, 22 November 1985 and 9 January 1986.
26. Baclagon, *op. cit.,* pp. 199-200.
27. *Ibid.*
28. Baclagon and Crisol, *Valor, op. cit.,* p. 91.

Chapter 10

1. *Philippine News* (New York), "New Evidence On Marcos War Record," by Bonifacio H. Gillego, January 12-18, 1983, p. 1.
2. Willoughby, *op. cit.,* p. 41.

3. Letter From Maharlika to United States Liberation Army Headquarters, dated 25 January 1945, (Washington, D.C.: National Archives, R.G. 407, File 60, Box 298).
4. Letter from Ferdinand Marcos to Colonel Volckmann, dated 1 May 1945, (Washington, D.C.: National Archives, R.G. 407, File 60, Box 298).
5. Letter from Ferdinand Marcos to Headquarters, Philippine Army, dated 18 August 1945, with endorsements, (Washington, D.C.: National Archives, R.G. 407, File 60, Box 298).
6. *Ibid.*
7. *Ibid.*
8. Report of Captain Elbert R. Curtis, dated 24 March 1948. (Washington, D.C.: National Archives, R.G. 407, File 60, Box 298).
9. Letter From Ferdinand Marcos to Guerrilla Affairs Section, dated 18 December 1945. (Washington, D.C.: National Archives, R.G. 407, File 60, Box 298).
10. Letter From Headquarters, Philippine-Ryukyus Command to Ferdinand Marcos, dated 7 June 1947. (Washington, D.C.: National Archives, R.G. 407, File 60, Box 298).
11. Letter From Ferdinand Marcos to Headquarters, Philippine Army, dated 18 August 1945, with endorsements, *op. cit.*
12. Report of Captain Elbert R. Curtis, dated 25 July 1947, *op. cit.*
13. Report of Lt. George Kemper, dated 27 March 1948, (Washington, D.C.: National Archives, R.G. 407, File 60, Box 298).
14. Letter From Headquarters, Philippine-Ryukyus Command to Ferdinand Marcos, dated 7 June 1947, *op. cit.*
15. Letter From Ferdinand Marcos to Commanding General, PHILRYCOM, dated 2 December 1947, *op. cit.*
16. Letter From Ferdinand Marcos to Headquarters, Philippine Army, dated 18 August 1945, with endorsements, *op. cit.*
17. Maharlika History, *op. cit.*
18. Report of Captain Elbert R. Curtis, dated 25 July 1947, *op. cit.*
19. Letter From Colonel Volckmann to Captain S.M. Valdez, dated 2 November 1944, (Washington, D.C.: National Archives, R.G. 407, File 60, Box 298).
20. Pobre, *op. cit.*
21. Report of Captain Elbert R. Curtis, dated 25 July 1947, *op. cit.*
22. Report of Lt. Pete C. Breaz, *op. cit.*
23. Letter From Ferdinand Marcos to Headquarters, Philippine-Ryukyus Command, dated 7 June 1947, *op. cit.*
24. Report of Lt. Kenneth Neubauer, dated 21 July 1947, (Washington, D.C.: National Archives, R.G. 407, File 140, Box 372).
25. Report of Lt. H.M. Velarde, dated 30 July 1945, (Washington, D.C.: National Archives, R.G. 407, Box 537).
26. Report on Allas Intelligence Unit, dated 17 July 1945, (Washington, D.C.: National Archives, R.G. 407, File 140, Box 372).
27. Letter From Ferdinand Marcos to Commanding General, PHILRYCOM, dated 2 December 1947, *op. cit.*
28. Report of Captain Elbert R. Curtis, dated 24 March 1948, *op. cit.*

29. Report of Maj. R.G. Langham, dated 31 May 1945, (Washington, D.C.:
    National Archives, R.G. 407, File 60, Box 298).
30. U.S. Court of Claims, Ferdinand E. Marcos versus The United States,
    Claim No. 50278.

Part II

Chapter 11

1. David J. Steinberg, *The Philippines: A Singular and Plural Place,*
   (Boulder, Colorado: Westview Press, 1982), p. 58.

Chapter 12

1. *San Francisco Examiner,* "Rebellions Mark Philippine History," 22 August
   1983, p. A3.
2. Interview with Jose Lukban, November 22, 1985, San Francisco.
3. Diosdado Macapagal, "The Stonehill Case," Radio-TV address on the program "President Macapagal Speaks to the Masses," August 14, 1962.
   (Manila: printed by Malacañan).
4. Central Intelligence Agency Memorandum, "Philippine Elections,"
   (Washington, D.C.: Directorate of Intelligence, Office of Current Intelligence, October 28, 1965).
5. Report of an Amnesty International Mission to the Republic of the Philippines, November 11-28, 1981, (London: Amnesty International Publications, 1982), p. 54.
6. *Atlanta Constitution* newspaper, Weekend magazine, "Philippine
   Documents Support Charges Marcos Stashed $229 Million Overseas," July
   26, 1986.
7. *Philippine Free Press* magazine (Manila), "Portraits of Senator and Congressman As Warlords," November 14, 1970, p. 1.
8. *Ibid.,* "Private Armies Legalized," January 23, 1971, p. 8.
9. Steinberg, *op. cit.,* p. 3.
10. *Philippine News* (Manila), "Probe of Plaza Miranda Starts," May 28-June
    3, 1986, p. 7.
11. Interview with Johnny Quijano, April 18, 1986, Manila.

Chapter 13

1. *Philippine Times* (Chicago), 24 December 1979.
2. *Ibid.*
3. David J. Steinberg, "Jose P. Laurel—A 'Collaborator' Misunderstood,"
   The Journal of Asian Studies, Volume XXIV, Number 4, August 1965, p.
   663.
4. *Ibid.,* p. 655.

5. *Ibid.*
6. Amnesty International Report, *op. cit.,* p. 56.
7. *Ibid.*
8. Primitivo Mijares, *The Conjugal Dictatorship,* (San Francisco: Union Square Publications, 1975), p. 337.
9. *Ibid.,* p. 335.
10. *Ibid.,* p. 325.
11. David J. Steinberg, *The Philippines: A Singular and Plural Place,* (Boulder, Colorado: Westview Press, 1982), p. 122.
12. Proclamation 1081, in *Notes on the New Society of the Philippines,* Copyright 1973 by Ferdinand E. Marcos, p. 228.
13. Mijares, *op. cit.,* p. 435.
14. Amnesty International Report, *op. cit.,* p. 56.
15. *Ibid.,* p. 15.
16. *Ibid.,* p. 59.
17. *Ibid.,* p. 52.
18. Mijares, *op. cit.,* p. 438.
19. *Ibid.*
20. Steinberg, *op. cit.,* p. 122.
21. Amnesty International Report, *op. cit..* p. 63.
22. Mijares, *op. cit.,* p. 418.
23. "The Extradiction Treaty Between the Philippines and the United States: Facts and Implications," Philippine Occasional Studies Paper No. 5, Philippine Studies Program, (Honolulu: University of Hawaii, Center for Asia and Pacific Studies, August 1982), pp. 51-53.

Chapter 14

1. *Far Eastern Economic Review* magazine (Hong Kong), "Liberated — But Tied to Old Loyalties," January 5, 1984, pp. 32-37.
2. Mijares, *op. cit.,* p. 224.
3. *Ibid.,* p. 225.
4. *Fortune* magazine, "The High Flying First Lady of the Philippines," July 2, 1979, p. 95.
5. Mijares, *op. cit.,* p. 226.
6. *Newsweek* magazine, "The Iron Butterfly," August 12, 1974.
7. *Philippine Times* (Chicago), December 24, 1979.
8. *Ibid.*
9. William H. Sullivan, *Obbligato,* (New York: W.M. Norton & Co., 1984), p. 256.
10. *Ibid.,* p. 257.
11. *Philippine Daily Inquirer,* "Meldy Tagged In New Fund Mess," April 6, 1986, p. 1.
12. *Newsweek* magazine, "The Iron Butterfly," August 12, 1974.
13. *Cosmopolitan* magazine, "The Ten Richest Women In the World," December 1975.
14. *San Francisco Chronicle,* Herb Caen's column, March 11, 1975, p. 22.

15. *Pacific Stars and Stripes* newspaper, "Marcos Family—Study Core of Philippine Life," November 9, 1975, p. 8.
16. *The New York Times Magazine,* "Creating A Dynasty In the Philippines," May 24, 1981, p. 16.
17. *Fortune* magazine, "The High-Flying First Lady of the Philippines," July 2, 1979, pp. 93-96.
18. *Ibid.,* p. 94.
19. *People* magazine, "The Imelda Marcos Shopping Guide: A Cache 'N' Carry Way To Spend the Fortunes of A Nation," April 7, 1986, pp. 139-141.
20. *New York Times,* "Manila Inner Circle Gains Under Marcos," January 15, 1978, p. 1.
21. *Far Eastern Economic Review* magazine (Hong Kong), "Out of the Muddle, A Promise of Bliss," February 16, 1979, p. 44.
22. *Ibid.,* p. 46.
23. *We Forum* newspaper (Manila), "Experts Question Imelda's Spending," November 15-17, 1982, p. 1.
24. *People* magazine, *op. cit.*
25. *Life* magazine, "Silver Anniversary For the Iron Butterfly," July 1979, pp. 29-36.
26. *Far Eastern Economic Review* magazine (Hong Kong), "A Political Factor In the KKK Equation," October 29, 1982, p. 34.
27. *Ibid.*
28. *Daiy Inquirer,* newspaper (Manila), "Fictitious Contractors Got ₱198M," June 28, 1986, p. 1.
29. *Manila Times* newspaper, "Intelligence Fund Used for FM Trips," April 1, 1986, p. 1.
30. *People* magazine, *op. cit.*
31. *Far Eastern Economic Review* magazine (Hong Kong), " A Political Base Grows From A Military Base," October 29, 1982, p. 38.
32. *Ibid,* "How Did It Happen? What Can Be Done?" December 15, 1983, p. 77.
33. *Ibid,* "Creditors In Manila," November 5, 1982, p. 58.
34. *Ibid,* "MIFF sin miffs Sin," February 17, 1983, p. 30.
35. *Ibid.,* p. 31.
36. Fred Poole and Max Vanzi, *Revolution In the Philippines: The United States In A Hall of Cracked Mirrors,* (New York: McGraw-Hill Book Company, 1984), p. 308.
37. *Far Eastern Economic Review* magazine (Hong Kong), "Life-Raft For Manila's Hotels," October 21, 1977, p. 53.
38. *Los Angeles Times,* "Imelda: The Philippine 'Eva Peron,' " October 24, 1980.
39. *Newsweek* magazine, "The Iron Butterfly," August 12, 1974.
40. *Daily Inquirer* newspaper (Manila), "Imelda, Kokoy Grabbed ₱200 M Tourism Fund," April 14, 1986, p. 1.
41. *Fortune* magazine, *op. cit.,* p. 93.
42. *Philippine News* newspaper (San Francisco), "Imelda's M. Manila Commission In Hock," December 11-17, 1985, p. 6.

Chapter 15

1. Steinberg, *op. cit.*, p. 78.
2. Amnesty International pamphlet, "Arrest, Dentention, and Political killing of Priests and Church Workers In the Philippines," (New York: Amnesty International USA, December 31, 1982), p. 3.
3. *Ibid*, p. 4.
4. *Ibid.*
5. Amnesty International Report, *op. cit.*, p. 63.
6. Mijares, *op. cit.*, p. 418.
7. *Far Eastern Economic Review* magazine (Hong Kong), "Church Forms A United Front," February 25, 1977, p. 20.
8. *Ibid.*
9. *Business Day* newspaper (Manila), "Sin Calls For Gov't Reforms," July 16, 1984, p. 12.
10. *New York Times,* "Pope, With Marcos Beside Him, Delivers Human Rights Talk," February 18, 1981.
11. *Ibid.*
12. Amnesty International pamphlet, *op. cit.*, p. 5
13. *Ibid*, p. 4.
14. *Ibid.*
15. *San Francisco Chronicle,* "Behind the Wave of Fear In the Philippines," May 18, 1983, p. F4.
16. *Pacific Stars and Stripes* newspaper, "Philippine Cardinal: The Church Will Survive Official Persecution," October 23, 1982.
17. *San Francisco Chronicle,* "Marcos, Defiant Clergy Are Uneasy Adversaries," January 30, 1983, p. A13.
18. *Washington Post,* "Crackdown On 'Rebel Priests' Widens Church-State Rift In Manila," February 18, 1983, p. A28.
19. *San Francisco Chronicle, op. cit.*
20. *Far Eastern Econimic Review* magazine (Hong Kong), "The Gun and the Crucifix," December 10, 1982, p. 38.
21. Amnesty International pamphlet, *op. cit.*, p. 2.
22. *Ibid.*, p. 5.
23. *Ibid.*, p. 2.
24. *Asiaweek* magazine (Hong Kong), "In Sugar Country, Priests On Trial," March 9, 1984, p. 20.
25. *Ibid.*
26. *Ibid.*
27. Amnesty International pamphlet, *op. cit.*
28. *Veritas* newspaper (Manila), "Why Brian Gore Was Tried," August 12, 1984, p. 14.
29. Amnesty International amphlet, *op. cit.*
30. *San Francisco Examiner,* "Pope To Workers: Fight Exploiters," February 20, 1981.
31. *Aisaweek* magazine (Hong Kong), " 'Injustice Reigns' In Sugar Country," December 3, 1982, p. 47.
32. *Ibid,* "In Sugar Country, Priests On Trial," March 9, 1984, p. 20.

33. *Veritas, op. cit.*
34. Amnesty International pamphlet, *op. cit.,* p. 3.
35. *Ibid.*
36. *Asiaweek* magazine (Hong Kong). "In Sugar Country, Priests On Trial," March 9, 1984, p. 20.
37. *Ibid.*
38. *Ibid.*
39. *Veritas, op. cit.*
40. *Manila Times* newspaper, "No Coverup On Court-Martial of PC Men—Ramos," September 1, 1984, p. 2.

Chapter 16

1. *Far Eastern Economic Review* magazine (Hong Kong), "All the President's Men," March 10, 1983, p. 15.
2. Mjiares, *op. cit.,* p. 454.
3. *Washington Post,* "Government Abuses Toughen Philippine Guerrilla Movement," August 12, 1982, p. A20.
4. *Time* magazine, " 'Red Areas' In the Hills," May 14, 1984, p. 14.
5. U.S. Senate Staff Report For the Committee On Foreign Relations, "The Situation In the Philippines," (Washington, D.C., October 1984), p. 24.
6. *Ibid.,* pp. 22-23.
7. *Far Eastern Economic Review* magazine (Hong Kong), "Red 'Army' On the March," June 28, 1984, p. 40.
8. Steinberg, *op. cit.,* pp. 112-113.
9. *San Francisco Chronicle,* "Philippines Wants More U.S. Aid To Fight Rebels," January 19, 1985, p. 8.
10. U.S. Senate Staff Report, *op. cit.,* p. 17.
11. *Far Eastern Economic Review* magazine (Hong Kong), "The Ethnic Pot Begins To Boil—Manila's Misery," June 27, 1975, p. 21.
12. *Philippine News* newspaper (San Francisco), "Focus: Interview With MNLF Reformist Leaders," September 11-17, 1985, p. 1.
13. *Far Eastern Economic Review* magazine (Hong Kong), "Calm On the Moro Front," August 9, 1984, p. 29.
14. *Philippine News, op. cit.*
15. *Far Eastern Economic Review, op. cit.*
16. Amnesty International Report, *op. cit.,* p. 57.
17. U.S. Senate Staff Report, *op. cit.,* pp. 22-23.
18. Steve Psinakis, *Two 'Terrorists' Meet,* (San Francisco: Alchemy Books, 1981), p. 312.
19. *Ibid.,* p. 20.
20. *Philippine News* newspaper (San Francisco), "Doris Baffrey, Accused Bomber, Ordred Released," February 27-March 5, 1985, p. 1.
21. Amnesty International Report, *op. cit.,* p. 57.
22. *Ibid.,* p. 62.
23. *Ibid.,* p. 64.
24. U.S. Senate Staff Report, *op. cit.,* p. 27.
25. *Ibid.*

26. *Far Eastern Economic Review* magazine (Hong Kong), "The Military Card In Play," October 13, 1983, p. 15.
27. *Ibid.*
28. Amnesty International Report, *op. cit.,* p. 5.
29. *Ibid,* p. 3.
30. *Ibid,* p. 58.
31. *Aisaweek* magazine (Hong Kong), "Hope Fades For the Detainees," March 25, 1983, p. 17.
32. *Ibid.*
33. Amnesty International Report, *op. cit.,* p. 5.
34. *Ibid.,* p. 7.
35. *Ibid.,* p. 52.
36. *Philippine News* newspaper (San Francisco), "Marcos Amends Death Decres," May 1-7, 1985.
37. Amnesty International Report, *op. cit.,* p. 71.
38. *Far Eastern Economic Review* magazine (Hong Kong), "The Rot In the Writ," June 2, 1983, pp. 38-39.
39. Amnesty International Report, *op. cit.,* p. 17.
40. *Ibid.,* p. 2.
41. *Ibid.,* pp. 17-18.
42. *Far Eastern Economic Review, op. cit.*
43. *Ibid.*
44. *Ibid,* "Law of the Juggle," August 25, 1983, p. 14.
45. Fred Poole and Max Vanzi, *op. cit.,* p. 75.

Chapter 17

1. *Far Eastern Economic Review* magazine (Hong Kong), "The party's Over," November 18, 1972.
2. Mijares, *op. cit.,* p. 350.
3. *Ibid.,* p. 351.
4. *Ibid.,* p. 358.
5. *Ibid.,* p. 366.
6. "Some Are Smarter Than Others," by Ricardo Manapat, unpublished report, 1979, p. 5.
7. Mijares, *op. cit.,* p. 328.
8. *San Francisco Chronicle,* "A President Who's Above Criticism," June 29, 1976.
9. *San Francisco Chronicle,* "New Bribe Offer In Philippine Case," by Jack Anderson, July 14, 1975.
10. Steve Psinakis, *op. cit.,* p. 188.
11. *New York Times,* "Son of Strong Critic of Marcos Reportedly Slain In Manila," June 14, 1977.
12. *Far Eastern Economic Review* magazine (Hong Kong), "After Zeitlin, Assurances," November 19, 1976, pp. 18-19.
13. Mijares, *op. cit.,* pp. 352-355.
14. *Ibid.*

15. *Far Eastern Economic Review* magazine (Hong Kong), "Journalist Vindicated," March 11, 1977.
16. "Country Reports on Human Rights Practices for 1981," by U.S. Department of State, Washington, D.C., February 1982.
17. *South China Morning Post* newspaper (Hong Kong), "Marcos Attacks 'Half-Hearted' Press." September 8, 1982.
18. *Asiaweek* magazine (Hong Kong), "Quit: Letty Jimenez-Magsanoc," July 24, 1981, p. 19.
19. *Bulletin Today* newspaper (Manila), "What Exactly Is Press Freedom?" by Arlene Babst, September 17, 1982.
20. *We Forum* newspaper (Manila), "Lady Newscaster Pressured to Quit?" October 29-31, 1982, p. 1.
21. *Pacific Stars and Stripes* newspaper, "RP Military Closes Opposition Paper," December 9, 1982.
22. *Bulletin Today* newspaper (Manila), "Link 'Forum' Editor to Urban Guerrillas," December 14, 1982, p. 1.
23. *Pacific Stars and Stripes* newspaper, "Manila Claiming Jailed Writers Not Legitimate Members of the Media," December 10, 1982.
24. "Artists, Writers and Intellectuals and the Culture of Crisis," by Doreen G. Fernandez. Paper presented at Association for Asian Studies Annual Meeting, March 22-24, 1985, Philadelphia, p. 15.
25. Doreen G. Fernandez, *op. cit.,* p. 12.
26. *San Francisco Chronicle,* "Marcos Orders Journalist Held," April 14, 1983.
27. *Bulletin Today* newspaper (Manila), "Enrile Says Reds Using Media As A 'Propaganda Tool,' " December 11, 1982, p. 1.
28. *Washington Post,* "Opposition Sees Journalist Trial As Sign of New Marcos Crackdown," February 20, 1983, p. A40.

Chapter 18

1. Ferdinand E. Marcos, *Today's Revolution,* (Manila, 1971).
2. Ferdinand E. Marcos, *Notes On the New Society of the Philippines,* (Manila, 1973).
3. *Bulletin Today* newspaper (Manila), Jesus E. Bigornia column, May 25, 1982, p. 4.

Chapter 19

1. *New York Times,* "Marcos Defends His War Record; Aquino Accuses Him of Deception," January 25, 1986, p. 6.
2. *Philippine News* newspaper (San Francisco), "Monuments To A Frivolous Regime," August 21-27, 1985, p. 6.
3. *Reports of the Fact-Finding Board on the Assassination of Senator Benigno S. Aquino, Jr.,* (Metro Manila: Mr. & Mrs. Publishing Company, 1984), p. 177.
4. *San Francisco Chronicle,* "Marcos and the Maharishi," October 28, 1984, p. 7.

5. *San Francisco Chronicle,* "From the Desk of Ferdinand Marcos," March 12, 1986, p. 13.
6. Mijares, *op. cit.,* p. 252.

Chapter 20

1. "Who Controls the Philippine Economy?" by John F. Doherty, unpublished report (Metro Manila: Ateneo University, 1980).
2. "Some Are Smarter Than Others," *op. cit.,* pp. 19-21.
3. *Ibid.*
4. *Ibid.*
5. *Ibid.*
6. *Ibid.*
7. *Washington Post,* Parade Magazine, "Extortion In High Places," March 2, 1975.
8. *San Francisco Examiner,* "Poverty, Debt, Joblessness: Aquino's Fight Just Starting," March 10, 1986, p. A-5.
9. *Pacific Stars and Stripes* newspaper, "Marcos Family—Study Core of Philippine Life," November 9, 1975, p. 8.
10. *Far Eastern Economic Review* magazine (Hong Kong), "Letter From Manila," December 24, 1976, p. 110.
11. "Some Are Smarter Than Others," *op. cit.,* p. 17.
12. *Ibid.,* p. 18.
13. *Asian Wall Street Journal,* "Philippine Fugitive's Testimony Said To Link Marcos to U.S. Deals," January 30, 1986, p. 1.
14. *Ibid.*
15. *San Francisco Examiner,* "A Marcos 'Front' Tells His Side," March 23, 1986, p. 1.
16. *Asian Wall Street Journal, op. cit.*
17. *Philippine News* newspaper (San Francisco), "Marcos Crony Central Figure In Seattle Fight For Housing," January 30-February 5, 1985, p. 1.
18. *Manila Chronicle,* "Valasco Accused Of Oil Kickbacks," July 2, 1986, p. 9.

Chapter 21

1. "An Analysis of the Philippine Economic Crisis." A Workshop Report, by University of the Philippines, School of Economics, June 1984.
2. Walden Bello, David Kinley, and Elaine Elinson, *Development Debacle: The World Bank In the Philippines,* (San Francisco: Institute For Food and Development Policy, 1982), p. 24.
3. *Ibid.,* p. 96.
4. *Ibid.,* p. 50.
5. *Wall Street Journal,* "Ties To The Top: In the Philippines, It's Whom You Know That Counts," January 12, 1978.
6. *New York Times,* "Manila Inner Circle Gains Under Marcos," January 15, 1978, p. 1.
7. *Time* magazine, "Tales From Disiniland," January 23, 1978.

8. *Fortune* magazine, "The $2.2 Billion Nuclear Fiasco," September, 1986, pp. 39-46.
9. *Asiaweek* magazine (Hong Kong), "After Disaster, A New Beginning," December 11, 1981, p. 39.
10. "Some Are Smarter Than Others," *op. cit.*
11. *Fortune* magazine, "The Philippines Veers Toward Crisis," July 27, 1981, pp. 34-38.
12. *Ibid.*
13. *Ibid.*
14. *Far Eastern Econimic Review* magazine (Hong Kong), "Delta's Dire Straits," April 16, 1982.
15. *Business Day* newspaper (Manila), "Philfinance Violations Confirmed," June 21, 1981, p. 11.
16. *Far Eastern Economic Review, op. cit.*
17. *Asian Wall Stree Journal,* "Philippine Fugitive's Testimony Said To Link Marcos To US Deals," January 30, 1986, p. 1.
18. *San Francisco Examiner,* "Founder Quizzed In Bank Probe," February 5, 1986, p. 1.
19. *Far Eastern Economic Review* magazine (Hong Kong), "Wanted: Financier Dewey Dee," February 13, 1981.
20. *Asian Wall Street Journal, op. cit.*
21. C.P. Fitzgerald, *A Concise History of East Asia,* (Sydney: Halsted Press, 1966), p. 265.
22. *Asian Wall Street Journal, op. cit.*
23. *Asiaweek* magazine, *op. cit.*
24. *Far Eastern Economic Review* magazine (Hong Kong), "A bailed Out Case." March 24, 1983, p. 78.
25. *Ibid.,* "Following the Deltic Oracle," January 6, 1983, p. 61.
26. *Fortune* magazine, *op. cit.*
27. *Far Eastern Economic Review* magazine (Hong Kong), "Delta's Dire Straits," April 16, 1982.
28. *Business Day* newspaper (Manila), "Silverio Gives 10-Year Forecast For Delta," March 26, 1983, p. 8.
29. *Daily Express* newspaper (Manila), "Private Sector Urged To Study CDCP Case," March 17, 1983.
30. *Outlook* magazine (Manila), "Filipino-Foreign Bank Marriages, Why the High Divorce Rate?," April 1979, p. 22.
31. Memo For Concerned Citizens, #4 (Metro Manila, December 1983), p. 12.

Chapter 22

1. Memo For Concerned Citizens, #4, *op. cit.,* p. 21.
2. "The Bureaucratic Crunch: Are We Ready To Pay Its Price?" Senior Staff Memo, Center for Research and Comminication (Manila, March 1979).
3. *Business Day* newspaper (Manila), "When Economists Speak," August 27, 1984, p. 4.
4. Memo For Concerned Citizens, #4, *op. cit.*

5. *Far Eastern Economic Review* magazine (Hong Kong), "Time For A Real Debate," June 9, 1983, p. 63.
6. Memo For Concerned Citizens, #4, *op. cit.*
7. *Business Day* newspaper (Manila), "Government Direct Shift In Capital Flow," January 4, 1980, p. 7.
8. *Bulletin Today* newspaper (Manila), "Rely On Investments, Not Loans – Armacost," December 17, 1983.
9. "The Government's Role In Improving Philippine Productivity," by Bernie Villegas. Senior Staff Memo, Center for Research and Communication, (Manila, December 1981).
10. Richard D. Robinson, *Foreign Investment In the Third World: A Comparative Study of Selected Developing Country Investment Promotion Programs,* (Washington, D.C.: Chamber of Commerce of the United States, International Division, 1980), pp. 27 & 33.
11. *San Francisco Examiner,* "Poverty, Debt, Joblessness: Aquino's Fight Just Starting," March 10, 1986, p. A-5.
12. "Negative Productivity Behavior In the Philippines," by Ledivinia V. Cariño and Raul P. de Guzman, University of the Philippines, College of Public Administration, 1982. Paper presented at the National Conference on Public Administration.

Chapter 23

1. *Far Eastern Economic Review* magazine (Hong Kong), "Cracks In the Coconut Shell," January 8, 1982, pp. 42-47.
2. "Some Are Smarter Than Others," *op. cit.*
3. *Observer* magazine (Manila), "The Quarrel Over Coconuts," December 6, 1981, pp. 8-12.
4. *Ibid.*
5. *Far Eastern Economic Review* magazine, *op. cit.*
6. *Observer* magazine, *op. cit.*
7. *Far Eastern Economic Review* magazine, *op. cit.*
8. *Ibid.*
9. *Ibid.*
10. *Observer* magazine, *op. cit.*
11. *Business Day* newspaper (Manila), "Palaez Slay Try," July 23, 1982, p. 1.
12. *Ibid.*
13. "Effects Of Recent Developments On the Coconut Farmers," Report by United States Agency For International Development (Manila, January 9, 1984).
14. *Far Eastern Economic Review* magazine, *op. cit.*
15. *Ibid.,* "Favouritism Still In Favour," June 30, 1983, p. 51.
16. *Ibid,* "Cracks In the Coconut Shell," January 9, 1982, p. 42.
17. *Fortune* magazine, "The Philippines Veers Toward Crisis," July 27, 1981, p. 36.
18. *Far Eastern Economic Review* magazine, *op. cit.*
19. "Effects of Recent Developments on the Coconut Farmers," *op. cit.*

20. *Weekend* magazine (Manila), "Uncovering the Coconut Bomb." November 8, 1981, p. 7.
21. "An Analysis Of the Economic Policies Affecting the Philippine Coconut Industry," by Ramon L. Clarete and James A. Roumasset. Philippine Institute for Development Studies, Working Paper 83-08 (Makati, Metro Manila, 1983).
22. *Far Eastern Economic Review* magazine, *op. cit.*
23. *Ibid.*, "Beer and Coconut Milk," June 7, 1984, p. 61.
24. *Philippine News* newspaper (San Francisco), "Marcos' Special Crony Flew With Him To Exile," March 5-11, 1986, p. 7.

Chapter 24

1. Steinberg, *op. cit.,* p. 88.
2. "Impact Of Government Policies On Philippine Sugar," by Gerald C. Nelson and Mercedita Agcaoili. Philippine Institute For Development Studies, Working Paper 83-04 (Makati, Metro Manila, 1983).
3. *Far Eastern Economic Review* magazine (Hong Kong), "Philex Still In Sugar Business," July 22, 1977, p. 53.
4. *Ibid.*, "Manila: Aid For Growers," July 1, 1977, p. 42.
5. *Ibid.*, "The Monopoly Game," March 1984, p. 42.
6. *Manila Bulletin* newspaper (Manila), "Benedicto Controls 50 Firms, Only 4 Sequestered So Far," April 13, 1986, p. 25.
7. *Ibid.*
8. *Philippine News* newspaper (San Francisco), "ABS-CBN Owners Reclaiming Seized Property," January 30-February 5, 1986, p. 7.
9. *Manila Bulletin* newspaper, *op. cit.*
10. *Far Eastern Economic Review* magazine (Hong Kong), "Favouritism Still In Favour," June 30, 1983, pp. 50-51.
11. "Sugar Shortage In A Sugar Country." Senior Staff Memo, Center For Research and Communication (Manila, December 1981).
12. *Bulletin Today* newspaper (Manila), "CB Tightening Credit Further," October 1, 1983, p. 1.
13. *Business Day* newspaper (Manila), "Nasutra Wants Both Domestic, Export Sugar, NASP Claims," August 14, 1984, p. 18.
14. *Far Eastern Economic Review* magazine (Hong Kong), "No Pain, No Gain," July 26, 1984, p. 48.
15. *Ibid.*, "Manila: Aid For Growers," July 1, 1977, p. 42.
16. *Times Journal* newspaper (Manila), "Business Sector Wants NFA, Nasutra Abolished," October 31, 1981, p. 8.
17. "Sugar Shortage In A Sugar Country," *op. cit.*
18. "Towards A More Stable Philippine Sugar Industry." Senior Staff Memo, Center For Research and Communication (Manila, May 1982).
19. *We Forum* newspaper (Manila), "Nasutra Hit On Huge Profits From Sugar," November 8-9, 1982, p. 1.
20. *Far East Economic Review* magazine (Hong Kong), "Optimism Gives Way to Gloom in the Countryside," December 15, 1983, p. 74.

21. "Liquidity Problems In the Sugar Industry." Senior Staff Memo, Center For Research and Communication (Manila, March 1981).
22. "An Analysis Of the Philippine Economic Crisis," *op. cit.*, p. 85.
23. *Philippine News* newspaper (San Francisco), "Focus: Graft, Corruption Sour RP Sugar Industry," February 20-26, 1985, p. 1.
24. "An Analysis of the Philippine Economic Crisis," *op. cit.*, p. 82.

Chapter 25

1. Psinakis, *op. cit.*, p. 292.
2. Steinberg, *op. cit.*, p. 123.
3. Psinakis, *op. cit.*, p. 331.
4. *Los Angeles Times,* Editorial: "Where Has Bush Been?," July 2, 1981.
5. "U.S. Perceptions and Policies Toward the Philippines: Has A Transition Begun?," by Larry Niksch, U.S. Congressional Research Service, Library of Congress. Prepared for the Joint Seminar on United States – Philippines Relations, December 6-7, 1983.
6. *We Forum* newspaper (Manila), "U.S. Senators Hit Reagan For Coddling FM," October 8-10, 1982, p. 1.
7. *Far Eastern Economic Review* magazine (Hong Kong), "The No-Credit Risk," July 16, 1982, p. 40.
8. *Washington Post,* "Millions For Marcos?," September 14, 1982, p. B-1.
9. *Washington Post,* "Marcos Said To Consider U.S. Trip A Major Milestone Of His Rule," September 13, 1982, p. A21.
10. *Time* magazine, "Rolling Out His Own Red Carpet," September 20, 1982, p. 20.
11. *Washington Post, op. cit.*
12. *Time* magazine, *op. cit.*
13. *Asiaweek* magazine (Hong Kong), "Travelling In Grand Style," October 1, 1982, p. 26.
14. *Washington Post,* Mary McGrory's column, September 19, 1982.
15. *Philippine Times* newspaper (Chicago), "The New Oligarchs," December 24, 1979, p. 1.
16. Amnesty International Report, *op. cit.*
17. *Seattle Times,* "$30-M Lawsuit vs. FM, FL," September 18, 1982, p. 1.
18. *Ibid.,* "Marcos Welcomed With Warm Praise," September 17, 1982, p. A17.
19. *Ibid.,* "Dinner, Dancing & Demonstration," September 17, 1982, p. D1.
20. *Asiaweek* magazine (Hong Kong), "A Meeting Of Friends," October 1, 1982, pp. 23-26.
21. *Washington Post,* "His Regime Has Improved Rights, Marcos Tells Congressional Panel," September 18, 1982, p. A19.
22. *Ibid.,* "Marcos Welcomed With Warm Praise," September 17, 1982, p. A17.
23. *Asiaweek* magazine, *op. cit.*
24. *Ibid.*
25. *Bulletin Today* newspaper (Manila), "FM & US Media Attitude To RP," October 7, 1982, p. 1.

26. *Pacific Stars and Stripes* newspaper, "Prelate Condems Rights Abuses In Philippines," October 16, 1982.
27. *Bulletin Today* newspaper, *op. cit.*
28. *We Forum* newspaper (Manila), "Marcos US State Visit: A Pyrrhic Success," October 22-24, 1982, p. B9.
29. *Asiaweek* magazine, *op. cit.*
30. *Ibid.*

Chapter 26

1. *Asiaweek* magazine, *op. cit.*
2. *U.S. News & World Report* magazine, "Third World: Uncle Sam's Tough New Stand," October 26, 1981, p. 20.
3. *Asiaweek* magazine (Hong Kong), "Wooing & Wowing Wall Street," October 8, 1982, pp. 40-41.
4. *Ibid.*
5. *Ibid.*
6. "An Analysis of the Philippine Economic Crisis," *op. cit.*, p. 61.
7. *Asian Wall Street Journal,* "Time For the Philippines To Face the Music," by Jaime V. Ongpin, August 9, 1984, p. 7.
8. *Bulletin Today* newspaper (Manila), "Foreign Debt Total Restated," May 5, 1982.
9. *Far Eastern Economic Review* magazine, (Hong Kong), "Virata Fights Back," May 21, 1982, p. 66
10. Memo For Concerned Citizens, #2, (Metro Manila, November 1983), p. 2.
11. *Observer* magazine (Manila), "The Incredible Shrinking Peso," October 31, 1982, p. 16.
12. Memo For Concerned Citizens, #4, (Metro Manila, December 1983), p. 17.
13. *Ibid.*, p. 32.
14. Walden Bello, David Kinley and Elaine Elinson, *op. cit.*, p. 43.
15. *Ibid.*, p. 192.
16. *Asiaweek* magazine (Hong Kong), "Learning To Live With the IMF," December 10, 1982, p. 40.
17. *Far Eastern Economic Review* magazine (Hong Kong), "Creditors In Manila," November 5, 1982, p. 58.
18. *Business Day* newspaper (Manila), "Reserves Overstated Since 1981," August 9, 1984, p. 3.
19. "The Philippine Economy: Recent Events." A Report prepared by U.S. Agency For International Development, OD/PE (Manila, April 1984), p. 25.

Chapter 27

1. Benigno S. Aquino, Jr., *Testament From a Prison Cell,* (Metro Manila: Benigno S. Aquino, Jr. Foundation, 1984), p. xii.
2. Steinberg, *op. cit.*, p. 102.
3. *San Francisco Examiner,* "Doctors Say Marcos Had Transplants," November 10, 1985, p. 1.

4. *Newsweek* magazine, "Marcos Takes the Offensive," October 10, 1973, p. 8.

5. *San Francisco Chronicle*, "Marcos Accuses 33 Leaders of Sabotaging the Economy," November 15, 1983, p. 21.

6. *San Francisco Chronicle*, "U.S. Calls Aquino's Slaying a 'Cowardly, Despicable Act,'" August 22, 1983, p. 7.

7. *San Francisco Chronicle*, "U.S. Wants Arrest of All 'Responsible,'" October 24, 1984, p. 14.

8. *Far Eastern Economic Review* magazine (Hong Kong), "The President Regrets...," October 13, 1983, p. 14.

9. Steinberg, *op. cit.*, p. 60.

Chapter 28

1. *Business Day* newspaper (Manila), "Honorable Journalism," by Nines Cacho Olivres, may 2, 1984, p. 8.

2. *Bulletin Today* newspaper (Manila), "FM Assails Foreign Media," May 1, 1984, p. 1.

3. *Newsweek* magazine, "Marcos Takes the Offensive," October 10, 1983, pp. 8-9.

4. *San Francisco Examiner*, "Opposition Groups Sprout Up To Shape A New Philippines," November 16, 1983, p. A4.

5. *Ibid.*, "Imelda Marcos Blames News Media For Unrest In Philippines," September 19, 1983, p. A12.

6. *Bulletin Today* newspaper (Manila), "Delegate Hits Western Media," October 5, 1983, p. 5.

7. *Far Eastern Economic Review* magazine (Hong Kong), "Our Rich Uncle Sam," March 15, 1984, p. 44.

8. *Malaya* newspaper (Manila), "Sin Asails 'Extravagance' Of FM Regime," December 14-15, p. 1.

9. *San Francisco Examiner*, "Philippine Cardinal Urges Free Election," September 24, 1983, p. 1.

10. *Asiaweek* magazine (Hong Kong), "Church and State: Time For Detente," April 1, 1983, p. 13.

11. *South China Morning Post* newspaper (Hong Kong), "Marcos Gets Tough On Opposition Groups—Sin Describes Meeting," September 26, 1983.

12. *Newsweek* magazine, *op. cit.*

13. *South China Morning Post* newspaper, *op. cit.*

Chapter 29

1. *Bulletin Today* newspaper (Manila), "$9.9B Debt Maturing Next Year," December 18, 1983, p. 14.

2. *Ibid.*

3. Memo For Concerned Citizens, #2, (Metro Manila, November 1983), p. 3.

4. "The Philippine Economy: Policies and Development, 1975-1982." Published by Central Bank of the Philippines (Metro Manila, 1983).

5. *Asian Wall Street Journal,* "Bankers Say Manila Inflated Figures," December 19, 1983, p. 1.
6. *Far Eastern Economic Review* magazine (Hong Kong), "Optimism Gives Way To Gloom In the Countryside," December 15, 1983, p. 74.
7. *Malaya* newspaper (Manila), "Sin Assails 'Extravagance' of FM Regime," December 14-15, 1983, p. 1.
8. *Asiaweek* magazine (Hong Kong), "A 'Social Auditor' Speaks Out," January 6, 1984, p. 78.
9. *Veritas* newspaper (Manila), "The Gear Shifts To Crisis Management," January 1-7, 1984, p. 12.
10. *Business Day* newspaper (Manila), "Determining Poverty Thresholds," May 25, 1984, pp. 10-11.
11. *Ibid.*
12. *Ibid.,* "Filipinos Fearful of Future," June 14, 1984, p. 5.
13. *Ibid.*
14. "Income Distribution and Poverty In Selected Asian Countries," by J.M. Dowling, Jr., Asian Development Bank, unpublished report (Metro Manila), p. 10.
15. *Ibid.*
16. Steinberg, *op. cit.,* p. 114.
17. "What Happened To the Poor On the Way To the Next Development Plan?," by Mahar Mangahas. (Metro Manila: Development Academy of the Philippines, December 1981), p. 5.
18. *Business Day* newspaper (Manila), "Nasutra Wants Both Domestic, Export Sugar, NASP Claims," August 14, 1984, p. 18.
19. *Newsweek* magazine, "A Stinging Message To Marcos," May 28, 1984, p. 10.
20. "What Happened To the Poor On the Way To the Next Development Plan?," *op. cit.*
21. *Far Eastern Economic Review* magazine (Hong Kong), "The Military Card In Play," October 13, 1983, p. 15.
22. *Mr. & Mrs.* magazine (Manila), "Images '83 – '84," August 17, 1984, p. 44.
23. *Business Day* newspaper (Manila), *WorldPaper* Journal, "Facing Right and Left," August 1984, p. 12.
24. *Asiaweek* magazine (Hong Kong), "Passage – Charged: Fr. Jose Dizon," August 3, 1984, p. 55.
25. *Business Day* newspaper (Manila), "Sin Calls For Gov't Reforms," July 16, 1984, p. 12.
26. *Bulletin Today* newspaper (Manila), "FM Calls For Strong, Independent Courts," August 4, 1984, p. 1.
27. Amnesty International Report, *op. cit.,* p. 64.
28. *Times Journal* newspaper (Manila), "PC Details Communist Bid To Infiltrate Church," August 8, 1984, p. 1.
29. Supreme Court petition, *Renato Cañete vs. Brig. General Pedrito de Guzman et. al.,* G.R. No. 63776, dated August 17, 1984.
30. *San Francisco Examiner,* "Doctors Say Marcos Had Transplants," November 10, 1985, p. 1.

31. *Philippine News* newspaper (San Francisco). "$13 Billion Philippine Earnings Since 1965 Reported Missing," August 14-20, 1985, p. 4.
32. *San Francisco Chronicle,* "Manila's Spending Of Aid Criticized," December 6, 1985, p. 31.
33. *San Francisco Examiner,* "Philippines Diverted U.S. Schools Aid," December 8, 1985, p. 1.
34. *Philippine News* newspaper (San Francisco), "US Halts Fund Aid To NEA For Anomaly," January 8-14, 1986, p. 7.
35. *Ibid.,* "Reforms Made To Appease IMF," November 6-13, 1985, p. 1.
36. *Reports of the Fact-Finding Board on the Assassination of Senator Benigno S. Aquino, Jr., op. cit.*
37. *San Francisco Examiner,* "Laxalt's 'Secret' Trip Shows Up Tensions In U.S.-Philippine Tie," October 20, 1985, p. A-4.
38. *San Francisco Examiner,* "Doctors Say Marcos Had Transplants," November 10, 1985, p. 1.
39. *San Francisco Chronicle,* "Marcos Says He Wants An Election In January," November 4, 1985, p. 1.
40. *Far Eastern Economic Review* magazine (Hong Kong), "After All That Drama Look For Useful Reform," May 8, 1986, pp. 84-86.
41. Telephone conversation with secretary of Philip Habib, July 24, 1986.

Chapter 30

1. Patricia R. Mamot, *People Power,* (Quezon City, Philippines: New Day Publishers, 1986), p. 54.
2. *Time* magazine, "Rebelling Against Marcos," March 3, 1986, pp. 6-11.
3. *Mr. & Mrs.* magazine (Manila), "The Desperate 77 Hours," February 28-March 6, 1986, pp. 3-5.
4. Mamot, *op. cit.,* p. 64.
5. *Time* magazine, *op. cit.*
6. *Mr. & Mrs.* magazine (Manila), *op. cit.*
7. *Newsweek* magazine, "The Showdown," March 3, 1986, pp. 8-14.
8. *Manila Times* newspaper (Manila), "FM Ordered Arrest of 10,000—Enrile," June 21, 1986, p. 1.
9. *Manila Bulletin* newspaper (Manila), "The Courts and the Press," June 21, 1986, p. 5.
10. Mamot, *op. cit.,* p. 80.
11. *Ibid.,* p. 70.
12. *Newsweek* magazine, *op. cit.*
13. *Ibid.*
14. *Ibid.*
15. Mamot, *op. cit.,* pp. 78-79.
16. *San Francisco Examiner,* "The General's Confusion As Marcos Fell," March 10, 1986, p. A-4.
17. *Far East Economic Review* magazine (Hong Kong), "The Days That Shook Marcos Out of Power," March 6, 1986, pp. 18-19.
18. *Philippine News* newspaper (San Francisco), "Eyewitness To the Revolution of 1986," June 11-17, 1986, p. 12.

19. *Time* magazine, "Anatomy of a Revolution," March 10, 1986, pp. 28-34.
20. *San Francisco Examiner,* " 'Survivor' of Marcos Regime, " March 4, 1986, p. 1.
21. Mamot, *op. cit.,* pp. 90-91.
22. *Far East Economic Review* magazine (Hong Kong), *op. cit.*
23. *San Francisco Examiner,* "The General's Confusion As Marcos Fell," March 10, 1986, p. A-4.
24. *PC/INP Journal* (Manila), "Fighting Men In Their Flying Machines," by Col. Antonio Sotelo, Jan.-Feb. 1986, pp. 20-22.
25. *Ibid.*
26. *Far East Economic Review* magazine (Hong Kong), *op cit.*
27. *South China Morning Post* newspaper (Hong Kong), Spectrum magazine, "Swept Away By Stuff of Song and Legend," March 2, 1986, p. 2.
28. Mamot, *op cit.,* pp. 58-59.
29. *Far East Economic Review* magazine (Hong Kong, *op. cit.*
30. *Time* magazine, *op. cit.*
31. *Ibid.*
32. *San Francisco Examiner,* " 'Survivor' of Marcos Regime," March 4, 1986, p. 1.
33. Mamot, *op. cit.,* s p. 162-163.
34. *San Francisco Examiner, op. cit.*
35. "Investigation of the Costs Involved in Moving Former President Marcos and His Party from Manila to Hawaii," Report of the Readiness Subcommittee of the Committee On Armed Services, House of Representatives (Washington, D.C., May, 1986).
36. *San Francisco Examiner,* "Sin Tells Story of Revolt," May 7, 1986, p. A-3.

Other Readings

1. Teodoro A. Agoncillo and Milagros C. Guerrero, *History of the Filipino People,* Fifth Edition (Quezon City: Garcia Publishing Company, 1982).
2. "Aspects of Poverty in the Philippines: A Review and Assessment." Volume II of a report by the World Bank (Washington, D.C., 1 December 1980).
3. Richard J. Barnet & Ronald E. Muller, *Global Reach—The Power of the Multinational Corporations,* (New York: Simon and Shuster, 1974).
4. Romeo M. Bautista, John N. Power and associates, *Industrial Promotion Policies in the Philippines,* (Makati, Metro Manila: Philippine Institute For Developmental Studies, 1979).
5. Joachin G. Bernas, "Some Reflections on Eight Years Under Martial Rule," from *Not By Bread Alone,* edited by Fr. Pacifico A. Ortiz, S.J., Bishops-Businessmen's Conference Dialogue On Human Development Under Martial Law, (Manila, 1980).
6. Effects of Recent Developments on the Coconut Farmers. Report by U.S. Agency for International Development (Manila, 9 January 1984).

7. Augusto Caesar Espiritu, Merlin M. Magallona, Lilia R. Bautistal, Reuben D. Torres & Esteban B. Bautista, *Philippine Perspectives On Multinational Corporations,* (Quezon City: University of the Philippines Law Center, 1978).

8. Economic Profile and Causes of Poverty in Bicol. Report by U.S. Agency for International Development (Manila, May 1982).

9. Lewis E. Gleek, Jr., *American Business and Philippine Economic Development,* (Manila: Carmelo & Bauerman, 1975).

10. Iligan Integrated Steel Mill Incorporated Management Audit. Report of Business Research Foundation, Inc. (Quezon City: University of the Philippines, 1972).

11. Frank Isaiah, *Foreign Enterprises in Developing Countries,* (New York: John Hopkins University Press, 1980).

12. Charles C. McDougald, A Commentary On the Report Entitled "Multinational Corporations in the Philippines" Prepared By the Technology Resource Center. Prepared for the American Chamber of Commerce of the Philippines (Makati, Metro Manila, April 16, 1979).

13. *Ibid,* Multinational Corporations In the Philippines, 1978. Prepared for the American Chamber of Commerce of the Philippines (Makati, Metro Manila, December 1, 1980).

14. Anat R. Negandhi and S. Benjamin Prasad, *The Frightening Angels,* (Kent, Ohio: Kent State University Press, 1975).

15. Pacifico A. Ortiz, S.J. (editor), *Not By Bread Alone,* (Manila: Bishops-Businessmen's Conference, 1980).

16. "Overview of Developments in Public Expenditures, 1978 – 1983." Report by U.S. Agency For International Development (Manila, 1984).

17. Norman G. Owen, editor, *The Philippine Economy and the United States,* (University of Michigan: Center for South and Southeast Asia Studies, Number 22, 1983).

18. *Philippine Statistical Yearbook.* Prepared by the National Economic and Development Authority (Metro Manila, various years).

19. Niceto S. Poblador, *Socio-Cultural Environmental and Organizational Structure and Performance: A Cross Sectional Analysis,* (Quezon City: University of the Philippines, 1976).

20. *Poverty and Basic Needs.* World Bank brochure. (Washington, D.C., September 1980).

21. Poverty Profile, Bicol Region. Report by U.S. Agency for International Development (Manila, August 1982).

22. Poverty Profile, Eastern Visayas. Report by U.S. Agency for International Development (Manila, September 1982).

23. Poverty Profile, Western Visayas. Report by U.S. Agency for International Development (Manila, January 1981).

24. Anthony Sampson, *The Money Lenders,* (Middlesex, England, Penguin Books, 1981).

25. *Sharing In Development.* Report of Inter-Agency Team financed by the United Nations Development Program (Metro Manila: National Economic and Development Authority, 1974).

26. Raymond Vernon, *Storm Over Multinationals,* (Cambridge: Harvard University Press, 1977).

27. *Ibid., The Economic and Political Consequences of Multinational Enterprises: An Anthology,* (Boston: Harvard University Press, 1972).

28. *A White Paper On Philippine Industry.* Report of Philippine Chamber of Industries (Manila, 1977).

29. *The World Bank and the World's Poorest, 1980.* World Bank brochure (Washington, D.C., 1980).

30. Gregorio F. Zaide, *Jose Rizal — Life, Works, and Writings,* (Manila: C.F. Villanueva Publishers, Inc., 1981).

Index

ACCRA law firm, 227
Agatep, Zacarias, (Fr.), 152-153
Aglipayan Party, 7
Aglipay, Gregorio, 197
Agoncillo, Teodoro A., 10, 79-80
Agrava, Corazon J. (Judge), 275,
    283
Agrava Commission, 279
Aguinaldo, Emilio, 264-265
Allas, Cipriano, (Capt.), 103,
    104-105
Allen, Teddy (Brig. Gen.), 296
American Caesar, (Manchester),
    9-10
American Society of Travel Agents,
    bombing incident, 167
Amnesty International
  documents human rights abuses,
    167-168, 170-172, 246
  Enrile refuses to meet, 153
  objects to emergency powers, 130
  gives proof of oppression, 241,
    244-245
AMRSP, Association of Major
    Religious Superiors, 148, 281
Ancheta, Donato (Capt.), 103-104
Anderson, Bernard (Maj.), 63, 66,
    83-86
Andrews, Edwin D. (Lt. Col.),
    68-69
Ang Manga Maharlika. *See*
    Maharlika

Anido Case, 182n
apo (patron), 114
Apostol, Eugenia D., 184
April 6 Liberation Movement, 166
Aquino, Agapito (Butz) (brother of
    Ninoy), 295
Aquino, Antonio (Tony) (brother of
    Ninoy), 43
Aquino, Benigno S. (Ninoy)
  background, 262-264
  correspondent in Korea for *Manila
    Times* newspaper (1950), 178
  requests election-eve noise barrage,
    166
  excluded from running for election
    by age requirement, 240
  Huks surrender to, 116
  implicated in bombing plot,
    166-167
  leads demonstrators in
    Washington, 247
  petition to courts on jurisdiction
    of military tribunal, 148
  Plaza Miranda bombing and,
    120-121
  ran against Imelda for Interim
    National Assembly, 138
  ran for office from prison, 165
  return from exile, 2-3, 174, 267
Aquino, Corazon (Cory)
  announces candidacy, 286
  marriage, 226, 262

offers help to Enrile, 294
sworn in as President, 301
urges Marcos must step down,
    leave country, 287, 303
Armacost, Michael, 220, 300
Armed Forces of the Philippines
    (AFP), 14
Arnold, Robert H. (Lt.), 72, 76
Arrest, Search and Seizure Orders
    (ASSOs), 164-165
Art of War, The (Sun Tzu), 293
Asia Industries, 213
Asiaweek magazine, 179
Assassination
  Agrava Commission, 279, 283-285
  of Ninoy Aquino, 264-267
Associated Press news service, 180
Association of Major Religious
    Superiors (AMRSP), 148, 281
Association of Survivors of
    Japanese Prisons, 56
ATOM (August Twenty-One Move-
    ment), 295
August 21 rally, 281
Avedoso, Terry, 63

Babst, Arlene, 182-183
Baccay, Potencio, 285
Back pay, earned as guerrilla, 97
Baclagon, Uldarico (Col.), 15, 26,
    42, 65, 91-93
Baffrey, Doris, 167
Bagong Lipunan Site and Services,
    (BLISS),139-141
Balweg, Conrado (Fr.), 153
BANDILA (flag), 295
Bangsa Moro (Muslim Nation)
    Army, 164
Bank Advisory Committee, 274
Banking
  banking system, 214
  bank loans to directors' relatives,
    214
  Central Bank, 273-275
  corruption in, 208
  financial scandal causes crisis, 213
  see also Cronyism, Economy,
    Finance

Barangays, 129
Barba, Fortuna Marcos (sister of
    Marcos), 202
Barnett, George M. (Lt.), 71, 73,
    76-77
Bataan, surender of, 72
Bautista, Thelma H., 205
Beams, Dovie, 106
Benedicto, Roberto, 177, 181, 190,
    218, 234-235
Bernas, Joachin G., 188
Biographies of Marcos, claims in-
    consistent, unconfirmed by con-
    temporary accounts, 14-16, 26,
    65, 81, 90, 93, 97, 106
Blackburn, Don (Capt.), 76
BLISS (Bagong Lipunan Site and
    Services), 139-141
"Blue Book," The, 117
Blue Ladies, 136
Bluemel, Clifford (Brig. Gen.),
    39-42
Booms, Albert (Fr.), 149
Bosworth, Stephen (U.S. Amb),
    296, 300, 301
Breaz, Pete C. (Lt.), 89
Broadcast Media Council, 177
Brocka, Lino, 176
Bronstein, Phil, 270
Bulletin Today newspaper, 138,
    178, 182-184, 247, 270
Burgos, Jose G., 183-184, 269
Bush, George (U.S. Vice President),
    240
Business Day, 219, 291
But Not in Shame: The Six Months
    After Pearl Harbor (Toland), 15
Butterfield, Fox, 165

Cacho-Olivarez, Ninez, 183, 269
Caen, Herb, 138
Calvert, Parker (Capt.), 75
Campos, Jose Y., 205, 212
Cancun economic summit, 249-250
Cañete, Renato, 281
Capinpin, Mateo (Brig. Gen.), 28,
    31, 33-35, 40, 46, 48, 85, 87
Casey, Hugh G. "Pat" (Maj. Gen.),
    62, 96

Catholic Bishops Conference, 147-148

CDCP (Construction and Development Corporation of the Philippines), 210, 213-214

Chammag, Isidoro, 184

Chinese Anti-Japanese Guerrilla Force. *See* Guerrilla units

Chua, Antonio Roxas, 120

Church
Amendment 6 and, 150
KKK members murdered, 154
"Liberation Theology" and, 154
Marcos regime and adversary role of, 143, 147-148
military liason committees and, 148
organizations in, 147-148
relations with Marcos worsen, 275

Church, clergy
active in non-violent ouster of Marcos, 296-297, 302
clergy-bourgeois clique, 275
harassment of, 148-149, 151-152, 157-158, 280
promoted Basic Christian Communities, 154
as representative of the people, 131, 147
taking up arms, 152-153
teaches about human rights, 154

Civil Intelligence and Security Authority (CISA), 169-170

Clark Air Base, 241

Climate of Philippines, 111-112

Cocofed, 225

Coconut levy, 225, 226, 227, 230

Cocopec scandal, 229

Cojuangco, Corazon. *See* Aquino, Corazon (Cory)

Cojuangco, Eduardo Jr. (Danding), 218, 226-229, 279

Collaborators, 9-10, 85-86, 89

Commission on Social Action of the Bishops Conference, 152

Communist Party of the Philippines (CPP), 161-162

"Compadres" system, 113-115

Concepcion, Jose, 278

Conjugal Distatorships, The (Mijares), 178

Constitution
Amendment Six and, 149
approved by hastily called referendum (1973), 128-129
convention of 1970
eliminated separation of powers (1973), 125, 127-128
further amendments to (1976), 149
Marcos dissatisfied with (1972), 121
Marcos granted lifetime immunity from legal action, 240
plebiscite (1981), 239

Constitutional Authoritarianism
described, 123-126
expands military's police powers, 127

Construction and Development Corporation of the Philippines (CDCP), 210, 213-214

Consumer Price Index, 253

Corregidor, surrender of, 72

Corro, Rommell, 270

Corruption, 207, 222
see also Graft

Courts
independence undermined, 130
judges required to submit resignations, 129
Lansing Doctrine and, 173-174
Marcos appointees, courts controlled by, 126-127, 280
Marcos granted immunity from legal action, 129

Cronyism
access to bail-out funds, 254
cause of loss of faith in government, 147
crony capitalism, 191n, 201-215, 277
the grand coalition and, 187-191, 219, 239
law, immunity from, granted cronies, 188
self-enrichment as goal, 188-189
see also Graft

Cruz, Emigdio, 16-17, 80
Cruz, Roman, 205
Cuenca, Rodolfo, 207, 210-211,
    213-214, 218
Curtis, Elbert R. (Capt.), 70, 83,
    102, 103-104
Cushing, Walter M., 72

Daily Express newspaper, 177, 270
Daily Inquirer, 290
Dangan, Vicente (Fr.), 156
Death Decrees, 171
Death March, 55-56
Debt service ratio, 252
Decorations
  AFP investigations of not through,
    14
  often given for support of AFP
    appropriations bills, 14
  proper procedures for awarding,
    13, 33
  US-Philippine equivalents, 23n
Decorations, Marcos'
  based on affidavits after the fact,
    13-14, 28, 102
  discrepancies in accounts and doc-
    umentation of, 15, 26, 33-34
  Philippine Distinguished Conduct
    Star, 28, 56, 91
  Philippine Distinguished Service
    Stars, 58-59, 95, 99
  Philippine Gold Crosses, 23, 25,
    42, 48, 50, 93, 99
  Philippine Medal for Valor, 31-41
  U.S. Distinguished Service Cross,
    27-28
  U.S. Purple Heart, 91
  U.S. Silver Stars, 25, 93
  U.S. Medal of Honor, 39
  unconfirmed by contemporary
    accounts, 13, 15-17, 22, 26, 28,
    40, 43, 48, 51-52, 106
Wounded Personnel Medals, 90
De Jesus, Simeon (Maj. Gen.), 62
de la Torre, Edicio (Fr.), 151
Dee, Dewey, 212-214, 254-255
Del Rosario, Ramon, 275
Delta Motors Corporation, 211

Dictatorship
  affirmed by Supreme Court, 148
  peaceful end to, 1-2, 301-303
Dimalinao village, bombing of, 152
Diokno, Jose W. (Sen.), 121
Disini, Herminio, 207, 209-210
Dizon, Jose (Fr.), 280
Documents on the Marcos War
    Medals, 31, 33-35, 93
Doherty, John (Fr.), 176, 201
Dollar salting, 252

East Central Luzon Guerrillas. See
    Guerrilla units
Economy
  crony capitalism and widespread
    corruption in, 222-223
  faulty government projections for,
    255
  foreign investment in, 208, 211,
    219-221, 242, 249-250
  free market vs managed,
    217-218, 223
  government spending freeze and,
    255
  growth rate, disputed by IMF,
    255
  IMF applies pressure to cut spend-
    ing, 142
  indebtedness and, 251
  industrial projects in, increase
    income inequality, 276
  monopolies and, 205-206, 217-219
  multinational corporations and,
    221
  nationalization of industries and,
    218, 236
  overpricing, protectionism and leg-
    islative favoritism in, 218-219,
    251
  recession in, and reduced demand
    for exports, 208
  red tape tradition and, 220, 222,
    255-256
  strikes and, 243
  see also Infrastructure
Edifice complex, 190

Elections
announced (1985), 285
campaign of 1969, 119
faud in, 2, 10-11, 119-120, 138,
165, 278, 278, 286
observed by foreign media, 278
presidential (1981), 240
Enrile, Juan Ponce
background of, 225-226
chairman of United Coconut
Planters Bank, 227
chairman of Philippine National
Bank, 233
denies anti-clergy campaign, 150
goes to Washington, 249
heads Mass Media Council and
crackdown on media, 177, 184
joins the reformists and opposition, 291-298
leads revolt against Marcos purge
of military ranks, 159-160
meets with Catholic Bishops, 153
power eclipsed by Ver, 170
refuses to meet with Amnesty
International, 171
survives ambush attempt, 121
urges trial of Gore and Dangan,
156
Enriquez, Manuel P. (Lt. Col.),
73-74
Escobar, Emilio, (Sagad, The
Broom), 77
Escolta Guerrillas, 97
Espino, Romeo, (Gen.), 163, 169
Estancio, Jesus (Jess), 218
Exiles
Aquino, Benigno S. (Ninoy), 263
de la Torre, 151
Quijano and Yuyitung, 121-122
Salonga, 131
Extradition treaty, 245-246

Fall of the Philippines, The
(Morton), 20
Far Eastern Economic Review, The,
139-140, 175
Favoritism, 141
in government and business,
decried, 118
journalists and, 177
Marcos advocates Walang
Palakasan (No special favors),
123
Presidential Center for Special
Studies, plush appointments to,
176-177
through legislation, 209
see also Cronyism; Graft
Fernandez, Doreen, 176
Fernando, Enrique (Supreme Crt.
Chief Justice), 174, 274
Fertig, Wendell (Lt. Col.), 60,
65-66, 67-70, 80, 82
Filipino Heroes of World War II
(Baclagon), 15
Filipinos, traits of. See Society
Film Festival, 142-143
Filtrona, 209
Finance
debt-service ratio redefined, 252
excessive indebtedness, 210-213
foreign debt, 249
fraud, counterfeit commercial
paper, 211-212
government bail-outs of crony
corporations, 214-215
government cash crisis caused by
election spending, 286
government defaults on foreign
debt, 271, 273
government indebtedness, spending, and Imelda, 208, 251
IMF delays/refuses to loan more,
254-256, 282
international reserves drained and
mistated, 253
lack of public accountability,
190, 206, 214, 251
misuse of funds, 137-138, 140,
142-143, 144-145, 277
Monetary Board controlled by
Marcos, 254
overpriced projects, 252
peso devalued, 275
rescue of troubled crony companies, 254

revolving credits and debt figure,
   252, 273
World Bank and, 142-143, 208,
   242, 282
see also Banking; Cronyism,
   Ecomony
Floirendo, Antonio, 204
Folk Arts Theatre, 138, 144
For Every Tear a Victory (Spence),
   14, 106, 118
Fortich, Antonio Y. (Msr.),
   154-157
Fortune magazine, 137
Francisco, Vicente, 10, 115
Free Philippines. See Guerrilla units
Free Press, 291

Galman, Rolando, 265, 279, 283
Gapud, Rolando, 205, 212, 274
Gerlock, Eduardo (Fr.), 149
Gillego, Bonifacio, 14, 26, 97,
   183-184
Golden Buddha scandal, 202
Gore, Brian (Fr.), 152, 154-157
Graft, 119
   "Blue Book" scandal, 117
   bribery, 120, 255-256
   corruption, 207, 222
   dollar salting, 252
   extortion, 209
   favorable legislation, extortion,
      crony capitalism, 191
   forced sale of manila Electric and
      Philippine Airlines, 203
   "ghost project" with fictitious
      contractors, 141
   illegal government loans, 203
   Import Control Board, Marcos
      and, 116
   import tax avoidance, 252
   kickbacks, 189, 203, 206, 210,
      251-252
   overpricing, 251-252
   Marcos' Swiss bank accounts, 119
   proceeds of sugar monopoly, 190
   stock dumping, 209
   ten-percenter schemes, Marcos
      and, 116

Grand Coalition, The. See
   Cronyism
"Great Cheese Scandal", 143
Guerrilla Resistance Movement in
   the Philippines, The
   (Willoughby), 59
Guerrilla units
   Marcos falsely claims leadership
      of, 100
   1st Provisional Guerrilla Regiment,
      73
   11th, 14th, 15th, 43rd, 66th &
      121st Infantry groups, 71-76,
      94
   Chinese Anti-Japanese Guerrillas,
      Force, 82
   Cushing's, 72
   East Central Luzon Guerrillas,
      63, 82
   Fil-American Irregular Troups, 59
   Free Philippines, 62, 71, 74, 82
   Hukbalahaps, 63
   Hunters, 57, 58-59, 63, 71, 82
   LOD Sabotage Unit, 82
   Major Bernard Anderson's group,
      63
   Marking's, 59, 63, 67, 71
   Philippine Scouts, 75
   President Quezon's Own Guerrillas
      (PQOG), 58-61, 67, 82
   U.S. Armed Forces in Philippines
      —Northern Luzon (USAFIP NL),
      76-77, 79, 88-89, 92, 94-96
   U.S. Forces in Phil., No. Luzon—
      USFIP NL, 75
   Yay Panlilio, 63
   see also Maharlika

Habib, Philip, 288, 292, 300
Haig, Alexander, 240
History of the 21st Division
   from Capinpin, 26, 28
   by O'Day, 27, 28, 32, 39
History of the Philippines
   American occupation, 112-113,
      264-265
   early settlers, 111
   independence, 113

Rizal, 261-262
Spanish occupation, 1, 111-112
Homma, Masaharu (Lt. Gen.), 37,
   45, 46, 71
Hooley, Richard, 219
Horan, John P. (Lt. Col.), 71-73,
   75
Huks, 116, 162
   see also Guerrilla units,
   Hukbalahaps
Human rights abuses
   arrest without warrant, 172
   attract international attention, 164
   American vs Philippine, 131
   Amnesty International investigates,
   170-172
   investigators arrested, 151
   Irregular Civilian Home Defense
   Force (ICHDF) and, 168
   murder, 153-154, 157-158, 281
   pervasive surveillance of citizens,
   127
   reported, 244-246
   "salvaging", 172
   torture, 127, 158, 172, 281
   U.N. declarations signed, 118,
   170
   worsen, 157
   writ of habeas corpus, 150
   see also Amnesty International,
   Opponents/critics, Press
Hunt, Ray (Capt.), 89
Hunters. See Resistance/guerrilla
   units

Imai, Takeo (Col.), 35-36, 41
Imelda
   birth and family, 134-135
   Rose of Tacloban, 134-135
   Muse of Manila, 135
   met Marcos, 135-136
   25th Wedding Anniversary celebration, 140
   allows pronographic films, 143
   ambition, 136
   ancestral estate, 137
   announces Sariling Sikap (Self
   Reliance), 276

appointed governor of Manila,
   138, 141
appointed head of BLISS (Bagong
   Lipunan Site and Services),
   139, 141
appointed head of Economic
   Support Fund (ESF), 142
appointed Minister of Human
   Settlements, 138, 141
appointed to Executive Committee,
   141-142
belief in "hole in the sky", 145
called "richest woman in the world
   (Cosmopolitan magazine), 138
distributed cash to Constitutional
   Convention delegates, 120
"edifice complex", 144, 190
elected to Interim National
   Assembly, 138, 141
extravagance and shopping sprees,
   133, 137-144, 190
famous reply on wealth of her
   family: "Some smarter than
   others", 137
foreign trips, 138-141, 143
Iron Butterfly, 134, 145
need for illusions, 3
nervous breakdown, 136
public image, 133
resigns from Executive Committee
   (1984), 278
will not run for re-election, 278
leaves the Philippines, 302
IMF (International Monetary Fund,
   142, 208, 254-256, 273, 282
Import Control Law, 115
Income inequality, 276
Infrastructure
   early modernization of for sugar
   export, 233
   outlays for, 251
   poor condition of, 220, 221
Ingles, Gustavo (Col.), 58
Interim National Assembly, 165
International Film Festival, 142-143
International reserves, definition,
   253
Iron Butterfly (Imelda), 134

Irregular Civilian Home Defense Force (ICHDF), 168
I Saw the Fall of the Philippines (Romulo), 17
I Walked With Heroes (Romulo), 17

Jabidah massacre, 163
Jacinto, Fernando, 204
Judiciary Reorganization Act, 280

Kalibapi, 124, 129
Kangleon, Edgardo (Fr.), 153
Kabataang Barangay, 272
Katipunan ng Kristianong Katilingban (KKK), 154, 281
Keithley, June, 297
Kempetai, 56-58,
Kennedy, Edward (Sen.), 241
Kickbacks. *See* Graft
Kilusang Bagong Lipunan (KBL) party, 165
Kilusang Kabuhayan at Kaunlaran (KKK), 140-141
Kilusang Mayo Uno (KMU), 184
King, Edward P. (Maj. Gen.), 52, 55
KKK (Katipunan ng Kristianong Katilingban, 154
KKK (Kilusang Kabuhayan at Kaunlaran), 140-141
Kokoy, *See* Romualdez, Kokoy

Laban Party, 166
Lacson, Arsenio H., 115, 135
Lacson, Raphael, 113
Lademora, Carlos, (Lt. Col.), 168-169
Landlords, 154
Land reform, 277
Langham, R.G. (Maj.), 105
Lansing Doctrine, 173-174
Lapham, Robert (Maj.), 76
Lapus, Ismael, D. (Captain), 18, 26, 28
Last Farewell, The, 261
Laurel, Jose P., 8-11, 65, 85, 87, 123-124
Laurel, Salvadore, 11, 301
Laurel-Langley Act, 233
Laxalt, Paul, 285, 300, 301
Lazaro, Lupino, 279
Ledesma, Oscar, (Sen.), 117
Life magazine, 140, 179
Light-A-Fire Movement, 166
Lim, Vicente (Brig. Gen.), 46
Limon, Fredrico (Archbishop), 152
Locsin, Teodoro, 115-116
Lopez, Eugenio (Geny), 203
Lopez, Fernando, 203
Lost Command, 168-169
Lough, Maxon (Gen.), 37, 39-41, 45
Lovely, Victor Burns, 166-167
Lucero, Aurelio (Maj.), 25-28, 31-34, 102
Lukban, Jose (Lt. Col.), 117, 118

Macapagal, Diosdado, 118
MacArthur, Arthur (Gen.), 264
MacArthur, Douglas (Gen.), 16, 36, 45, 67, 73, 87, 105-106, 159
MacKenzie, Harry (Maj.), 100
MacMillan, William D. (Lt.), 83, 101
Magsanoc, Letty, 182
Magsaysay, Ramon, 116, 136
Maharlika
  Duplicates information on Japanese troop strength, 69
  exploits unconfirmed by contemporary accounts, 78, 81
  formed, 59, 65
  Marcos' claims of size and control disputed, 63, 66, 67-68, 80, 83, 87-88, 98, 103
  movie made of, 106
  recognition requests and denials, 70-71, 98-101, 105
  records and exploits confused and contradictory, 81, 103-105
Malacañang Palace, 8, 9
Malaya, 269, 290
Malaya newspaper, 184
"Mambo Magsaysay", 297
Management by illusion, 256, 276

Manchester, William, 9
Mangahas, Mahar, 176, 277, 278
Manglapus, Raul, 57
Manila Bay Enterprises, 203
Manila Chronicle newspaper, 177
Manila Daily Bulletin newspaper, 178
Manila Electric Company, 203
Manila Times newspaper, 178
Manotoc Case, 182n
Manriquez, Romulo (Maj.), 74, 76, 79, 87, 88, 90-95, 99, 102
Manzano, Narciso, (Col.), 61-63, 66, 81, 96, 97, 178
Mapua, Angel, (Brig. Gen.), 299
Marbella Beach resort, 140
Marcos, Doña Josepha (mother of Marcos), 202
Marcos, Ferdinand E., historical highlights
birth (1917), 3
claims sports awards (disputed), 7
bar topnotcher (1939), 8
arrested for murder of Nalondasan (1939), 8
murder conviction overturned (1940), 8
early celebrity status (1941), 8
joins army (1941), 13
wartime exploits
assigned to 21st Infantry Div (1941), 17
sporty Oldsmobile, 43
prisoner of war (1942), 56
wounds, 50
promotions, 50
duties, 60
offered rank of General (disputed), 60
joins 14th Infantry (1944), 87
ordered executed as collaborator (1945), 89
father executed as collaborator (1945), 2, 89, 98
leaves 14th Infantry (1945), 95
postwar duties (1945-46), 96
leaves army (1946), 13, 101
see also Decorations, Maharlika

as politician (1946), 114-122
joins law firm (1946), 115
early political prestige (1947), 11, 102
claims reparations for cattle commandeered by Army (1948), 106
elected to Congress)1949), 115
elected Senator (1959), 117
elected Senate president (1963), 117-118
elected President (1965), 14, 118
declares martial law (1972), 121, 123
harassment of Church, 147-157
attempts purge of military ranks (1975), 159-160
re-elected president (1981), 240
announces end of martial law (1981), 150
announces new constitution (1981), 239
state visit to Washington (1982), 239-247
kidney transplants, 263, 282
re-elected (1986), 287
threatens bases, 267
refuses to resign, 285, 297
attempts deal with Laxalt, 300
leaves the Philippines, 302
greed uncovered, 189, 303
Marcos, Ferdinand E., personal characteristics:
"clairvoyant", 196
dynastic ambitions, 120, 190, 243
greedy, 198
illnesses, 65, 81, 90, 263, 282, 285
illusionist, 3, 276
paranoid, 3, 272, 275, 292
psychology of, 195-199
superstitious, 2, 196, 257
Marcos Foundation, 205
Marcos, Mariano (father), 7, 89
Marcos, Pacifico (Dr.) (brother), 202
Marcos Park and bust of Marcos, 196
Marcos, Pio (uncle), 202

Marcos, Barba-Fortuna (sister), 202
Marcos of the Philippines, 14
    Marcos relatives' and friends'
        peosperity , 202-206
Marcos-Valdez, Simeon (uncle), 202
Martial law, 121, 124-125, 150
Mass Media Council, 177
McCoy, Alfred W., 26
Media Advisory Council, 177
Menzi, Hans, 178, 182-183
Metro Manila Commission, 145
Mijares, Primitivo, 177-178
Military
  as arm of executive, 127
  clampdown on "subversives" of
    "Christian Left", 152
  courts created, 127
  discredited by lack of profes-
    sionalism, 289
  implicated in human rights abuses,
    281
  medals, *see* Decorations
  officer group calls for reforms, 290
  officers overdue for retirement,
    159, 289
  Philippine Constabulary members
    charged with murder, 155, 157
  powers expanded, 131, 164-165,
    167
  procurements, kickbacks for, 161
  protection given landowners, 169
  ranks and promotions expanded,
    159, 168-169
  reform movement, 290
  reformists revolt, 292-295
  resort to brutallity, 162
  secret marshalls, 243, 280
  spending increased, 160
  troops accused of human rights
    abuses, 159, 166
  units defect to revolutionaries,
    297-299
Military-Church adversarial
    relationship, 153
Miracle, on E. de los Santos, 2
Miss Universe Pageant, 138
Monetary Board, 254
Monopolies, coconut

alleged price manipulation, cor-
    ruption in, 231
Cocopec scandal, 229
dominated by large landowners,
    225
farmers' bank, 227
  farmers minimally benefitted
    from, 230
  stock manipulations in, 228-229
favoritism in, 227
lack of public accountability for
    funds, 230
land reform, crony-owned farms
    exempt from, 277
levy on copra, 225, 226-227, 230
replanting program, 226-227,
    229-230
Monopolies, sugar
  dismantling announced, 278
  domestic distribution system
    criticized, 236
  excessive trading costs in, 237-238
  farmers
    aided by Church, 238
    forced into poverty, 238
  land reform, crony-owned farms
    exempt from, 277
  legislative favoritism in, 235
  nationalization, 236
  price fixing in, 233-234, 238
  production decline, 235
  system inefficiency prevalent, 236
Morgan, Luis, 60
Moro National Liberation Front
    (MNLF), 163-164
Moros, 163-164
Morton, Louis, 20, 27
Moses, Martin (Lt. Col.), 75
Movement for Free Philippines, 167
Mr. & Ms. magazine, 184, 269, 290
*Multinational Corporations In the
    Philippines,* 221
Muse of Manila (Imelda), 135
Muslims, 163-164
"My Country" (film) banned, 176

Nacionalista party, 7, 240

Nakar, Guillermo, P. (Lt. Col.), 58, 73-75, 75
Nalundasan, Julio, 8, 88
NAMFREL (National Movement For Free Elections), 278, 286
Nara, Akira (Lt. Gen.), 35, 37, 39, 46
Nasutra (National Sugar Trading Corporation), 234-278
National Alliance for Justice, Freedom and Democracy, 280
National Democratic Front (NDF), 163
National Intelligence and Security Authority (NISA), 169-170
National Security Code, 150
National Sugar Trading Corporation (Nasutra), 234
Natural resources, 112
Negritos, 111
Neri, Jaime (Fr.), 58
Neubauer, Kenneth H. (Lt.), 104
New Manila Times, 290-291
New People's Army (NPA), 153, 155, 161-162
New Society, 123, 125
Newsweek, 138-139, 179
New York Times, The, 138, 139, 165, 195, 247
Nieva, Antonio, 184
Niksch, Larry, 240
Noble, Arthur K. (Lt. Col.), 75
Nuclear power plant, 210

O'Brien, Niall (Fr.), 154
Ocampo, Saturnino, 179-180
Ocampo-Kalfors, Sheila, 134
O'Day, John Patrick, 77
O'Day, Ray M. (Col.), 27-28, 33, 39, 50
Olaguer, Eduardo, 166
Oligarchy
  military protecting landlords, 157
  sugar bloc, 233
Ongpin, Jaime, 252
Ongpin, Roberto, 249, 292
"Operation Mad Dog", 165
Ople, Blas, 300

Opponents/critics, treatment of, 3
  Anido, 182n
  Apostol, 184
  Aquino, 120-121, 125, 262, 264-267
  Babst, 182-183
  Baccay, 285
  Burgos, 183-184
  Cacho-Olivarez, 183
  Chammag, 184
  Church, clergy, 147-148, 151
  "communism", 161
  de la Torre, 151
  demonstrators, 266
  Diokno, Jose W., 121
  Dizon, 279-280
  Doherty, 176, 201
  Gillego, 183-184
  Gore, Dangan and O'Brien, 154-157
  journalists, 125, 270
  KKK "communists", 154
  Lukban, 118
  Magsanoc, 182
  Mangahas, 176, 278
  Manruquez, 92
  Mijares, 178
  military reformists, 292
  Moros/Muslims, 163-164
  Ocampo, 179
  "Operation Mad Dog", 165
  Palaez, 182n, 228
  Pedrosa, 135
  plans to squelch opposition, 290
  Presidential Commitment Orders (PCOs), 174
  Preventive Detention Action (PDA), 174
  Quijano and Yuyitung, 121-122
  Roces, 178
  Salonga, 131
  "subversives", 14, 131, 151-152, 172, 183-184
  trade unionists, 244
  Wideman, 181
  Zeitlin, 180-181
  see also Exiles
Opposition
  April 6 Liberation Movement, 166

becomes a revolution, 295
boycotts, 288
demonstrations, 287
grows, 166, 266, 281, 285
Light-A-Fire Movement, 166
Movement for free Philippines, 167
Ortega, Carmen, 116
Ortigas, Gaston, 166
Osmeña, Sergio, 119
Overpricing, see Graft

Padilla, Ambrosio (Senator), 7
Pelaez Case, 182n, 228
Panorama magazine, 138, 182, 279
Parker, George (Maj. Gen.), 20
Parsons, "Chick", 86
Patajo, Lino (Lt.), 89
Paterno, Vicente T., 220
Patron, 113-114
Payola exposé, 120
Pedrosa, Carmen Navarro, 135
People's Victory rally, 287
Philex, Philippine Exchange Corp-
    oration, 233, 237
Philippine Airlines, 204, 219
Philippine Coconut Authority, 227
Philippine Coconut Producers
    Federation (Cocofed), 225
Philippine Exchange Corporation
    (Philex), 233, 237
Philippine Free Press newspaper,
    119
Philippine Herald newspaper, 178
Philippine National Oil Company,
    206
Philippine people. See Society
Philippine Perspectives on Multi-
    national Corporations, 221
Philippine Sugar Commission
    Philsucom), 234
Philippine Times, 270
Philippine Tobacco Filters Corp-
    oration, 209
Philippine Underwriters Finance
    Corporation, 211-212
Philsucom, Philippine Sugar
    Commission, 234
Pittsburgh Press, 285

Plaza Miranda bombing, 120-121,
    173, 274
Pobre, Cesar P. (Capt.), 79
"Political banks", 208
Political parties
  Aglipayan party, 7
  Kilusang Bagong Lipunan (KBL),
    165
  Laban, 166
  Nacionalista party, 7
Pope
  lectures Marcos, 150-151
  urges unionization of sugar cane
    workers, 155
  visit of, 140, 150
Poverty line, 276, 277
Praeger, Ralph, B. (Maj.), 72, 75
Presidential Center for Special
    Studies, 176-177
Presidential Commitment Orders
    (PCOs), 174, 281
President Quezon's Own Guerillas
    (PQOG). See Resistance/guerilla
    units
Press boycott of pro-Marcos news-
    papers, 270
  censorship, 136-37, 139, 140,
    143, 175-185, 267, 270-271
  censorship reported by U.S. State
    Department, 181
  freedoms curtailed, 125-126, 131
  lack of freedom noted by Inter-
    national Press Institute, 177
  propaganda, Marcos' use of, 3,
    195
  reaction to Marcos' Washington
    visit, 247
Preventive Detention Action (PDA),
    174
Print Media Council, 177
Private armies, 159
Propaganda
  film of official version of
    assasination, 270
  Marcos' use of, 195
  in textbooks, 175
Protestant National Council of
    Churches, 148

Psinakis, Steve, 167
Public Order Act. 150
Puyat, Gil (Sen. Pres.), 117, 128

Quezon, Manuel L., 7, 9, 10, 16-17
Quiet Diplomacy, 241, 266
Quijano, J.G. (Johnny), 115, 120-121
Quintero, Eduardo, 120
Quiriño, Elpidio, 10

"Radio Bandido", 297
Radio smuggled to Luzon, 66-67
Radio Veritas, 295-299
Ramos, Fidel (Gen.), 157, 170, 292, 301, 302
Ramsey, Edwin (Maj.), 63
Ranis, Gustav, 217
Ranis Report, 217
Redwood Bank, 212
Rescue-of-troubled-companies fund, 254
"Resistance Movement in Northern Luzon (1942-1945), The", 79
Reuter, James (Fr.), 296
Revere Sugar Corporation, 204
Revolution, 292-304
Reyes, Franco Vera, 74-75
Reyes, Jose B.L. (Sup. Ct. Justice), 130
Ricarte, Artemio (Gen.), 267
Rigor, Conrado B. (Maj.), 80
Rising Sun, The (Toland), 15
Rivera, Vincente (Capt.), 88-89, 91-95
Rizal, Jose, 261-262
Robinson, Richard, 222
Roces, Joachin (Chino), 178
Rock Christ group, 168
Romualdez, Alfredo (Bejo) (brother of Imelda), 203
Romualdez, Alita (sister of Imelda), 203
Romualdez, Benjamin (Kokoy) (brother of Imelda), 137, 177-178, 202, 242, 255, 300
Romualdez, Eduardo (cousin of Imelda), 203-204

Romualdez, Imelda. *See* Imelda
Romulo, Carlos P., 16-17, 34, 57, 249
Rose of Tacloban (Imelda), 134, 135
Rowan, Roy, 137
Roxas, Manuel (Brig. Gen. and President), 10, 11, 62, 87, 89, 102
Ryan, Jane, 119

Sabotage. *See* Guerilla units
Salonga, Jovito R., (Rep., later Sen.), 117, 120, 131, 245
salvaging, 166
San Agustin, Marcos Villa, 67
San Agustin, Primitivo (Cap.), 65, 66, 67, 69, 80
San Francisco Examiner, 270
Santos, Jose Abad (Supreme Court Justice), 9, 267
Sariling Sikap, 276
Sato, Gempachi (Col.), 48
Saunders, William, 85, 119, 189
Schouten, Anthony (Fr.), 151-152
Seafront Scandal, 209
Secret marshals, 243, 280, *see also* Military
Shaman, 3, 198
Sharkey, John, 26, 28
Shultz, George (Sec. of State), 174, 300
Silverio, Ricardo, 207, 211, 212
Sin, Archbishop Jaime Cardinal
   accuses Marcos of extravagance, 275
   asks people for support of reformists, 295
   asserts harassment of clergy not a coincidence, 152
   calls for end of authoritatianism, 280
   calls for return to democracy, 271
   criticizes showing of pornographic films, 143
   describes confrontation as "between good and evil", 174
   doubts official version of

assassination, 275
likens Marcos to a man on a tiger,
  303
proposes national council, 271
says priests must act, 147
speaks out against deception, 247
urges vigilance, 279-280
Singson, Fidel (Gen.), 294, 297
Snyder, Gerald S., 15
Society, Philippine
Chinese minority, 212n-213n
class/income disparities, 118-119
comunism, reasons for growth of,
  162
"compadres" system, 113-115
conspicuous consumption
  accepted, 239
corruption a way of life, 222
described in United States CIA
  memorandum, 118
ethnic origin, 111
favoritism and graft in, 118
"Filipino time", 265
Filipino traits, short memory and
  forgiveness, 274
force, rediness to use, 113, 119-120
oligarchical, 123, 189
poverty, Pope comments on, 155
poverty in, 118, 239, 276-277
status, excessive concern for, 113
traits of Filipina described, 134
violence, history of, 112, 120
warlords, private armies and
  security forces, 113, 115, 119, 231
wealth as measure of social value,
  113
see also Church
Sola, Pablo, 154-155
Soriano, Emmanuel V. (Noel), 176,
  304
Sotelo, Antonio (Col.), 298
Spence, Hartzell, 14, 43, 198
State visit to Washington
extravagance of, 242-243
purposes of, 242, 245
Steinberg, David Joel, 113, 119,
  123-124, 267
Stonehill, Harry S., 117-118, 205

Straughn, Hugh (Col.), 58-60
Subic Navel Base, 241
Sugar barons, 154
Sugar, paper traders, 236, 238
Sugar, trading costs, 237, 238
Sullivan, William, 137
Sun Tzu, 293
Surveillance of citizens. See Human
  rights

Tadhana (Fate), 195, 198
Tadiar, Artemio (Brig. Gen.), 296,
  297
Takechi, Susumu (Col.), 35-36, 41
Tañada, Lorenzo, 10, 62, 126, 280
Taniguchi, Kureo (Lt. Gen.), 46, 48
Task Force Detainees, 148, 281
Tatad, Francisco, 177
Technology Resource Center, 221
Teehankee, Claudio (Supreme Crt.
  Chief Justice), 173, 281, 301
TESCO (The Ex-Serviceman's
  Company), 83
The Iron Butterfly, 145
Thetaventures Limited, 204
They Never Surrendered (Snyder),
  15
They Served with Honor
  (Baclagon), 15
Thorpe, Claude (Col.), 82
Time magazine, 179
Times-Journal newspaper, 178, 270
Toda, Benigno, 204
Toland, John, 15, 37, 40, 42
Topography of Philippines, 111
Torture. See Human rights
Transitory Provisions, 127-129
Tripoli Agreement, 164

Ultimo Adios (The Last Farewell),
  261
Umali, Vicente, 59-60, 102
Unichem, United Coconut
  Chemicals, 228
Unicom, United Coconut Mills, 228
United Coconut Chemicals
  (Unichem), 228-229

United Coconut Mills (Unicom), 228

United Coconut Planters' Bank, 227

United Nations, Declaration Against Torture, 170

United States
appeals to Marcos to step down peacefully, 296-297, 300
bases, concern for, 142, 160, 240, 246
cancels Reagan visit, 266
censorship reported by State Department, 181
government support of Marcos, 239
helps against Huk insurgency, 116
House of Rep., passes press freedom resolution, 271
Justice Department suit, Cocopec scandal, 229
military institutions in, many Philippine officers attended, 159
"Quiet Diplomacy" policy, 241, 266
reports misuse of aid, 282
Schultz shows support for Marcos, 174
Senate condemns election result, 288
sends Habib, 288
sends Laxalt, 285
V.P. Bush praises Marcos, 240

University of Life, 144

Untold Story of Imelda Marcos, The (Pedrosa), 135

Utang na loob (debt of gratitude), 85, 114, 190

Valdez, Basilio J. (Maj. Gen.), 100-101

Valdez, Simeon, (Màj.), 103

Valor, (Baclagon & Crisol), 16, 25, 26, 51, 65, 96, 106

Vance, John R. (Col.), 34

Velarde, Hospicio M. (Lt.), 105

Velasco, Geronimo, 205, 218

Ver, 160, 169-170, 279, 283-284, 286, 289, 292, 294, 298, 302

Veritas, 269, 290

Villamor, Jesus (Col.), 15-17, 68, 80

Villanueva, Melecio, 157

Villegas, Bernardo (Bernie), 191n, 217-218, 221-222

Virata, Cesar, 249, 250, 273, 279

Volckmann, Russell W. (Col.), 76, 79, 85, 88, 90, 99

Wainwright, 28, 33-34, 45, 52

Wakamiya, Kiyoshi, 279

Walang Palakasan, 123

Warner, Everett L. (Lt. Col.), 73

Wartime exploits, Marcos'
army organization described, 17-18, 90
"buy and sell" activities, with Japanese, 83
imprisonment by Japanese, 57
military duties, conflicts in accounts of, 95-96
promotions, conflicts in accounts of, 84
restores civil government (disputed), 96
seen in Japanese uniform, 85
unconfirmed by contemporary accounts, 57, 59, 66, 68, 91-94

Washington, State visit to, 243-247

Washington Post newspaper, 181, 185

Weaver, James R.N. (Gen.), 41

We Forum newspaper, 14, 183, 185, 247, 269, 290

We Remained (Volckmann), 78

Westinghouse, 210

Wideman, Bernard, 181

William Saunders, 189

Willoughby, Charles W. (Lt. Col.), 59, 67, 73, 79-81, 97

World Bank, 142-143, 208, 254-255, 282

Yamashita, Tomoyoki (Gen.), 94

Yuyitung incident, 120-121

Zeitlin, Arnold, 180-181